PRAEGER SECURITY INTERNATIONAL ADVISORY BOARD

Board Cochairs

Loch K. Johnson, Regents Professor of Public and International Affairs, School of Public and International Affairs, University of Georgia (U.S.A.)

Paul Wilkinson, Professor of International Relations and Chairman of the Advisory Board, Centre for the Study of Terrorism and Political Violence, University of St. Andrews (U.K.)

Members

Anthony H. Cordesman, Arleigh A. Burke Chair in Strategy, Center for Strategic and International Studies (U.S.A.)

Thérèse Delpech, Director of Strategic Affairs, Atomic Energy Commission, and Senior Research Fellow, CERI (Fondation Nationale des Sciences Politiques), Paris (France)

Sir Michael Howard, former Chichele Professor of the History of War and Regis Professor of Modern History, Oxford University, and Robert A. Lovett Professor of Military and Naval History, Yale University (U.K.)

Lieutenant General Claudia J. Kennedy, USA (Ret.), former Deputy Chief of Staff for Intelligence, Department of the Army (U.S.A.)

Paul M. Kennedy, J. Richardson Dilworth Professor of History and Director, International Security Studies, Yale University (U.S.A.)

Robert J. O'Neill, former Chichele Professor of the History of War, All Souls College, Oxford University (Australia)

Shibley Telhami, Anwar Sadat Chair for Peace and Development, Department of Government and Politics, University of Maryland (U.S.A.)

Fareed Zakaria, Editor, Newsweek International (U.S.A.)

HOMELAND SECURITY AND FEDERALISM

Praeger Security International Advisory Board

Board Cochairs

Loch K. Johnson, Regents Professor of Public and International Affairs, School of Public and International Affairs, University of Georgia (U.S.A.)

Paul Wilkinson, Professor of International Relations and Chairman of the Advisory Board, Centre for the Study of Terrorism and Political Violence, University of St. Andrews (U.K.)

Members

Anthony H. Cordesman, Arleigh A. Burke Chair in Strategy, Center for Strategic and International Studies (U.S.A.)

Thérèse Delpech, Director of Strategic Affairs, Atomic Energy Commission, and Senior Research Fellow, CERI (Fondation Nationale des Sciences Politiques), Paris (France)

Sir Michael Howard, former Chichele Professor of the History of War and Regis Professor of Modern History, Oxford University, and Robert A. Lovett Professor of Military and Naval History, Yale University (U.K.)

Lieutenant General Claudia J. Kennedy, USA (Ret.), former Deputy Chief of Staff for Intelligence, Department of the Army (U.S.A.)

Paul M. Kennedy, J. Richardson Dilworth Professor of History and Director, International Security Studies, Yale University (U.S.A.)

Robert J. O'Neill, former Chichele Professor of the History of War, All Souls College, Oxford University (Australia)

Shibley Telhami, Anwar Sadat Chair for Peace and Development, Department of Government and Politics, University of Maryland (U.S.A.)

Fareed Zakaria, Editor, Newsweek International (U.S.A.)

HOMELAND SECURITY AND FEDERALISM

Protecting America from Outside the Beltway

MATT A. MAYER

Foreword by the Honorable Edwin Meese III

PRAEGER SECURITY INTERNATIONAL
An Imprint of ABC-CLIO, LLC

Santa Barbara, California • Denver, Colorado • Oxford, England

Copyright 2009 by Matt A. Mayer

All rights reserved. No part of this publication may be reproduced, stored in a retrieval system, or transmitted, in any form or by any means, electronic, mechanical, photocopying, recording, or otherwise, except for the inclusion of brief quotations in a review, without priorpermission in writing from the publisher.

Library of Congress Catalog Card Number

Mayer, Matt A.
   Homeland security and federalism : protecting America from outside the Beltway / Matt A. Mayer; foreword by the Honorable Edwin Meese III.
     p. cm.
   Includes bibliographical references and index.
   ISBN 978-0-313-35522-6 (hard copy : alk. paper) — ISBN 978-0-313-35523-3 (ebook)
1. National security—United States. 2. Civil defense—United States. 3. Terrorism—United States—Prevention. 4. Internal security—United States. 5. Federal government. I. Title.
   UA23.M395 2009
   363.350973—dc22   2009011642

13 12 11 10 9   1 2 3 4 5

This book is also available on the World Wide Web as an eBook.

Visit www.abc-clio.com for details.

ABC-CLIO, LLC
130 Cremona Drive, P.O. Box 1911
Santa Barbara, California 93116-1911

This book is printed on acid-free paper ∞

Manufactured in the United States of America

To the men and women fighting on the front lines today and to the countless men and women who paid the ultimate price throughout our nation's history to ensure that America remains the shining city on the hill.

To Jessica, Madeleine, and Genevieve—for whose love and security this book is dedicated.

Contents

Foreword *by the Honorable Edwin Meese III*		ix
Preface		xiii
Abbreviations		xvii
Part I	**How We Got Here**	1
1	A New Kind of War	3
2	A Short History of Civilian Defense in the United States	13
3	The Limitations of Today's Washington-centric Model	25
Part II	**Where We Should Go from Here**	41
4	Where Are All of the Federalists?	43
	Case Study 1: *Don't Mess with Texas*	51
5	The Role of Risk in Determining Where to Allocate Limited Resources	55
	Case Study 2: *A Tale of Two Cities*	67
6	The Importance of Local Preparedness	71
	Case Study 3: *Lessons Learned from SARS Elevates Seattle/King County Preparedness Efforts*	88
7	Decentralizing Disaster Management	91
	Case Study 4: *An Honest Approach to Disasters in Ohio*	104

8	Illegal Immigration and the Laboratories of Democracy	109
	Case Study 5: *Arizonians Say "Enough!"*	122
9	Counterterrorism from the Bottom Up	125
	Case Study 6: *Los Angeles' Counterterrorism Innovation*	137
10	The Role of the Community	141
	Case Study 7: *Training Tomorrow's Prevention Forces Today at Michigan State University*	150
Afterword		153
Notes		157
Bibliography		189
Index		203

Foreword

For four decades I have been part of the national debate on the size of the federal government and the importance of federalism. It seems that every time America faces a new challenge or a new threat, too many people reflexively turn to Washington, D.C., for the answer. That shouldn't always be the case.

In some situations, like the threat from the Soviet Union and communism, only the moral clarity of the Presidency, the strength of the military, and the vibrancy of a national economy unleashed could defeat such a global, nation-state threat. In other cases, like the challenge of welfare dependency, the federal government's "one size fits all" approach failed miserably. In that case, federalism provided America with an alternative choice, which was to decentralize power and responsibility to states and localities so that they could tailor their approaches to meet the specific and unique challenges the various jurisdictions faced.

After the September 11, 2001, attack, Americans correctly viewed the threat to be a foreign one. In response, we created a new federal department and centralized more power and responsibility in Washington, D.C. The problem with this response is that the blunt instrument of federal power aimed at a stateless foreign threat fails to possess the flexibility and manpower to effectively deal with that asymmetric threat once it arrives on our shores and embeds itself in our cities.

As I have said many times before, the states are where the ideas are formed. Our states have led the way on issue after issue: tort reform, welfare reform, tax reform, education reform, health care reform, and, as this book argues, homeland security reform.

We know from history that the federal bureaucracy is often hostile to federalism and will not reform itself or easily give up power. The Constitution of the United States established a central government of limited powers, having the authority necessary to deal with truly national matters. Our founders believed that the road to tyranny is paved by a federal government that usurps state and local power. The only way America is going to regain control over the federal government is if states and localities, and the elected officials who govern them, find their federalist voices and fight for the power that is rightfully theirs to begin with.

We must acknowledge that the agencies serving on the front lines in our domestic war against Islamic jihadists must include those at the local level. Even on September 11, 2001, when the greatest symbol of federal power—the Pentagon—was attacked inside the Beltway, it was local responders from Arlington County and Fairfax County, Virginia, and Montgomery County, Maryland, who saved the day. Yet, in the last eight years, we have centralized more and more of our homeland security efforts in the federal government.

In my role with The Heritage Foundation, I have had the opportunity to travel the country and talk with police and fire chiefs, mayors, and other local officials and first responders. These brave men and women all tell me the same thing: the roles and responsibilities between state and local governments and the federal government remain blurred. The federal government makes decisions impacting state and local governments without sufficient input from them, and thus there is a growing disconnect between the federal government and the states. To protect our citizens, we must correct this situation.

This book represents the opening thrust in a new battle, but is part of an intellectual war that has raged from the moment our founding fathers gathered in Philadelphia during the summer of 1787 to draft a new constitution. As retold in the second chapter, America possesses a rich history of relying on civilians to defend the nation. This strong tradition becomes vital in defeating an enemy that does not wear uniforms, uses our freedoms to exploit us, and targets innocent civilians. All our tanks and jet fighters are useless once our enemies manage to infiltrate our communities. An approach dominated by those inside the Beltway will cost a lot and achieve little.

We need a new approach.

The strategies articulated in this book recognize the limitations of federal power and, more critically, seek to reinvigorate the constitutional powers possessed by state and local governments. They aim to create a true partnership between the federal government and the states so that each focuses their finite resources on those activities in which they possess—not only the ability to succeed, but also the proper constitutional authority under which to act.

I don't think this book presents a compelling vision for a federalist approach to homeland security just because I believe in conservative values. Rather, as a former first responder myself, I think this book makes a strong case for changes in our approach to homeland security and disaster response. As a member of then-Governor Ronald Reagan's Cabinet in California, I had responsibility for the National Guard and the Office of Emergency Services, and I chaired Governor Reagan's Emergency Operations Council. I know firsthand the power and capabilities possessed by state and local governments to deal with major threats.

I also know firsthand the importance of local preparedness and the ability to control major incidents. We know that our enemies seek to inflict heavy consequences on us, and that they target urban centers with large densely packed populations and severely exposed by the vulnerabilities that exist in such places. More than ever, we must ensure that our higher risk urban areas possess the critical capabilities they will need to intercept and prevent an attack or, should an attack succeed, to adequately respond and recover from it.

A preparedness strategy focused on building critical capabilities in our high-risk urban centers sends an unequivocal message to terrorists that we will not make it easy for them to attempt or engage in their acts of cowardice. A nation prepared for terrorist attacks is the strongest means of deterrence we can engage in domestically. Our states and localities are ideally suited to lead in this effort.

The responsibility for preventing and responding to terrorism is shared between the federal government and the states. But in many other areas of emergency response, the Founders' concept of constitutional federalism—which has served our nation well throughout its history—requires the states to shoulder their responsibility to handle incidents occurring within their jurisdictions that are within their capabilities. Accordingly, the federal government must enforce this discipline by declining to intervene in local situations unless state resources are insufficient *and* when assistance is requested on that basis by the governor involved.

As the federal government involves itself more and more in the response to disasters across the United States, it creates a false public perception that disaster management is primarily the responsibility of the federal government. As this perception takes hold, there is less accountability of state and local officials, who divert their finite resources away from disaster response to other pressing issues. With insufficient state or local funding, disaster management capabilities become atrophied and entirely dependent on federal largesse. The federal government should step in to support state government only where the incident is beyond the capabilities of state and local resources and thus has national implications.

As with the September 11, 2001, attack and all disasters, our local and state emergency workers are the backbone of a successful response. Rather than seeking federal aid for every disaster, no matter how small, states and localities must develop the capabilities needed to handle the routine disasters that make up the vast majority of incidents that strike America. This local acceptance of responsibility will allow the federal government to focus on building disaster capabilities for truly catastrophic situations like Hurricane Katrina.

The federal government has the major responsibility for protecting our nation against external threats, while state and local authorities have the primary obligation to protect their citizens against crime, disorder, and other conditions that endanger public safety. Thus, both elements of our governmental system are directly involved in homeland security.

But the fact that the federal government has such a role should not diminish the critical involvement of the states. For good reason, the Founders expressly placed the responsibility for local public safety in the hands of state government, establishing our constitutional tradition of decentralized law enforcement. As Alexander Hamilton noted in *The Federalist* Number 17, "There is one transcendent advantage belonging to the province of the state governments, which alone suffices to place the matter in a clear and satisfactory light. I mean the ordinary administration of criminal and civil justice."

That is why state and local agencies must have a major role in both the determination of homeland security policy and strategies and in the prevention of and operational responses to terrorism. Our approach to counterterrorism must unleash the power and creativity of state and local governments. Experience during the history of our republic has shown that experimentation among the states has led to the discovery of the most effective ways to deal with complex issues.

Further, the involvement of local agencies is essential to gathering the intelligence needed to identify terrorist activity and prevent future attacks. Federal law enforcement resources are limited and cannot cover the "retail" gathering of information. More critically, federal agents lack the meaningful connection with local communities that enable the police officers who patrol neighborhood beats to relate to the citizens who have information about what is going on in their areas.

The answer to the critical needs of homeland security is for the federal and state governments to work together, each operating within their own sphere of constitutional authority, but cooperating to advance the public safety.

This book provides a detailed analysis of how the advancement of our historic concepts of constitutional federalism can provide a strong framework for protecting our nation against terrorism. The historical information and current case studies provide a wealth of data on what works and how violations of constitutional doctrines have been dangerous to liberty while unsuccessful in practice. It explains why lapses in following the federalist tradition have been detrimental to our citizens' best interests and provides a brightly lit pathway for the states to reclaim their rightful roles in protecting and preserving America.

Edwin Meese III
Attorney General of the United States (1985–1988)

Preface

They are everywhere in factories, offices, butcher shops, on street corners, in private businesses—and each carries with him the germ of death for society.

U.S. Attorney General Tom Clark[1]

Those who would give up essential Liberty, to purchase a little temporary Safety, deserve neither Liberty nor Safety.

Benjamin Franklin[2]

The risk of a terrorist attack in Anywhere, America, is always a possibility. The likelihood, however, of such an attack in most cities across America is—even today—remote. Without a doubt the terrorist attack on September 11, 2001, fundamentally altered the security under which Americans live. For much of our history, the expanse of both the Pacific and Atlantic Oceans made us much safer than many of our allies. Whether the enemy was a fascist regime led by a madman or a communist machine led by a cold-blooded killer, a strike on American soil proved challenging.

As America pushed further into the frontier of innovative technology, however, the world became smaller. Modern air travel greatly reduced the challenges posed by those two natural barriers that had protected us for so long. It was only a matter of time before a creative and driven enemy took advantage of the shrunken natural barriers to land a strike on our shores.

Surprisingly, that strike came not from a modern military with cutting-edge weaponry, but from a group of frustrated jihadists operating out of caves who had failed to bring change to their home countries. Instead of guns and rockets, they used first a van and explosives and then box-cutters and passenger airplanes.

In the course of two hours and fourteen minutes, they killed 2,973 innocent people, brought down over fifteen and a half million square feet of buildings in New York City, and destroyed a large segment of our military headquarters in Arlington, Virginia. That single-day death toll represented the largest number of deaths on American soil since another September morning in 1862 when over 3,000 Americans died at the Battle of Antietam during our Civil War. Such a blow was sure to alter the calculus of America's security posture for many years to come.

In the seven years since al Qaeda and Osama Bin Laden became household names in America, our response externally involved fighting wars in Afghanistan and Iraq and using all means necessary to push our functional borders as far from our actual borders as possible. Domestically, we created the U.S. Department of Homeland Security (DHS) and launched many new programs and initiatives to increase the security of our homeland.

While the success of our military efforts abroad will not be known for many years, our domestic efforts, when audited by independent entities, have proved to be less than stellar. Serious questions remain. Was creating DHS really a good decision? Did it make sense to combine twenty-two agencies into one department despite the seventy-five percent failure rate of one-to-one mergers in the private sector? Could bureaucrats in Washington really succeed at such a complex and broad set of missions? Is a Washington-centric approach ultimately the best way to secure America? And, as Franklin noted, would greater security require a loss of not just aspects of our liberty that border on convenience, but of our essential liberty?

There is a better way.

Historically, on issue after issue, change did not start inside the Beltway. Rather, trailblazers in America's states and cities burned the path to success. Washington did not launch welfare reform, Wisconsin did. Washington did not launch education reform, Florida did. Washington did not launch health care reform, Massachusetts did. Washington did not launch the privatization of government services, Indianapolis did. It has been and will continue to be Justice Louis Brandeis' "laboratories of democracy" that will tackle America's hardest problems and most complex challenges. Rarely, if ever, has Washington led the way. Why do politicians and policymakers in Washington think it will be different with homeland security?

It is one thing for the federal government to take the lead on cargo security, border security, and maritime security; it is altogether another thing for the federal government to take the lead on preparedness, disaster management, interior illegal immigration enforcement, and domestic intelligence. As statements ripe for inclusion in a "Restatement of the Obvious," if our enemies are in America, they are living in our states. If they execute an attack, it will occur in a city. If they succeed, the disaster response will come from first responders from cities and states. In all cases, the federal government lacks the resources (time, people, and assets) to be everywhere and do everything.

Our success and survival depends on the ability of states and localities to rise to the occasion, redirect resources where appropriate, build critical capabilities where needed, and tell the federal government to stay inside the Beltway, on the border, in the ports, and on the water keeping the enemy and its weapons out. In many cases, the federal government should act as the coordinator of national efforts, consolidator of best practices and lessons learned, and broad policy arbiter. Too often, the federal government has acted by fiat and mandate with nothing more than lip service given to the principle of federalism.

This book lays out an alternative to today's failed model, and aims to restore power to our nation's governors and mayors. Some of those governors and mayors may not want the power because it is far easier to blame Washington for all of today's ills than it is to take ownership of protecting the people. The Founding Fathers rightfully knew that keeping government as close to the people as possible would increase accountability, require transparency, and ensure that those entrusted with promoting our security would do so in a manner best suited to preserve our liberty.

This book takes a more reasoned position on the risk faced by America. Meaningful risk simply does not exist everywhere in America. We must do a better job of determining where meaningful risk does exist and then allocate resources to those places to minimize vulnerabilities and consequences. With over $210 billion spent on DHS and far too few success stories, this books attempts to allocate the responsibilities for securing America in a manner that should cost less and result in more successes.

As with most efforts, a great deal of thanks is owed to a few men and women who contributed in both large and small, but always critical, ways to this book. First, no words of thanks can ever repay Corey Gruber (Lt. Col., Ret.) for the years of service to our country, the guidance and mentorship offered during my time inside DHS and since I left, and the contributions to this book. Corey truly is a national treasure whose efforts have helped make us more secure and whose work and writings will influence generations to come.

Next, special thanks to the Honorable Edwin Meese III, James Carafano, Diem Nguyen, and The Heritage Foundation for supporting my work and giving me the opportunity to shape our homeland security policy. I also would be remiss if I didn't thank Rick O'Donnell, Joel Harris, Kristina Dorville, Ivette Fernandez, and Betsy Foster for your friendship, thoughts, and laughter during and after my DHS days—especially during the rough days following Hurricane Katrina. To Benjamin Atkins, Ingrid Babri, Veronique De Rugy, and Tom Karako for your early reviews and comments on this book, as well as my research assistants Jessica Zuckerman and Alexa Noruk for your support and all of the digging, analysis, and work you did to support this book.

Lastly, and, most importantly, thank you to Representative Russell Pearce and Treasurer Dean Martin from Arizona, Lt. John Sullivan from Los Angeles, Dr. David Carter from Michigan State University, Nancy Dragani and her outstanding team from Ohio, Carina Elsenboss and her colleagues from Seattle/King County Public Health, and Steve McCraw from Texas whose work is highlighted in the case studies following most of the chapters. The case studies highlight some of the great work being done across the United States to make us more secure.

I hope you enjoy reading this book as much as I enjoyed writing it.

Matt A. Mayer
September 11, 2008

Abbreviations

CBO	Congressional Budget Office
CBP	Custom and Border Protection
CIS	Citizenship and Immigration Services
CRS	Congressional Research Service
DHS	U.S. Department of Homeland Security
DOJ	U.S. Department of Justice
FBI	Federal Bureau of Investigation
FEMA	Federal Emergency Management Agency
FY	Fiscal Year
GAO	Government Accountability Office
HSPD	Homeland Security Presidential Directive
IC	Intelligence Community
ICE	Immigration and Customs Enforcement
IG	Inspector General
INA	Immigration and Nationality Act
IRCA	Immigration Reform and Control Act
JRIC	Joint Regional Intelligence Center
JTTF	Joint Terrorism Task Force
LAPD	Los Angeles Police Department
LASO	Los Angeles Sheriff's Office
LAWA	Legal Arizona Workers Act
MSU	Michigan State University
NPG	National Preparedness Goal
NPS	National Preparedness System
NYPD	New York Police Department
ODP	Office for Domestic Preparedness
OEMA	Ohio Emergency Management Agency
SAR	Suspicious Activity Report

SARS	Severe Acute Respiratory Syndrome
SHSP	State Homeland Security Program
TCL	Target Capabilities List
TEW	Terrorism Early Warning
TSA	Transportation Security Administration
UASI	Urban Areas Security Initiative
WMD	Weapons of Mass Destruction
WTC	World Trade Center

PART I

How We Got Here

1

A New Kind of War

> Islam cannot accept any compromise with jahiliyyah (the state of ignorance outside of Islam), either in its concept or in the modes of living derived from this concept. Either Islam will remain, or jahiliyyah; Islam cannot accept or agree to a situation which is half-Islam and half-jahiliyyah. In this respect Islam's stand is very clear.
>
> Sayyid Qutb[1]

> We hold these truths to be self-evident, that all men are created equal, that they are endowed by their Creator with certain unalienable Rights, that among these are Life, Liberty and the pursuit of Happiness.
>
> The Declaration of Independence[2]

This war is not a new war for America. It simply represents yet another battle in the ageless war on behalf of liberty. The intolerance and systematic oppression of freedom represented by Islamic jihadism differs only in degrees to the ideologies we have fought and defeated over the last two hundred and thirty-two years. While the battle is ours to fight today, many nations throughout history have fought freedom's battles. From the Spartans' courageous clash with the Persians at the Battle of Thermopylae in 480 B.C. to William Wallace and the Scottish rebellion in the Wars of Scottish Independence from 1297 to 1305 A.D., this war between freedom and oppression is as old as time.

Americans first joined the epic struggle in its own War for Independence from a tyrannical king. We later fought a battle among ourselves over the shameful institution of slavery during the Civil War. Later, the rise of foreign militarism required our steadfast efforts in the First World War. Soon thereafter, fascism reared its ugly head and led to the death of millions of people during the Second World War, including the extermination of six million men, women, and children simply because they were Jewish. Finally, we fought communism during the Cold War for over four decades until it, too, joined the other bankrupt belief systems on the "ash heap of history."[3]

We will win this battle—not because it is our destiny, but because freedom is an idea no man, government, army, or oppressor can defeat. It may take many years and the costs may be high in both life and treasure, but ultimately man's own yearning for freedom will prevail. The seeds of freedom can take root in the harshest of conditions and in the hardest soil. Eventually, freedom will take root among a few of our enemy's fighters and it will spread. Once it does, Islamic jihadism, like communism before it, will rot from within as those surrounded by it fight for a better life for themselves and their families.

America must recognize that the battle with Islamic jihadism is, however, different from the other battles it has fought. America's previous battles involved opponents who represented defined political jurisdictions. The soldiers in those battles wore uniforms, used traditional means of warfare, and mostly kept the killing on the fields of battle. Islamic jihadism rejects a political jurisdiction. It is represented by a loose collection of true believers who hide themselves across the world. Their "nation" is a hypothetical nirvana where the world's peoples submit to their warped version of Islam. Its "soldiers" don't wear uniforms, and they use non-traditional means of warfare. The greatest difference is that Islamic jihadists mostly seek to kill civilians.

With military and diplomatic efforts, we can take the fight to the enemy so that they cannot find the refuge in which to plan and launch new attacks on free nations. Even with those efforts, however, we likely cannot defeat Islamic jihadism; rather, we can only weaken it until freedom once again conquers oppression. As military historian Caleb Carr notes:

> There can be little question that both that strategy (targeting civilians) and those tactics will prove self-defeating: the current agents of terror have unwisely chosen to ignore the lessons of similar campaigns (although it is perhaps unrealistic to think that people who spend their time immersed in medieval religious rumination and bomb schematics would do anything else). Instead, they have elected to deliberately victimize civilians in a manner and on a scale not seen in generations, perhaps centuries. In so doing, the organizers, sponsors, and foot soldiers of every terrorist group involved in the September 11 attacks have unwittingly ensured that their extremist cause will be discredited among many of their sympathizers, disowned by most of their former sponsors, and finally defeated by their enemies: two thousand years of the lessons of terror dictate that this is the ultimate fate that awaits the attackers, no matter how many noncombatants they manage to kill along the way.[4]

America and the West must do everything possible to foment this abandonment, and tread cautiously so as not to extend the timeframe of this unwinding with counterproductive actions.

While the use of terror tactics is not new, other than minor skirmishes in our history, America has never fought enemies who used *primarily* terror as its means of fighting. As Carr notes, "terrorism, in other words, is simply the contemporary name given to, and the modern permutation of, warfare deliberatively waged against civilians with the purpose of destroying their will to support either leaders or policies that the agents of such violence find objectionable."[5] Knowing it cannot match America's military on a field of battle, Islamic jihadists take the fight to the streets and alleys of cities where it can win the Long War by inflicting death and destruction on the innocent.

Critically, America must be prepared to fight this war. At times, that fight may occur in American cities. It must show the enemy and those who sympathize and support it that democracy and capitalism have not turned America into the "weak horse." Americans may have been late in seeing the rise of modern terrorism—just as America was late in entering the Second World War—but ultimately we will see the fight through to victory because, our very way of life—our lives—are directly at stake.

FROM ISMAILIA TO NEW YORK CITY[6]

At the height of the Roaring Twenties in America, a future enemy half a world away arose in an unremarkable town in Egypt that eventually would give rise to events far beyond what could have been imagined at the time. In March 1928, Hassan al-Banna, a Sufi schoolteacher living in Ismailia, founded the Muslim Brotherhood in reaction to what he and others believed was a loss of original Islam due to Western influences.[7] The Muslim Brotherhood was a religious, political, and social organization in Egypt that subscribed to the founding belief statement that "Allah is our objective; the messenger is our leader; the Quran is our law; Jihad is our way; dying in the way of Allah is our highest hope."[8] Al-Banna did not believe in freedom; rather, he believed that it was "the nature of Islam to dominate, not to be dominated, to impose its law on all nations, and to extend its powers to the entire planet."[9]

In just over twenty years, the Muslim Brotherhood grew so rapidly that its membership swelled to roughly two million members by 1948.[10] Due to some of its secret activities, the Egyptian government dissolved the Muslim Brotherhood in December 1948.[11] In reaction, a member of the Muslim Brotherhood assassinated Egyptian Prime Minister Mahmud Fahmi Nokrashi on December 28, 1948.[12] A short time later, al-Banna was killed and instantly became a martyr to the cause.

At around the same time, in November 1948, on his first trip outside of Egypt, a middle-aged government bureaucrat named Sayyid Qutb traveled to America where he spent time in New York City, Washington, DC, Colorado, and California.[13] Qutb would stay for only nineteen months, but, in that time, he saw America as "a spiritual wasteland."[14] Instead of appreciating the benefits of freedom and becoming more moderate, Qutb reacted to the excesses of freedom that he saw and left a more radical man.[15] He returned to Egypt believing that "only by restoring Islam to the center of their lives, their laws, and their governments could Muslims hope to recapture their rightful place as the dominant culture in the world."[16]

Over the next fifteen years, Qutb became the intellectual leader for the Muslim Brotherhood and other Islamic jihadists. His literary work has become the foundation for today's radical interpretation of the Quran, especially his book *Ma'alim fi-l-Tariq* (*Milestones*) and his commentary *Fi Zilial al-Qur'an* (*In the Shades of the Qur'an*) that redefined the concept of jihad for Muslims. Qutb wrote both *Milestones* and *In the Shades of the Qur'an* while in prison following the attempted assassination of Egyptian President Gamal Abdel Nasser.[17]

Prior to Qutb's interpretations, many Muslims at that time believed jihad involved a personal struggle (the English translation of jihad is "to struggle") or required armed resistance in defense of Islam. Qutb moved beyond this interpretation and wrote that "J'haad in Islam is simply a name for striving to make this system of life dominant in the world ... Thus, wherever an Islamic community exists which is a concrete example of the Divinely-ordained system of life, it has a God-given right to step forward and take control of the political authority so that it may establish the Divine system on earth."[18] Qutb gave Islamic jihadists the Quranic interpretation to use jihad offensively to conquer others on behalf of Islam.

After almost ten years in prison, the Egyptian government released Qutb, but rearrested him only six months later.[19] After being tried for plotting to overthrow the government, the court found Qutb guilty and sentenced him to death.[20] Just before being hanged, Qutb's sister tried to get him to appeal his sentence to which Qutb prophetically responded, "My words will be stronger if they kill me."[21] On August 29, 1966, Qutb was executed by hanging and, like al-Banna, immediately became a martyr for the cause.[22]

Qutb's legacy grew larger over the course of time and was carried forward by his brother, Muhammad Qubt. The Egyptian government imprisoned Muhammad at the same time as Qutb, but it did not try him; instead, he spent the next seven years in prison.[23] When released, he went to Saudi Arabia where he became a Professor of Islamic Studies, and where he lectured on Qutb's writings and beliefs, as well as his own thoughts on Islam.[24] One of his students was a young man named Ayman al-Zawahiri.[25]

Zawahiri's path to radicalism started at a young age when he joined with other young men to form an underground group aimed at putting "Qutb's vision into action."[26] Over the next fifteen years, Zawahiri led the Egyptian Islamic Jihad, and worked secretly to overthrow Egypt's government so that an Islamic state could be established.[27] After the assassination of Egyptian President Anwar Sadat, Zawahiri was imprisoned, tried, and convicted of trafficking in weapons.[28] While in prison, in what was a surprise to many, he turned on his brothers and revealed the location of one of the most wanted men in Egypt, Essam al-Qamari.[29] Shortly after getting out of prison, Zawahiri moved to Saudi Arabia where he met Muhammad Qutb.[30]

Eventually, Zawahiri went to Pakistan in the late-1980s to help the Mujahideen in Afghanistan fight the Soviet Union.[31] In Pakistan, Zawahiri became a close associate of Saudi Osama bin Laden.[32] It was in Pakistan that Zawahiri seemed to turn his focus from overthrowing the Egyptian government to supporting *takfir* (excommunication), which is a declaration against those who have committed apostasy.[33] The punishment for committing apostasy is death.

During this time, Zawahiri battled with Sheikh Abdullah Azzam for bin Laden's attention.[34] Unlike Zawahiri's growing belief in takfir, Azzam believed that the "struggle was against nonbelievers ... not within the community of faith," and he explicitly did not think it was consistent with Islam to engage in "the intentional killing of civilians, especially women and children."[35] Azzam did, however, subscribe to Qutb's call for the establishment of an aggressive *qaeda* (base) on which to build a new Islamic nation.[36] As events would come to show, Zawahiri's support for takfir would defeat Azzam's more moderate views.

Zawahiri then went to Sudan to continue plotting against the Egyptian government.[37] At one point, consistent with our enemy's past exploitation of our freedoms and open borders, Zawahiri—a convicted Egyptian with known ties to terrorists—traveled to the United States in 1993 where he raised money to support the activities of Egyptian Islamic Jihad.[38] This trip occurred one month *after* the first World Trade Center (WTC) attack in 1993.[39]

After a botched attack on an Egyptian official in 1993 that caused the death of a young girl, the Muslim Street turned against Zawahiri and the Egyptian Islamic Jihad.[40] Zawahiri left Sudan in 1996 and "became a phantom."[41] In mid-1997, Zawahiri ended up in Afghanistan where he formally joined forces with bin Laden and launched today's version of al Qaeda.[42]

The road to Afghanistan for bin Laden started in Saudi Arabia. Even though he was the son of one of Saudi Arabia's wealthiest citizens, bin Laden grew up in a modest environment, and went to a school populated by students from across Saudi society who gained admittance by way of a merit-based competitive examination.[43] When bin Laden was fourteen, he became more religious and sympathetic to the plight of the Palestinian people in Israel.[44] During this time, bin Laden began his lifelong commitment to fasting two days a week as the Prophet Mohammed had done.[45]

In his later teens and college years, bin Laden joined the Muslim Brotherhood and began reading Qutb's famous works, as well as attending lectures by Mohammed Qutb.[46] During this period, bin Laden became a close associate of Azzam who urged many young Muslims to go to Afghanistan to fight with the Mujahideen against the Soviets.[47] In support of Azzam's efforts, bin Laden housed recruits and began to develop the fundraising skills and connections that would prove invaluable in funding al Qaeda activities after 1996.[48]

By 1986, bin Laden was fully engaged in the Afghan War, and oversaw the construction of massive tunnels and caves to serve as weapon depots in an unknown area that later would become known around the world as Tora Bora.[49] At the conclusion of the Afghan War, bin Laden, along with a cohort of other jidahist groups, established a loose collection of al Qaeda training camps and networks.[50]

On returning to Saudi Arabia in late-1989, bin Laden continued raising money for his Afghan jihadist network, and exercised increasing levels of independence from the Saudi government until his activities in Yemen created so many problems that the Saudi government took his passport.[51] The foundation for bin Laden's growing hatred of America began with the presence of American soldiers in Saudi Arabia during the first Gulf War in 1990 and 1991.[52] After turning down bin Laden's offer to protect Saudi Arabia from Iraq, King Fahd bin Abdul Aziz Al Saud allowed the United States to base operations from Saudi Arabia.[53] It angered many Muslims and enraged bin Laden that King Fahd had allowed non-Muslims into the heart of Islam so that they could attack other Muslims.[54]

The final break with the Saudi government came after bin Laden got back his passport and went back to Pakistan in the spring of 1992. Contrary to expectations, he expressly opposed the Saudi government's action in Afghanistan by undermining the efforts of Saudi Prince Turki al-Faisal, the head of Saudi Arabia's intelligence service.[55] Unable to return to Saudi Arabia, bin Laden accepted the invitation of the Sudanese government and moved his family and operations to Sudan by the end of 1992.[56]

In Sudan, al Qaeda's mission changed when, following the bombing in Aden, Yemen that was aimed at American soldiers and killed two innocent bystanders, bin Laden's imam, Abu Hajer al-Iraqi, issued two *fatwas* (religious opinions issued by an Islamic scholar)—one authorized the killing of American soldiers and the other permitted the killing of innocent civilians.[57] As Lawrence Wright noted:

> Al-Qaeda would concentrate not on fighting armies but on killing civilians. The former conception of al-Qaeda as a mobile army of mujahideen that would defend Muslim lands wherever they were threatened was now cast aside in favor of a policy of permanent subversion of the West. The Soviet Union was dead and communism no longer menaced the margins of the Islamic world. America was the only power capable of blocking the restoration of the ancient Islamic caliphate, and it would have to be confronted and defeated.[58]

In bin Laden's view, America was not a mighty hegemon; rather, it was weak.[59]

Due to Egyptian pressure because of jihadist violence coming across its border with Sudan, the Saudi government finally stripped bin Laden of his citizenship and cut him off from his inheritance in the spring of 1994.[60] He was now a man without a country and without the family fortune that had allowed him to build the far-flung al Qaeda empire. The final insult came when the Sudanese government confiscated his remaining assets and, under pressure from the United States, told bin Laden to leave.[61] On May 18, 1996, bin Laden, his family, and his fellow jihadists left Sudan and flew to Afghanistan where he would eventually partner with the Taliban and become a household name in America.[62]

In August of 1996, bin Laden issued his first fatwa against America titled, "Declaration of War against the Americans Occupying the Land of the Two

Holy Places."[63] The fatwa seemed focused on expelling the U.S. military from Saudi Arabia and not on a broader war with America.[64] Specifically, bin Laden states:

> Clearly after Belief (Imaan) there is no more important duty than pushing the American enemy out of the holy land ...
>
> Terrorising you, while you are carrying arms on our land, is a legitimate and morally demanded duty. It is a legitimate right well known to all humans and other creatures. Your example and our example is like a snake which entered into a house of a man and got killed by him ...
>
> It is a duty now on every tribe in the Arab Peninsula to fight, Jihad, in the cause of Allah and to cleanse the land from those occupiers. Allah knows that there [sic] blood is permitted (to be spilled).[65]

In the fatwa, bin Laden casts the obligation to jihad in defensive terms, not in the more controversial offensive terms laid out by Qutb.

After joining forces in 1997, Zawahiri and bin Laden waged a broader war on America. On February 23, 1998, they issued a fatwa against America that stated: "To kill the Americans and their allies—civilians and military—is an individual duty for every Muslim who can do it *in any country in which it is possible to do it*" (emphasis added).[66] In quoting from the Quran, the fatwa noted the legitimacy of killing apostates: "But when the forbidden months are past, then fight and slay the pagans wherever ye find them, seize them, beleaguer them, and lie in wait for them in every stratagem (of war)."[67]

In encouraging Muslims to rise against the Americans and become martyrs for Islam, the fatwa, citing the Quran, included this threat of eternal punishment for failure to act:

> O ye who believe, what is the matter with you, that when ye are asked to go forth in the cause of Allah, ye cling so heavily to the earth! Do ye prefer the life of this world to the hereafter? But little is the comfort of this life, as compared with the hereafter. Unless ye go forth, He will punish you with a grievous penalty, and put others in your place; but Him ye would not harm in the least. For Allah hath power over all things.[68]

Ultimately, the fatwa laid the groundwork that inspired young, middle class Muslims to become suicide bombers, including the nineteen terrorists who executed the September 11 attack.

In the seventy years from al Banna's founding of the Muslim Brotherhood and Qutb's radical interpretation of the Quran to Zawahiri's and bin Laden's declared war against America, this new enemy, hardened in the rough terrain of Afghanistan against an overwhelmingly superior military force, challenged America and its institutions that had been built to fight traditional wars against traditional enemies using traditional weapons and subject to traditional warfare restrictions and traditional diplomatic pressures. Traditions would be of little use in this new era of terrorism.

THE GATHERING STORM

For almost ten years before the September 11 attack, bin Laden repeatedly attacked and killed Americans. Critically, bin Laden had come to believe that while America appeared strong militarily, in reality, that military strength concealed a fundamental weakness.[69] This belief was alluded to several times in the 1996 fatwa when bin Laden asked, "[W]here was this false courage of yours when the explosion in Beirut took place on 1983 A.D. (1403 A.H.). You were turned into scattered pits and pieces at that time; 241 mainly marines soldiers were killed."[70] This weakness is what led bin Laden to believe that America could be driven from the Middle East.

The first known bombing conducted by al Qaeda occurred on December 29, 1992, when terrorists detonated a bomb in the Gold Mohur Hotel in Aden, Yemen.[71] The hotel housed American soldiers en route to Somalia.[72] America did not respond to the bombing. Based on his 1996 fatwa, the Aden bombing was another example to bin Laden of America's unwillingness to incur casualties. The fatwa posed a rhetorical question to Secretary of Defense William Perry: "And where was this courage of yours when two explosions made you to leave Aden in lees [sic] than twenty four hours!"[73]

Shortly thereafter, on February 26, 1993, in an attempt to bring down two buildings and kill thousands of Americans, terrorists financed by al Qaeda via Khalid Sheikh Mohammed and led by his nephew Ramsi Yousef drove a van packed with explosives into the parking garage of Tower One of the WTC.[74] The explosion damaged Tower One, killed six people, and injured 1,042 victims.[75] This bombing represented the first modern-era large-scale terrorist attack on America soil. Other than law enforcement operations to apprehend and try the perpetrators, the United States did not militarily respond to the attack.

Later that year, in June 1993, the Federal Bureau of Investigation (FBI) stopped a plot targeting "major New York landmarks, including the Holland and Lincoln Tunnels."[76] The Farouq mosque in Brooklyn and its cleric, Sheikh Omar Abdel Rahman, served as common links between the first WTC attack and the "landmark" plot.[77] Rahman had served in prison with Zawahiri in Egypt the early-1980s following the Sadat assassination where the two fought over the correct way to foment an Islamic revolution.[78] The rivalry continued in the late-1980s in Pakistan over bin Laden's attention.[79]

While never directly linked to al Qaeda, the downing of two Black Hawk helicopters during the First Battle of Mogadishu in Somalia on October 3 and 4, 1993, again confirmed in bin Laden's mind his belief that America could not sustain casualties.[80] In the 1996 fatwa, bin Laden referred to the event as follows:

> But your most disgraceful case was in Somalia; where—after vigorous propaganda about the power of the USA and its post cold war leadership of the new world order—you moved tens of thousands of international force, including twenty eight thousands American solders into Somalia. However, when tens of your solders were killed in minor battles and one American Pilot was dragged in the streets of

Mogadishu you left the area carrying disappointment, humiliation, defeat and your dead with you. Clinton appeared in front of the whole world threatening and promising revenge, but these threats were merely a preparation for withdrawal. You have been disgraced by Allah and you withdrew; the extent of your impotence and weaknesses became very clear.[81]

Whether right or wrong, bin Laden believed that the perceived American response to Beirut, Aden, the first WTC attacks, and Mogadishu showed that the United States was a "weak horse."

In January 1995, another plot involving Mohammed and Yousef came to light via Philippine authorities.[82] The Manila plot involved simultaneously blowing up twelve airplanes heading toward America in mid-flight.[83] Although authorities eventually captured Yousef, Mohammed fatefully eluded the police and later served as the mastermind behind the September 11 attack.[84]

On November 13, 1995, al Qaeda disciples exploded a truck bomb at a Saudi Arabian National Guard center where Americans were training Saudi soldiers in Riyadh, Saudi Arabia.[85] The attack killed five American soldiers.[86] America did not respond.

Seven months later, on June 25, 1996, terrorists likely affiliated with al Qaeda detonated another truck bomb at the Khobar Towers complex in Dharhan, Saudi Arabia.[87] The attack killed nineteen American soldiers.[88] America did not respond to the Khobar Towers attack despite knowledge of al Qaeda connections to the attacks in Aden and Mogadishu, as well as the Manila incident.[89]

Then, on August 7, 1998, al Qaeda suicide bombers launched near-simultaneous truck bombs on the U.S. embassies in Nairobi, Kenya, and Dar es Salaam, Tanzania.[90] The bombs killed 240 people, including twelve American citizens.[91] The response from the United States consisted of bombing a pharmaceutical plant in Khartoum, Sudan, and two al Qaeda camps near Khost, Afghanistan.[92]

In December 1999, authorities in Jordan detected and stopped planned millennium attacks at three locations in Jordan aimed at American tourists.[93] Authorities in the United States also intercepted a planned millennium attack aimed at Los Angeles, California.[94]

Finally, just eleven months before the September 11 attack, on October 12, 2000, seventeen American soldiers were killed and massive damages were inflicted on a military ship when two al Qaeda terrorists exploded a bomb-laden boat next to the *U.S.S. Cole* in the harbor in Aden, Yemen.[95] Despite such a direct and damaging attack on a military target, America did not respond to the *U.S.S. Cole* attack. The failure to respond was best characterized by the State Department's Counterterrorism Coordinator Michael Sheehan's prophetic question posed to Department of Defense officials, "Does al Qaeda have to attack the Pentagon to get their attention?"[96]

In hindsight, these attacks represented a gathering storm to which America failed to recognize. As George Friedman pointed out: "Before September 11, there was a tendency to vastly underestimate Al Qaeda's capabilities. This was particularly true because of Al Qaeda's efficient use of simple technologies. After September 11, the United States flipped its evaluation, vastly overestimating them."[97]

THE SLEEPING GIANT AWAKENS

In January 2000, the first two of the nineteen al Qaeda members who would hijack the four jetliners arrived in Los Angeles, California.[98] Over the course of the next twenty months, the remaining seventeen al Qaeda members made their way to the United States and began the final phase of preparations. During this time, the terrorists lived among Americans in many different cities such as San Diego, California; Phoenix, Arizona; Alexandria, Virginia; Paterson, New Jersey; and Fort Lauderdale, Florida.[99] The terrorists attended flight schools where they learned to fly commercial airliners, and conducted multiple surveillance trips on coast-to-coast flights in preparation for the attack.[100] They had adopted Western dress and shaved their beards, and blended into the American "melting pot."

On September 11, 2001, al Qaeda finally got the attention it deserved when it struck America and killed 2,973 people.[101] As one government worker stated at 10:02 A.M. that morning, "This is a new type of war."[102] In his address to the American people that fateful day, President George W. Bush enunciated what would come to be known as the centerpiece of the Bush Doctrine: "We will make no distinction between the terrorists who committed these acts and those who harbor them."[103] Nine days later, President Bush remarked, "Tonight we are a country awakened to danger."[104] As the trail of attacks highlighted above indicates, that awakening should have occurred much sooner than September 2001, and the doctrine should have been known as the Clinton Doctrine.

Although the National Commission on Terrorist Attacks upon the United States (the 9/11 Commission) equivocated on the issue of whether the federal government could have prevented the September 11 attack, it seems fairly straightforward that it did too little based on what it knew. After all, if the federal government had enough information that allowed it on four separate occasions (1998, late-1999, fall 2000, and July 2001) to warn the Taliban "that they would be held accountable for further attacks by Bin Ladin," then certainly the *U.S.S. Cole* attack should have resulted in military strikes on the Taliban to demonstrate to them in a language they could understand that the United States was deadly serious.[105] As the 9/11 Commission noted about our warnings to the Taliban, "delivering it repeatedly did not make it more effective."[106] It simply fed into bin Laden's theory of the weak horse.

Just sixteen days after the September 11 attack, Secretary of Defense Donald Rumsfeld gave a speech titled, "A New Kind of War." Rumsfeld, a veteran of three presidents and holder of the distinction as both the youngest and oldest Secretary of Defense in America's history, stated flatly: "This will be a war like none other our nation has faced."[107] Within twenty-six days, American troops were in Afghanistan routing the Taliban and searching for bin Laden.

Although the enemy was new, America's history held lessons on how it should respond to this new kind of war.

2

A Short History of Civilian Defense in the United States

> In the councils of government, we must guard against the acquisition of unwarranted influence, whether sought or unsought, by the military-industrial complex. The potential for the disastrous rise of misplaced power exists and will persist.
> President Dwight D. Eisenhower[1]

> The powers not delegated to the United States by the Constitution, nor prohibited by it to the States, are reserved to the States respectively, or to the people.
> U.S. Constitution[2]

Throughout its history, Americans have faced many kinds of enemies. While the response to these enemies involved a military component, often times it also involved a civilian defense component. From colonial days to the Cold War, the civilian defense component combined centralized and decentralized elements. Importantly, it evolved from every home keeping and bearing arms to a professionalized force of first preventers and first responders. With this new kind of war, the role for these decentralized civilian defenders becomes significant.

In constructing the most effective and efficient means by which to prevent and to protect and, God forbid, respond to and recover from a terrorist attack within the United States, history holds lessons that we have heretofore failed to heed. From the Colonial period through the Cold War, citizens, in their own capacity and through states and localities, have answered the call time and time again to defend their rights to "Life, Liberty, and pursuit of Happiness."[3] Whether they shed blood, sweat, or tears, Americans have always been willing to "pay any price, bear any burden, meet any hardship, support any friend, oppose any foe, in order to assure the survival and the success of liberty."[4]

While critics certainly misstated President Bush's call to action on September 20, 2001, by claiming that all he asked Americans to do following the attack on September 11 was to "go shopping," the Bush Administration's record on civilian participation over the last eight years is thin. Other than a few grossly underfunded programs such as the Citizen Corps and the Community Emergency Response Team, as well as the Ready.gov Web site, very little has been done to meaningfully engage Americans in this Long War.

America repeatedly has faced threats to its existence. Its own birth arose violently from the bravery and commitment our Founding Fathers had in throwing off the shackles of the English King. We must look back at what has happened in our history, so that we can incorporate the lessons learned. Islamic jihadism, like monarchy, fascism, and communism before it, seeks a world in direct conflict with the American way of life. We have defeated those threats with arms, economic vitality, and a citizenry willing to serve and to sacrifice. This time should be no different.

THE COLONIAL PERIOD

On the colonization of North America, the early focus of civilian defense centered on settlers protecting themselves from attacks by Native Americans, which ranged from minor skirmishes to major conflicts such as the Pequot War.[5] One of the earliest and most famous attacks occurred on March 22, 1622, when the Powhatan Indians attacked the Jamestown settlement.[6]

Ignoring Laocoön's famous and unheeded warning as immortalized in Virgil's *Aeneid*—"Do not trust the horse, Trojans! Whatever it is, I fear the Greeks even bringing gifts"—the attackers entered the settlement on the previous day by bearing gifts.[7] The next day, in the midst of walking freely among the settlers, the attackers began their brutal and indiscriminate slaughter of 347 men, women, and children.[8]

In 1705, Robert Beverley, an early historian of Virginia, wrote that "all men were lulled into a fatal security and became everywhere familiar with the Indians—eating, drinking, and sleeping amongst them, by which means they became perfectly acquainted with all our English strength and the use of our arms, knowing at all times when and where to find our people, whether at home or in the woods, in bodies or dispersed, in condition of defense or indefensible."[9] This description is eerily reminiscent of the *modus operandi* of the September 11 attackers who carefully lived among us to learn our vulnerabilities. In response, the settlers organized and launched several attacks of their own against the Powhatan tribe.

When one colonial government failed to protect the settlers from the Native Americans, a group of small farmers led by Nathaniel Bacon took matters into their own hands and rebelled against the government and fought with the Native

Americans.[10] History recorded this act as Bacon's Rebellion. Civilian defense against the Native Americans throughout the thirteen colonies became the norm.

Eventually, oppression by the British government replaced the Native Americans as the focus of frustration among the colonists. Without the benefits of a professional army, each colony had its own militia composed of citizen soldiers. After the Battles of Lexington and Concord, the Second Continental Congress issued the following resolution:

> Resolved, That it be recommended to the inhabitants of all the united English Colonies in North America, that all able bodied effective men, between sixteen and fifty years of age in each colony, immediately form themselves into regular companies of Militia, to consist of one Captn, two lieutenants, one ensign, four serjeants, four corporals, one clerk, one drummer, one fifer, and about sixty-eight privates ...
>
> That each colony, at their own expense, make such provisions by armed vessels or otherwise, as their respective assemblies, conventions, or committees of safety shall judge expedient and suitable to their circumstance and situation, for the protection of their harbours and navigation on their sea coasts, against all unlawful invasions, attacks, and depredations, from cutters and ships of war ...
>
> Where in any colony a militia is already formed under regulations approved of by the convention of such colony, or by such assemblies as are annually elective, we refer to the discretion of such conventions or assembly, either to adopt the foregoing regulations in the whole or in part, or to continue their former, as they, on consideration of all circumstances, shall think best.[11]

Although this resolution predates the establishment of the United States under the Constitution where a much stronger federal role was established, it evidenced a firm commitment to decentralizing powers to the colonies. Most of the local organization of the citizenry within the colonies occurred through the various Committees of Correspondence and Safety, which acted as counter-governmental entities to the official British entities within the colonies.[12]

Throughout the Revolutionary War, the Continental Army itself largely consisted of men from across the colonies that answered Thomas Paine's call to revolution in *On Common Sense*, but at "no point did [Washington's] total forces number more than 60,000 men ... [who were] always short of everything."[13] Both the Second Continental Congress and the various colonial governments funded and supplied the Continental Army.[14]

After ratification of the Constitution, in recognition of the importance of each citizen taking responsibility for the security of the country, George Washington, in his *Letter to the Annual Meeting of Quakers* in September 1789, noted that "your principles and conduct are well known to me; and it is doing the people called Quakers no more than justice to say, that (*except their declining to share with others the burden of the common defense*) there is no denomination among us, who are more exemplary and useful citizens" (emphasis added). Washington knew that the very underpinnings of America's newly established rights, including religious freedom, were dependent on the willingness of the people to defend those rights. All citizens, therefore, were obliged to participate in the common defense of America.

Naturally, this obligation on the part of all Americans to engage in its common defense started with the Second Amendment and the right to bear arms preserved for the people therein. Although it may seem unthinkable today that Americans would have the need to bear arms against the government, the Founding Fathers understood all too well that government is only as good as those possessing its reins. The Second Amendment, as timeless as each of the other amendments within the Bill of Rights, ensures that America will not slip easily back into bondage.

As important, in support of the people's rights, on December 15, 1791, the ratification of the Tenth Amendment ensured that the states and the people would retain their historical powers over most aspects of their lives. Specifically, the Tenth Amendment clearly established that the states and the people would retain the powers that were not expressly granted to the federal government. This simple amendment is the cornerstone of American federalism, and provided state and local leaders the strongest basis on which to exert their inherent powers over their respective jurisdictions. For a majority of America's history, the Tenth Amendment surrounded the District of Columbia and countered the impulses of Washington politicians to federalize our lives.

Over the next hundred years, the primary components of defense included military forts along the frontier and civilians protecting themselves from Native Americans. Throughout this period of time, while certain areas within the United States faced external threats during the War of 1812 and the Mexican-American War, the rest of the country remained internally focused on westward expansion. The very nature of the Civil War involved civilian defense, but lessons from that war are difficult to discern given that it involved Americans fighting Americans.

WORLD WAR I

Despite the fact that World War I was the first truly global war, the fighting occurred mostly in Europe. The American homeland was not in much danger of being invaded or bombed. Nonetheless, on August 29, 1916, in the U.S. Army Appropriation Act of 1916, the Congress established the Council of National Defense.[15] The aim of the Council of National Defense was to gain the support of citizens by creating "anti-saboteur vigilance, encourag[ing] men to join the armed forces, facilitat[ing] the implementation of the draft, participat[ing] in Liberty Bond drives, and help[ing] to maintain the morale of the soldiers."[16]

In response to the federal Council of National Defense, states and localities created similar organizations, which became conduits through which government and the people communicated about the war.[17] These state and local councils directed "volunteer activities in the fields of public health, welfare, morale, economic stability, Americanization, and conservation and production of critical material."[18] The Council of National Defense provided guidance to state and local councils. By October of 1918, about 120,000 local councils and another 14,000 women Field Divisions existed across the United States. In addition, nineteen states started militia-like home guards for active defense in the event of an invasion by enemy forces.

This tri-level system with the federal level on top set a "precedent [that] greatly influenced subsequent civil defense planning."[19] Once the war ended on November 11, 1918, there was a quick dissolution of the state and local councils.

WORLD WAR II

With the onset of the Great Depression and the massive expansion of the federal government in response to that economic threat, questions remained as to what role states and localities would have in protecting the homeland during increasingly likely global conflicts. On July 31, 1940, Franklin D. Roosevelt's administration launched the Division of State and Local Cooperation to assist with the mobilization of the civilian population and its resources for war.

Many state and local leaders found the Division of State and Local Cooperation a useless bureaucracy, so they argued for the creation of an agency that possessed real powers. A report from the U.S. Conference of Mayors in 1940 noted that weapons did not "recognize State political boundaries any more than microbes do... for efficient organization it is simply out of the question to expect state agencies, restricted in their functioning to obsolete and archaic political boundaries, to handle the task."[20] While many states already had established state councils, President Roosevelt "advised state governors to re-establish state and local councils if they considered such action warranted."[21]

In response to pressure from states and localities, President Roosevelt issued Executive Order 8757 on May 20, 1941, that created the Office of Civilian Defense.[22] The Office of Civilian Defense was charged with "assisting States and through State Defense Councils... giving advice and suggestions to local communities about problems of organization and about programs."[23] The first leader was Fiorello La Guardia who agreed to the position only if he also could retain his job as Mayor of New York City.[24] Mayor La Guardia "immediately proceeded to organize on the basis that protection was the only important aspect of civilian defense; he dismissed the health, welfare, nutrition, child-care, housing, physical fitness, and similar programs as 'sissy stuff.'"[25]

In terms of communicating with states and localities, Mayor La Guardia sent substantial information to lower councils on a variety of issues, including "warning systems, protective shelter, and the training of air raid wardens, first-aid workers, rescue squads, auxiliary medical personnel, decontamination squads, auxiliary policeman, auxiliary firemen, and aircraft spotters."[26] Not surprisingly given the enduring nature of the capabilities, many of the capabilities Mayor La Guardia wanted states and localities to possess in 1941 became, after the September 2001 attack, critical capabilities in the Target Capabilities List (TCL). The TCL is a list of capabilities developed by first preventers, first responders, and officials from all levels of government that enables states and localities to prepare for a terrorist attack.

James M. Landis, Dean of the Harvard Law School, became the first full-time leader of the Office of Civilian Defense.[27] Approximately one month after the bombing of Pearl Harbor, Landis gave a speech on January 17, 1942, titled, "The Need for Civilian Protection."[28] In the speech, Landis stated:

> A second simple truth we must recognize is that the building of adequate civilian defense cannot be done overnight, and that we must prepare long in advance to meet new dangers that may rise from the shifting battle lines in the Pacific and Atlantic Oceans. Today we hold the enemy at a distance, by the Eternal, we shall continue to do so. But lines may change, battlegrounds shift fast, and we must now get ready to deal with whatever the swiftly-moving future may have in store.[29]

Noting the hard work that lay ahead, Landis then made the case for unified action based on federal control.

Landis acknowledged, "Subordination to unified authority and unified command has not hitherto characterized our political life [given that] we have distributed the political authority that we now must bring together among municipalities, counties, States, and the Federal government."[30] Because the enemy does not care for our political jurisdictions, Landis made the practical argument that blackout regulations (for example) could not change from jurisdiction to jurisdiction as such an approach would result in some areas being lit-up during an air raid.[31]

One of the key offices created to achieve preparedness goals was the Citizens Defense Corps.[32] The Citizens Defense Corps consisted of roughly ten million volunteers who learned such things as emergency firefighting, built shelters, and received training in evacuation and care of victims.[33] Another important program was the Civil Air Patrol,[34] which permitted civilian pilots to engage in coastal border patrol missions, as well as search and rescue operations.[35] The Civil Air Patrol continues to operate today with over 56,000 members who provide civil air support for special events and emergencies.

Throughout America, states, localities, and citizens organized many types of groups to help the war effort. One of the strongest was the Civilian War Services Branch, which was an agency of local government and funded entirely by local government.[36] These groups brought "together all elements of the community, all groups, agencies and individuals, so that the community as a whole [would], first, study, then plan and effect solutions of community problems created by the war; and second give maximum city-wide support to vital national war programs."[37] Unlike the customary low level of participation by citizens today, blackout drills occurred in most urban areas during World War II.[38]

The state groups also did not receive federal funds. By the end of 1943, it was estimated that there were over twelve million volunteers across America engaged in volunteer activities and "over 8,200 independent local Defense Councils, and in addition over 3,000 which are subsidiaries or branches of the others."[39] In his resignation letter in 1943, Landis noted that "the state and local defense councils could take responsibility for their civilian defense programs with *a minimum of national guidance*" (emphasis added).[40]

On May 4, 1945, President Harry Truman issued an executive order that abolished the Office of Civilian Defense as of June 30, 1945.[41] Shortly after the war ended, the state and local entities were discontinued as well.

THE COLD WAR

Just a year and a half later, due to the threat from the Soviet Union, the War Department launched a review of America's civilian defense capabilities.[42] One of the key findings from the *United States Strategic Bombing Survey Summary Report (Pacific War)* issued on July 1, 1946, was that the civilian defense measures that the Japanese put in place before the war "contributed substantially in minimizing casualties."[43] This finding spurred a review of America's civilian defense policies and capabilities.

In February 1948, the Civil Defense Board issued its report on America's civilian defense (referred to as the "Bull Report") containing, among others, three key assumptions:

1. The fundamental principle of civil defense is self-help;
2. Each level of government has responsibility for organizing, training, and equipping for civil defense including use of mutual aid devices; and
3. The major civil defense problems are not appropriately military responsibilities because such problems are civilian in nature and should be solved by civilian organization.[44]

With these assumptions, the Bull Report recommended that a separate Civil Defense Agency be established in the Department of Defense.[45] In response, the Secretary of Defense created the Office of Civil Defense Planning and charged it with preparing "a program of civil defense for the United States, including a plan for a permanent federal civilian defense agency."[46]

Contrary to the push for a federalized civilian defense capability, the Office of Civil Defense Planning issued a report (known as the "Hopley Report") that did "recommend the establishment of a national office," but only for providing "leadership and guidance in organizing and training the people" because the "basic operational responsibility [should] be placed on states and communities."[47] The Hopley Report included a model state civil defense act.[48] Hence, early on, the driving policy decision on civilian defense was to place the responsibility with governors and mayors.

Due to the recommendations in the Hopley Report, President Truman eliminated the Office of Civil Defense Planning and replaced it with an Assistant Secretary for Civil Defense Liaison who would coordinate civilian defense activities across the federal government, with states, localities, and the private sector.[49] Consistent with traditional defense activities and constitutional powers, the federal role in domestic protection focused on "detection, observation, and identification of aircraft, air raid warning systems, border patrol, anti-aircraft defense, civil air patrol, camouflage, and protection construction."[50] At the state and local level, many states enacted legislation to strengthen their civilian defense capabilities.[51]

Over the course of the Cold War, the federal agency charged with leading the civilian defense efforts became an alphabet soup of ever-changing names. In response to the detonation of the first nuclear device by the Soviet Union in 1949, President Truman created the Federal Civil Defense Administration, which took over the National Security Resources Board's mission.[52]

In the spring of 1950, the Congress held hearings on America's civilian defense capabilities, which concluded with a criticism from state and local leaders that is strikingly similar to the criticism heard today about the federal responses to the September 11 attack and Hurricane Katrina.[53] Namely, the state and local leaders leveled "their most emphatic criticism" at the delay in getting something done, as "they believed that too much time already had elapsed and that the Federal Government should release further information regarding the nature of the dangers to be faced and protection measures to be taken."[54]

In response, the Congress passed the Federal Civil Defense Act of 1950.[55] The Federal Civil Defense Act of 1950 gave the federal government the "authority for planning, sheltering, and evacuation and support to states and localities with planning, technical guidance and assistance, training, and a fifty-fifty matching grant for equipment."[56] As discussed later, the response to Islamic jihadists fifty-three years later was similar in some respects, but different in other respects. Those differences account for the current imbalance of power between the federal government and states and localities after September 11, 2001.

Rather than prioritizing civilian defense measures that could make some difference, the federal government aimed for the perfect solution. For example, knowing the loss of life that would occur if a nuclear weapon hit an American city, the federal government proposed building a nationwide system of shelters buried deep in the ground to hold the entire population of the United States.[57] The estimated cost of this one proposal was $300 billion, which in 1950 was an unfathomable amount of money.[58] As one commentator noted, "The disconnect between the perfect solution, what was possible, and the perception of how annual programs contributed to meeting either was to bedevil Civil Defense programs for the next three decades."[59] This struggle with making the perfect the enemy of the good also would hamper efforts after the September 11 attack in relation to the TCL and other critical programs.

During the 1950s, the building of bomb shelters, conducting citizen drills, and communicating information became the main focus of civilian defense actions. While psychologically reassuring, the popular drill that had schoolchildren hide under their desks would have done little to protect them from a nuclear attack. Other information came in the form of "Rules of Survival" as outlined in the 1950 issue of the *Bulletin of the Atomic Scientists*. The Rules of Survival were as follows:

1. Try to get shielded.
2. Drop flat on the ground or floor.
3. Bury your face in your arms.
4. Don't rush outside right after a bombing.
5. Don't take chances with food or water in open containers.
6. Don't start rumors.[60]

This information seems fairly basic today, but little was known about radiological exposure in 1950. The important point is that the government tried to provide citizens with some information on this emerging threat.

In 1961, the Office of Civil and Defense Mobilization became charged with the federal civilian defense mission.[61] The Congress later changed the name to the Office of Emergency Planning, which then became the Office of Emergency Preparedness. That entity changed names two additional times—first to the Office of Preparedness and then to the Federal Preparedness Agency.[62] Eventually, in 1979, President Jimmy Carter issued an executive order that merged many of the civilian defense disaster agencies and programs from across the federal government into Federal Emergency Management Agency (FEMA).[63]

The agencies and programs folded into FEMA included: the Federal Insurance Administration, the National Fire Prevention and Control Administration, the National Weather Service Community Preparedness Program, the Federal Preparedness Agency of the General Services Administration, the Federal Disaster Assistance Administration activities from Housing and Urban Development, and the Defense Department's Defense Civil Preparedness Agency.[64] As discussed in Chapter 3, this constant "reshuffling of the deck chairs" has its parallel in the federal responses to the September 11 attack and Hurricane Katrina as it relates to FEMA and the other primary federal entity—the Office for Domestic Preparedness (ODP)—charged with working with states and localities on civilian defense matters.

Throughout these name changes in the 1960s and early-1970s, the Vietnam War occupied the federal government and drained resources from other missions such as civilian defense. As a result, little was accomplished across the country in building a meaningful civilian defense capability.

Although the many name changes that occurred during the Cold War inject a certain level of levity to the issue, the reality was quite different. For the first time in almost two hundred years, Americans faced a clear and present danger to their lives and freedoms that required a viable civilian defense capability. As Soviet Premier Nikita Khrushchev famously uttered at a Moscow reception with western diplomats, "Whether you like it or not, history is on our side. We will bury you."[65]

Unlike the First and Second World Wars, the Cold War came with a very real possibility of a direct attack on the continental United States.[66] If it came, the attack would be in the form of nuclear weapons that would cause massive loss of life, physical destruction, and economic catastrophe. The stark truth facing Americans and the federal government during the Cold War was that we were largely unable to stop an attack once launched. Our civilian defense, therefore, focused solely on surviving the attack, minimizing the losses from an attack, and recovering from the effects of radiation.

THE ILLUSION OF PEACE

After the collapse of the Soviet Union in 1991, America spent the next decade on its "holiday from history" as it became the world's sole superpower. The economic boom of the 1990s caused most Americans to forget about the threats from outside of our borders and focus more on lattes and McMansions. Federal, state, and local budgets reached surpluses for the first time in decades, and government spending exploded.

As a reward for winning the Cold War, our military suffered substantial cuts under President Bill Clinton. The Clinton "peace dividend" resulted in defense spending of less than three percent of Gross Domestic Product.[67] As one expert noted: "The Clinton White House sent the military on a procurement 'holiday,' purchasing almost no new ships, tanks, or planes. The Army shrunk to its smallest size since World War II... Readiness levels were declared unacceptable."[68] Despite these massive cuts in defense spending, throughout the 1990s President Clinton deployed the military around the world—to Kosovo, Haiti, and the continued enforcement of the No Fly Zone over Iraq. Nonetheless, as the sole superpower with no challenger in sight, politicians with other spending priorities decided America just did not need to maintain its military strength.

We were warned that America's troubles were not over. Looking back, it is difficult to understand why the first WTC attack in 1993 did not serve as a sufficient warning that history had not gone on a holiday after all and that there would be no real peace for the United States. After all, Yousef and his fellow terrorists did try to bring down all 220 stories of the WTC. The mere fact that they actually were able to detonate a massive bomb in America was a success in itself. If they had used enough explosives or found a weaker structural element of the buildings, they would have been wildly successful.

In response to that successful attack, the federal government did little to nothing to restart our civilian defense activities. States and localities also failed to heed this warning. The federal government treated the 1993 WTC attack as a law enforcement/criminal justice matter, so failed to see it as a threshold event.

Demonstrative of our failure to comprehend the true threat, after the first WTC attack, New York City Mayor Rudy Giuliani made the fateful decision to relocate New York City's emergency operations center to the WTC complex, thereby ensuring that it would be without a command center "when it was needed most" for roughly seventy-two hours when the second strike came.[69] Specifically, as the 9/11 Commission noted in *The 9/11 Commission Report: Final Report of The National Commission on Terrorist Attacks upon the United States* (the *9/11 Commission Report*), "Some questioned locating it both so close to a previous terrorist target and on the 23rd floor of a building (difficult to access should elevators become inoperable). There was no backup site."[70]

So, roughly ten years after the end of the Cold War, the sleeping giant was stirred from its slumber by the September 11 attack. In response to the attack, the Congress created DHS, which absorbed FEMA and several other components charged with civilian defense missions. Policymakers faced many choices on how best to defend the homeland from the Islamic jihadists who were willing to die to inflict harm on Americans.

As America started to rebuild its civilian defense capability, would it heed the lessons from history and adapt the lessons for this new enemy and new kind of war? The answer came quickly.

3

The Limitations of Today's Washington-centric Model

> This Administration here and now declares unconditional war on poverty.
> President Lyndon B. Johnson[1]

> When government decides to solve something, we have learned to be wary. The cure may not always be worse than the disease, but it is usually bigger and it costs more.
> President Ronald W. Reagan[2]

The reaction to most crises today in the United States is increasingly to look to Washington for a solution. A flood occurs in Ohio. Where is FEMA? A bridge tragically collapses in Minnesota. Where is the Department of Transportation? Arizona's budget is bursting under the financial strain of illegal immigrants. Where is Immigration and Customs Enforcement (ICE)? Levies are growing old in California. Where is the Army Corps of Engineers? A family sadly lacks health care in West Virginia. Where is Medicaid? The list goes on and on.

Yet Washington's track record of success is poor. From education reform to welfare reform, the Washington-centric model has rarely led the way to a better tomorrow. If ever proof existed that the federal government possesses a structural inability to "get it right," the fact that over a year before the September 11 attack, the National Commission on Terrorism issued its report *Countering the Changing Threat of International Terrorism* in which "the Commission concluded that, although American strategies and policies are basically on the right track, significant aspects of implementation are seriously deficient."[3] Prophetically, the cover of the report contained a picture of the WTC.[4]

This finding that, but for implementation issues, American counterterrorism efforts were "basically on the right track"—just fifteen months later—would once again highlight the historical disconnect between perception and reality.

As the 9/11 Commission found: "We learned that the institutions charged with protecting our borders, civil aviation, and national security did not adjust their policies, plans, and practices to deter or defeat it."[5]

Even more revealing is that the report opened with this famous quote from Thomas C. Schelling:

> Surprise, when it happens to a government, is likely to be a complicated, diffuse, bureaucratic thing. It includes neglect of responsibility but also responsibility so poorly defined or so ambiguously delegated that action gets lost. It includes gaps in intelligence, but also intelligence that, like a string of pearls too precious to wear, is too sensitive to give to those who need it. It includes the alarm that fails to work, but also the alarm that has gone off so often it has been disconnected. It includes the unalert watchman, but also the one who knows he'll be chewed out by his superior if he gets higher authority out of bed. It includes the contingencies that occur to no one, but also those that everyone assumes somebody else is taking care of. It includes straightforward procrastination, but also decisions protracted by internal disagreement. It includes, in addition, the inability of individual human beings to rise to the occasion until they are sure it is the occasion—which is usually too late. (Unlike movies, real life provides no musical background to tip us off to the climax.) Finally, as at Pearl Harbor, surprise may include some measure of genuine novelty introduced by the enemy, and possibly some sheer bad luck.[6]

Schelling's remarks come from the Foreward in Roberta Wohlstetter's *Pearl Harbor: Warning and Decision*, which is one of the best reviews of America's capabilities leading up to the Pearl Harbor attack on December 7, 1941. This powerful quote applies with equal force to the events of September 11, 2001, as it did to the Pearl Harbor attack some sixty years earlier. Despite the singular use of explosives in the two terrorist attacks in the United States and the multiple terrorist attacks at American assets abroad, the 2000 report spends much of its time focused on an attack using chemical, biological, nuclear, or radiological weapons.

Some will argue that the federal government must be doing something right given the lack of an attack in America since the September 11 attack. On this point, history provides some guidance. Recall that prior to the September 11 attack, the last successful terrorist attack in America by a foreign terrorist organization occurred over *eight* years earlier. The enemy is patient. Very patient. Would anyone seriously argue that the lack of a successful terrorist attack in America during those eight years was due to efforts made by the federal government? The *9/11 Commission Report* undermines that argument.

That being said, the federal government has put in place some capabilities and programs that have made America more secure. Many of those capabilities and programs are discussed below. It should receive credit for those actions. In too many cases, however, the federal government is failing to perform as expected and successes seem few and far between. In other areas, however, a different approach than the one currently being taken is not only likely to achieve greater success, but frankly is the only way to honor the Constitution and secure America.

So, what happened domestically after the September 11 attack?

THE FEDERAL GOVERNMENT GROWS AND RESHUFFLES

Although the necessary changes did not occur in the ten years leading up to the September 11 attack, it did not take long following the attack for the federal government to respond domestically to this new kind of enemy and war. By early October 2001, the White House created the Homeland Security Council to coordinate the federal entities that had responsibilities for securing the homeland.[7] In his remarks to the Congress, President Bush named Pennsylvania Governor Tom Ridge as the head of the Homeland Security Council, which would serve in parallel to the National Security Council.[8]

On October 26, 2001, the Congress passed and President Bush signed into law the Uniting and Strengthening America by Providing Appropriate Tools Required to Intercept and Obstruct Terrorism Act of 2001 (PATRIOT Act).[9] The PATRIOT Act greatly enhanced the federal government's ability to prevent terrorism by using more aggressive surveillance techniques such as delayed notification search warrants, roving wiretaps, and National Security Letters.[10] The PATRIOT Act also included anti-money laundering provisions, increased resources for border security, and new intelligence activities.[11]

In July 2002, the federal government released the first version of the National Strategy for Homeland Security.[12] The strategy stated, "Homeland security is a concerted national effort to prevent terrorist attacks within the United States, reduce America's vulnerabilities to terrorism, and minimize the damage and recover from attacks that do occur."[13] It identified one purpose, three objectives, eight principles, six mission areas, forty-three major initiatives, and four foundations.[14]

Fourteen months after the September 11, 2001, attack, the Congress passed the Homeland Security Act of 2002 and President Bush, who first perhaps wisely opposed the creation of DHS, signed the legislation into law on November 25, 2002, which reorganized the federal government and created DHS.[15] This reorganization represented the largest shuffling of federal homeland security entities since the creation of FEMA in 1979.

As a precursor of things to come, FEMA and its head Joe Allbaugh fought to keep FEMA out of DHS and tried to takeover ODP. When Allbaugh lost those battles, he left FEMA, only to be replaced by his long-time friend, Michael Brown. Brown's sum total of emergency management experience consisted of his year and a half as Allbaugh's right-hand man. The early skirmishes and elevation of Brown laid the foundation for the troubled relationship between FEMA and DHS, which would come to a head during the response to Hurricane Katrina.

The twenty-two components that had been located in other departments or agencies included the Customs Service; the Immigration and Naturalization Service; the Federal Protective Service; the Transportation Security Administration (TSA); the Federal Law Enforcement Training Center; the Animal and Plant Health Inspection Service; ODP; FEMA; the Strategic National Stockpile/National Disaster Medical System; the Nuclear Incident Response Team; the Domestic Emergency Support Team; the National Domestic Preparedness Office; the Chemical, Biological, Radiological, and Nuclear Countermeasures Program; the Environmental Measures Laboratory; the National Bio-weapons Defense Analysis Center; the Plum Island Animal Disease Center; the Federal Computer Incident Response Center; the National Communications System; the National Infrastructure Protection Center; the Energy Security and Assurance Program; the Secret Service; and the Coast Guard.[16] These twenty-two entities would be merged and organized into four directorates or maintained as direct reports to the Secretary.

In January 2003, President Bush invoked his powers under section 872 of the Homeland Security Act of 2002 to "reconfigure the functions of certain border security agencies into two new components—the Bureau of Customs and Border Protection and the Bureau of Immigration and Customs Enforcement—within the department's Border and Transportation Security Directorate."[17] This use of section 872, much to the Congress's disdain, would establish a crucial mechanism for Executive Branch action.

On March 1, 2003, DHS started operating as the newest federal department. The new department consisted of 179,241 employees with a budget of $27.1 billion.[18] Although the Secret Service and the Coast Guard directly reported to the Secretary and the Citizenship and Immigration Services (CIS) office reported to the Deputy Secretary, the remaining entities became components in one of four directorates overseen by an Under Secretary.[19] The Border and Transportation Security Directorate included four key components: Customs and Border Protection (CBP), ICE, TSA, and ODP.[20] FEMA became the only major component of the Emergency Preparedness and Response Directorate.[21] The Information Analysis and Infrastructure Protection Directorate housed the Information Analysis and the Infrastructure Protection offices.[22] The remaining directorates were the Science and Technology Directorate and the Management Directorate, which were also led by Under Secretaries.[23]

Just under a year later, on January 26, 2004, Secretary Ridge reorganized DHS by taking ODP and its $3.5 billion budget from Border and Transportation Security and consolidating it with a small group of seventeen employees who served as the communication link to states and localities, as well as a few grant programs from FEMA and TSA.[24] The new entity—the Office of State and Local Government Coordination and Preparedness—reported directly to Secretary Ridge.[25] The purpose of the consolidation was to create a "one-stop-shop" for homeland security grants and terrorism preparedness programs so that states and localities would not have to navigate several DHS components for terrorism preparedness assistance.[26] Once again, FEMA, led by Brown, expended enormous effort fighting Secretary Ridge's actions, but lost.

A little over a year later, under the new leadership of Secretary Michael Chertoff, DHS launched the Second Stage Review in March 2005 as a "systemic evaluation of the Department's operations, policies, and structures."[27] Secretary Chertoff announced the results of the Second Stage Review on July 13, 2005, which would occur via the section 872 authority and statutory changes made by the Congress.[28] The proposed organizational changes included eliminating the Border and Transportation Security Directorate and making CPB, ICE, and CIS direct reports; unifying the department's preparedness functions centered around ODP under a new Under Secretary for Preparedness; making the Information Analysis component a direct report to the Secretary and moving the Infrastructure Protection piece to the Under Secretary for Preparedness; creating an Under Secretary for Policy; and eliminating the Emergency Preparedness and Response Directorate and making FEMA a direct report to the Secretary.[29]

As expected, FEMA and Brown spent considerable time and resources opposing the proposed changes. The outcome, however, remained the same. The changes were not scheduled to become effective until October 1, 2005.[30] Because of Hurricane Katrina and congressional interference, however, the full reorganization did not occur.

Following Hurricane Katrina, the Congress initiated yet another reorganization of DHS when it ironically validated Brown—who it had spent months vilifying—and moved all preparedness elements to FEMA except the IP element, which became effective on April 1, 2007.[31] The justification for the reorganization centered in part on a mistaken belief that FEMA's performance during Hurricane Katrina was due to the movement of preparedness programs out of FEMA. Because the Second Stage Review changes had not occurred as of the time Hurricane Katrina struck the Gulf Coast, nothing substantively had changed at FEMA.

As discussed more fully in Chapter 7, FEMA's poor response to Hurricane Katrina was entirely consistent with its history of poor responses to previous catastrophic disasters such as Hurricane Andrew in 1992 and Hurricane Floyd in 1999. The emergency management community and FEMA advocates in the Congress merely used the poor response to Hurricane Katrina to get what they had tried and failed to get in 2002–2003, which was ODP and its multibillion dollar grant, training, and exercise programs. Even today, almost eight years after September 11, 2001, and after getting control of ODP, FEMA advocates still aim to move FEMA out of DHS and make it once again report directly to the President.

More recently, in October 2007, the Homeland Security Council released the latest version of the National Strategy for Homeland Security.[32] Unfortunately, the new document reads more like a public relations piece than a true reformulation of America's national strategy after five years of experience. The document is short on innovation and creativity and long on recycled clichés.

For now, the reshuffling of the deck chairs at DHS seems to have subsided.

FIVE YEARS AND COUNTING

After five years, multiple reorganizations, and well over a $210 billion combined budget, the sober reality is that DHS still struggles to accomplish its mission of efficiently and effectively protecting America. Many attempt to defend the sluggish pace of progress by comparing the stand-up of DHS to the creation of the Department of Defense in 1947. The problem with this comparison is that it conveniently ignores the fifty years of technological progress that transpired, especially the arrival of the computer.

With the aid of the modern computer and related software capabilities, merging DHS arguably should have been substantially easier than the birth of the Department of Defense. The fact that that has not been the case should lead to one of three conclusions: there is simply widespread incompetence, the department as constructed is inherently unmanageable, or it is the result of a combination of both incompetence and unwieldiness. Based on the discussion that follows, option three seems to be the winner.

A recent report from the Inspector General (IG) for DHS noted "major management challenges" in nine key areas: "Catastrophic Disaster Response and Recovery; Acquisition Management; Grants Management; Financial Management; Information Technology Management; Infrastructure Protection; Border Security; Transportation Security; [and] Trade Operations and Security."[33] With so many moving pieces, it really should be no surprise that DHS remains a great idea theoretically, but far less in reality.

One of the key problems causing DHS to stumble in its various missions is that the current structure and missions are too broad for any one organization and leadership team to successfully manage. Between the substantive programs and the procedural requirements of running such a large enterprise, having so much to do ensures that very little gets done or gets done well. When political appointees with little or no experience are thrown into the mix and, at times, thrown in well above their competency level, success may be a bridge too far.

In terms of process problems, the IG noted several key areas where DHS faces challenges that simply require a dedication of time, resources, and, most importantly, competent leadership. For example, as noted, "financial management has been a significant challenge for DHS since its creation in 2003. This year, the independent auditors, KPMG LLP (KPMG), under contract with the OIG will be unable again to complete an audit of the DHS consolidated balance sheet and Statement of Custodial Activity as of and for the year ended September 30, 2007. In addition, KPMG noted that numerous material weaknesses in internal control continued to exist."[34] DHS finally took steps in late 2006 to fix these longstanding deficiencies.[35] It simply is inexcusable that it took three years of financial management failure and material weakness findings for necessary changes to be made.

In terms of procurement capabilities, the IG found that "DHS has made limited progress in ensuring financial oversight and accountability within the acquisition function. DHS financial information is generally unreliable, and financial systems do not have the internal controls and integration that acquisition personnel require. Also, the acquisition and finance offices have not successfully partnered on acquisition planning and strategic decision-making."[36] Without a functioning procurement system, DHS will not be able to leverage the technology and innovation necessary to perform its missions.

Finally, information technology limitations continue to undermine operational excellence. As the IG stated, "We continued to identify problems with outdated or stove-piped systems, at times supporting inefficient business processes. Planning to modernize IT was unfocused, often with inadequate requirements identification, analysis, and testing to support acquisition and deployment of the systems and other technologies needed to improve operations. We also found consideration of privacy matters to be lacking for some IT programs."[37]

In addition to the many destabilizing reorganizations and lack of progress in key management areas, the senior leadership turnover at DHS also contributes significantly to the functional limitations. A look at nine senior leadership positions illustrates the churn problem. Specifically, the number of people who served as Secretary, Deputy Secretary, TSA Administrator, Grants Director, CPB Commissioner, ICE Commissioner, CIS Commissioner, Chief Financial Officer, and Chief Procurement Officer for six months or more totals thirty-one as of August 2008, which translates to roughly six new leaders each year.

As anyone who has worked in Washington knows, each leadership change brings with it a new set of priorities and a "not invented here" mentality. As a result, the bureaucracy has adapted to the constant state of flux. This adaptation tends to take the form of benign neglect of new priorities, but also surfaces as intentional delay tactics and, on occasion, hostile opposition. After all, the civil service system, although good in many respects, protects even the most incompetent and belligerent employees.

In addition to these procedural problems, DHS has made too little progress in some key mission areas where it properly has the lead.

SOME MISSIONS ARE FEDERAL

Substantively, as the 9/11 Commission correctly noted, "The United States should consider *what to do*—the shape and objectives of a strategy. Americans should also consider *how to do it*—organizing their government in a different way."[38] In response to this call to reorganize the government to defeat this new enemy, a commitment to give true meaning to America's federalism principles must be made. That commitment requires us to assign roles and responsibilities in a manner that is most effective, efficient, and most closely adheres to the Constitution.

As to the federal government's roles and responsibilities, the Constitution expressly establishes the key roles and responsibilities vis-à-vis homeland security. First, in Article I, section 8, the Constitution states that the "Congress shall have the Power" to "regulate Commerce with foreign Nations," "establish an uniform Rule of Naturalization," "make Rules concerning Captures on Land and Water," and "make Rules for the Government and Regulation of the land and naval forces."[39] Secondly, the Fourteenth Amendment states that "all persons born or naturalized in the United States, and subject to the jurisdiction thereof, are citizens of the United States and of the State wherein they reside."[40] These powers include the regulation of international cargo security, citizenship and visa policy, border security, and control of America's waterways.

The 9/11 Commission also provides a road to follow; namely, it identifies that the "challenge for national security in an age of terrorism is to prevent the very few people who pose overwhelming risks from entering or remaining in the United States undetected."[41] A concomitant challenge is "to prevent the very few [things that] pose overwhelming risks from entering or remaining in the United States undetected."[42] These two interrelated challenges, therefore, should become the primary focus of DHS.

This focus places an emphasis on five key missions: securing borders and waterways, securing transportation modes, securing commerce, securing identities, and securing critical infrastructure. Operationally for DHS, these missions involve CBP, the Coast Guard, TSA, the Domestic Nuclear Detection Office, ICE, and CIS. By narrowing the focus of DHS to these five critical missions, DHS can dedicate its finite resources in a manner that ensures the proper level of funding, people, assets, and managerial oversight. As discussed below, the other mission areas should become secondary focuses of the federal government as states and localities take the lead.

In the Herculean task of securing America's borders and waterways, although much has been done, much remains to be done. After doing little to secure the northern and southern land borders, CBP finally received the funding it needed to hire additional border patrol agents, strengthen ports of entry, and build additional infrastructure, including fencing. With the rollout of the Secure Border Initiative program in 2006, CBP is seeking to leverage technology to build a virtual fence along the 6,000 miles of land border where a physical fence may be unworkable. The results so far, however, are not encouraging.

On the waterfront, the Coast Guard is attempting to recover from years of budget shortfalls to resupply its water and air assets. The Coast Guard's Integrated Deepwater program is already over budget and behind schedule in achieving that aim. The Coast Guard must control the "marine areas under U.S. jurisdiction [that] cover 3.5 million square miles of ocean, 95,000 miles of coastline, and 26,000 miles of commercial waters."[43] As the land border becomes harder to cross, enemies and criminals will attempt to reach the United States via the water. This heightened activity will require even greater effort and coordination between CBP and the Coast Guard.

The mission assigned to TSA to secure our transportation modes is enormous and difficult to do in a decentralized manner. Given the significant number of international airports across the United States that serve as the entry point for millions of foreign travelers every year, a federal lead is required. The 9/11 Commission summarized it best when it stated:

> The U.S. transportation system is vast and, in an open society, impossible to secure completely against terrorist attacks. There are hundreds of commercial airports, thousands of planes, and tens of thousands of daily flights carrying more than half a billion passengers a year....
>
> About 6,000 agencies provide transit services through buses, subways, ferries, and light-rail service to about 14 million Americans each weekday.[44]

Because transportation systems are inherently sums of the various parts that make up the system, a weakness in one part renders the entire system vulnerable. It is, therefore, critical that one entity oversees these complex and intricate systems. With its responsibility for air passenger, air cargo, rail, and mass transit security, TSA still must make enormous strides before those systems are secure. It alone presents its leadership and DHS's leadership with enough challenges to keep them busy.

A close partner of TSA in securing the U.S. transit systems is the Domestic Nuclear Detection Office. One of its key initiatives is to design and deploy a domestic nuclear detection capability in key high-risk areas, including transit systems and major trucking arteries. Unfortunately, this program is plagued with both technological and managerial problems. This effort, once the challenges are overcome and it is fully operational, will serve as a strong deterrent to terrorists seeking to acquire radioactive isotopes for release or detonation in a major American city.

In terms of the security of commerce, both CBP and the Coast Guard play vital roles. Shortly after the September 11 attack, CBP created, implemented, and expanded the Container Security Initiative and Customs-Trade Partnership Against Terrorism programs, which fundamentally allowed CBP to push America's borders from domestic ports to foreign ports.[45,46] This additional buffer gives CBP the opportunity to utilize the Advanced Targeting System to screen and inspect cargo containers before the containers are loaded onto container vessels and sent to the United States.[47]

With the addition of CBP's 24-hour rule requiring manifest data before a container can be loaded on a vessel and the Coast Guard's 96-hour Advance Notice of Arrival rule for vessels approaching American ports, the structure now exists to layer on technology. CBP must make progress on the faltering Secure Freight Initiative, including its 10 + 2 rule, and deploy working radiation portal monitors and other invasive and non-invasive screening capabilities to increase significantly the security of America's commerce. Such a task is no small feat given that America's ports "account for two billion tons and $800 billion of domestic and international freight annually. Approximately 8,000 foreign vessels, manned by 200,000 foreign sailors, make more than 50,000 ship visits to U.S. ports each year."[48] Between the security of America's borders and waterways and the security of its commerce, CBP and the Coast Guard, like TSA, require dedicated management teams and significant support from DHS leadership.

As for securing identities, nothing is more critical than first knowing who is in America living and working legally. Constitutionally, the federal government sets the requirements for citizenship, naturalization, refuge, asylum, and visa policies. The federal government's historical performance problems in executing in these areas must end. The problems include: (1) a backlog of applications and petitions; (2) a failure to enforce existing laws for those who overstay their visas and the employers who hire those individuals; and (3) a lack of control and visibility over who among us are citizens, visa recipients, and holders of green cards. The responsibility to fix these problems rests largely on CIS and ICE.

Although ICE has made some progress over the last two years in enforcing existing laws by cracking down on employers who employ illegal workers and by detaining and removing foreigners who overstay their visas, CIS remains dysfunctional. Nonetheless, it plays a vital role in fixing America's flawed legal immigration system. Beyond deploying technology to bring CIS into the twenty-first century, the Congress needs to provide the funds so that CIS can put in place the resources to eliminate backlogs and process all future applications and petitions in six months or less.

America cannot expect to compete in a competitive global environment if the world's best and brightest cannot easily come to America to fill unmet needs in our technology sectors. Similarly, ICE must continue to aggressively punish scofflaw employers, build detention facilities to house violators awaiting deportation, and utilize all means to simplify and shorten the removal process. The Congress needs to ensure that laws make it as easy as possible to deport illegal immigrants. Although we should ensure they receive minimal due process so as to meet constitutional requirements, we should not burden ICE, the judicial system, and our diplomatic corps by giving illegal immigrants due process that they are not entitled to receive.

With the continued strengthening of the U.S. VISIT program, the launch of the E-Verify system, the roll-out of the Transportation Worker Identification Credential, and the eventual implementation of the Real ID Act, a future in which the federal government knows who is in America as citizens or visitors and who is employed in America is not far off. These efforts will ensure that the security of our physical identities is strong.

The security of our critical information technology infrastructure is a beast unto itself. Current estimates set the number of cyber attacks on U.S. government information technology systems at roughly 12,986 in Fiscal Year (FY) 2007.[49] Many of those attacks originate in China on behalf of the Chinese government as espionage efforts.[50] Similarly, cyber thieves troll the Internet every day aiming to steal the personal and financial information of Americans so they can gain physical identification or buy goods illegally. Even more troubling is the rise of cyber jihadists who use the Internet to foment and to commit jihad.

In January 2008, British security services apprehended Younes Tsouli who operated under the *nom de plume* of *Irhabi* (terrorist) 007 and is believed to be one of the top cyber jihadists for al Qaeda.[51] Tsouli would hack into Web sites and unbeknown to the owners use those sites to post terrorist videos from Iraq.[52] He once hacked into and posted a video of bin Laden on a Web site owned by the state of Arkansas.[53] Experts continually note the increased use of the Internet to organize, plan, and launch terrorist attacks.[54]

In light of the risks, DHS's cyber security efforts thus far are troubling. As the DHS IG found:

> Specifically, the division has not (1) established priorities to ensure that its mission-critical tasks supporting its programs are completed timely; (2) developed enhanced performance measures that can be used to evaluate effectiveness in meeting its mission; (3) fully developed its information sharing and communications programs with the private sector; [or] (4) developed and implemented enhanced procedures to ensure that all known cyber incidents from across the federal government are reported.[55]

Greater progress must be made to secure America's information technology systems and the identities of its citizens online.

Another key area where a federal lead makes sense from both an efficiency and effectiveness standpoint, as well as from an interstate regulatory aspect, is the security of America's critical infrastructure and key resources. In February 2005, DHS released the Interim National Infrastructure Protection Plan, which "outlines how DHS and its stakeholders will develop and implement the national effort to protect infrastructures across all sectors."[56] The plan acknowledged the inability of the federal government to do it alone; specifically, the plan states that "this is an effort that requires the integrated, coordinated support of Federal departments and agencies; State, local, and tribal entities; and public and private sector asset owners and operators."[57]

Sixteen months later, DHS released the Final National Infrastructure Protection Plan, which "sets forth a comprehensive risk management framework and clearly defined roles and responsibilities for the Department of Homeland Security; Federal Sector-Specific Agencies; and other Federal, State, local, tribal, and private sector security partners."[58] More importantly, roughly one year later, the Secretary approved the seventeen sector-specific plans that address "the unique risk characteristics" of each sector.[59] The seventeen sectors are agriculture and food; banking and finance; chemical; commercial facilities; communications; dams; defense industrial base; government facilities; emergency services; energy; information technology; national monuments and icons; nuclear reactors, materials and waste; postal and shipping; public health and healthcare; transportation systems; and water.[60]

As auditors noted, DHS still needs to complete vital work in the chemical, transportation, and agriculture and food sectors.[61] Similarly, "DHS also could do more to prioritize resources and activities based on risk."[62] Nonetheless, DHS has made progress in securing America's critical infrastructures and key resources, largely due to the truly collaborative approach taken with the private sector with the drafting and release of the final plan and the sector-specific plans.

Under the leadership of the agencies, programs, and initiatives noted above, the federal government is making solid progress in securing America's borders and waterways, securing its transportation modes, securing commerce, securing identities, and securing critical infrastructure. Constitutionally, this federal lead is justified. Given all of the key programs and continued poor performance, it is critical that the leadership at the federal level focus on making sure that changes are made to get the ship righted.

Another well-publicized obstacle to success for DHS is the inefficient and burdensome oversight from the Congress. Even though accountability and transparency are a vital part of government, the Congress, despite the recommendation from the 9/11 Commission, has failed to reform its oversight of DHS. As a result, 86 different congressional committees have a role in monitoring DHS.[63] As Secretary Chertoff noted, "Over the last year my colleagues and I have been called to testify 224 times; that averages to about four times a week. Since the department's creation, DHS officials have testified 761 times, provided roughly 7,800 written reports and answered more than 13,000 questions for the record."[64] Each hearing, report, and question requires an elaborate review and preparation process involving countless staff and senior leadership input and countless hours.

There is only a finite amount of time, people, and money available to work on the complex and necessary programs noted above. A more constitutional distribution of work between the federal government and states and localities must be reached. In some areas, the current federal government lead is simply unjustified, unsustainable, and constitutionally weakest. States and localities are better positioned to make progress both in terms of resources, competencies, and constitutional authority.

SOME MISSIONS ARE BETTER SUITED FOR STATES AND LOCALITIES

There is an undeniable reality that makes a Washington-centric approach a bad choice in certain situations. Where wide variations in challenges and needs exist (i.e., "one size fits all" fits few well) and where urgency of action is vital (i.e., bureaucratic process kills), the ability of effective action and leadership from Washington is fatally impacted. The key deficiencies are due to the geographic size and diversity of the United States and the minimal manpower the federal government controls across America. This reality holds true when it comes to developing the right capabilities in the right places at the right levels, to responding to both natural and manmade disasters, to controlling illegal immigration in the interior of the country, and to gathering information and intelligence and acting on it operationally.

When it comes to capabilities, the sheer diversity in size, populations, population densities, presence of critical infrastructure and key resources, and threat levels in the urban, suburban, and rural areas across America is enormous, thereby creating massive variations in challenges faced by those areas and needs in this post-September 11 and Hurricane Katrina environment. Just think of the differences between Dyersville, Iowa, and New York City and you get the idea.

These profound deviations result in ineffective DHS interactions with states and localities. The Congress and DHS have passed down mandate after mandate, requirement after requirement, and half-baked measure after half-baked measure that show little respect for state and local partners. Even worse, the federal "one size fits all" approach fails to take into account these wide differences of challenges and needs across America.

The sum result of these inconsistent approaches and efforts is that states and localities have made too little progress in building capabilities. Why might you ask is that Washington's fault? As discussed more fully in Chapter 6, Washington is to blame because prior to forcing down all of those mandates, requirements, and half-baked ideas, it failed to develop sound programmatic grant management and financial oversight capabilities internally and failed to work closely with state and local partners to put in place similar capabilities. Shortly after the September 11 attack, Congress opened the floodgates and appropriated billions of federal funds for states and localities. Without any infrastructure or useful guidance from DHS on how to handle this massive influx of funds and requirements, they became overwhelmed.

As a result of these failures, precious time and resources have been wasted. As reported by the DHS IG in 2008, "Our audits have reported on the states' inability to effectively manage and monitor these funds and demonstrate and measure improvements in domestic security. Our reports also pointed out the need for DHS to monitor the preparedness of state and local governments, grant expenditures, and grantee adherence to the financial terms and conditions of the awards."[65] Five years of failure is too long, we must change how we build capabilities in the United States.

Fortunately, DHS did lay the foundation on which to build this new approach to building resiliency. Unfortunately, it then ignored that work. As described in full in Chapter 6, DHS spent a considerable amount of resources to work collaboratively with states and localities and other stakeholders to develop the TCL. Using the TCL as the foundation, a true partnership among levels of government to secure the homeland in a prioritized manner can be developed and implemented. Under this partnership, DHS can help build the programmatic and financial oversight infrastructure, provide guidance on technical issues, and coordinate cross-jurisdictional activities where necessary. Meanwhile, states and localities can take the lead in identifying what capabilities they need and get to work putting those capabilities in place.

As every emergency management professional has stated countless times, "all disasters are local." The point being made, of course, is that when a disaster hits, it hits a local community and the first responders by necessity come first from the local community, come next from neighboring communities, followed by the state, followed by the states in the region, and finally followed by the federal government. Of all types of disasters, only one—a hurricane—provides advance notice, allowing the federal government to be useful in the first hours of the disaster.

This mindset led to the all-hazards approach to disasters favored by the emergency management community. The problem, however, was that the all-hazards approach lacked a methodology or architecture. It offered no specifics as to what is or would be needed. After the September 11 attack, the nation needed a way to shape and size its homeland security efforts. The TCL provided the specifics of what is needed to perform the actions outlined in our strategies and plans.

Yet, as discussed in Chapter 7, over the last sixteen years, the push to federalize as many disasters as possible has gotten stronger and stronger with each passing year. This development has resulted in two key interrelated problems. First, the federalization of routine natural disasters has created a disincentive at the state and local level to invest in and build disaster capabilities. After all, if Washington will get involved and pay for it, why should governors and mayors not push for greater federal involvement? The reason, of course, is that should something beyond the routine occur, those states and localities will be woefully unprepared to deal with the disaster and Washington, as noted above, will not be able to do much when it really matters.

The second problem is that, as FEMA finds itself consumed by every disaster that has occurred in the United States no matter how routine, it squanders finite resources that are needed to build capabilities to deal with catastrophic disasters. As the IG concluded, "attempts to plan for an event such as Hurricane Katrina had been ongoing since 1998, but were never completed for a variety of reasons, including a lack of federal funding, other natural disasters occurring, and the terrorist attacks of September 11, 2001."[66] As a result, FEMA continues to be plagued by "major management challenges in preparing to meet future catastrophic disasters [in] the following areas: (1) coordination of disaster response efforts, (2) catastrophic planning, (3) logistics, (4) acquisitions, (5) housing, and (6) evacuation."[67]

Hurricane Katrina demonstrated these problems vividly.

We must reverse this centralization of disaster management and return to the more decentralized approach where states and localities are held entirely responsible for noncatastrophic disasters. The federal government then can focus its resources on the six areas noted above, which must be addressed before the next catastrophic disaster strikes the United States.

As discussed in Chapter 8, whether the city is Phoenix, Arizona, or Hazelton, Pennsylvania, once an illegal immigrant has evaded the federal capabilities at America's borders or in its visa processes, that illegal immigrant is living in a city in a state where he is working, taking from the public dole, or committing crimes. As we now know, instead of just one or two illegal immigrants, cities across the U.S. are filled with roughly twelve million illegal immigrants. The idea that the federal government alone has the constitutional authority to address this massive problem is nothing more than flawed progressive thinking.

With less than 6,000 ICE agents, the federal government simply has few too resources to meaningful enforce the laws. Rather than merely use ICE agents to plug the hole in the damn as the water pours over the lowered gates, the federal government should focus its finite resources on the detention and removal of criminals, the removal of visa violators, and the enforcement of federal laws on recalcitrant employers who employ illegal immigrants. ICE should continue to build detention facilities, and the State Department should get more aggressive with nations who refuse to take back their citizens through such tools as readmission accords and the revocation of visa privileges for embassy staff and their families.

Although some progress has been made under federal law to leverage the vastly superior numbers in state and local law enforcement to detain illegal immigrants, much more can and should be done. With over one million state and local law enforcement officers, the federal government should cede more authority to them to detain illegal immigrants. Governors and mayors also should increase their efforts to deal with the illegal immigrants who are in their jurisdictions by putting more laws on the books and more boots on the ground focused on this problem. As more states and localities enact laws to punish employers who hire illegal immigrants and landlords who house them, many illegal immigrants will make the purely economic decision to go home as the cost of staying becomes too high.

Finally, a special mention must be made of information and intelligence gathering, analysis, and dissemination. Before the creation of DHS, the FBI served as the lead federal agency on domestic information and intelligence activity, and had built relationships with state and local law enforcement. These relationships spanned decades. One of the outcomes of these relationships was the Joint Terrorism Task Force (JTTF) program where the FBI and state and local law enforcement jointly staffed operations centers dedicated to information and intelligence activities.[68]

As part of the Department of Justice (DOJ), the FBI worked closely with the various DOJ offices that provided funding, technical assistance, and support to state and local law enforcement. One of the key offices was ODP. When the Congress created DHS and shifted ODP from DOJ to DHS, and substantially increased the grant funding it received for states and localities, an inherent conflict arose between DOJ/FBI and DHS.

With the Information Analysis and Infrastructure Protection Directorate, DHS moved to create its own programs focused on state and local information and intelligence gathering, analysis, and dissemination. Not surprisingly, political appointees and bureaucrats interested in empire building used ODP's funds to support DHS-led initiatives such as the Homeland Security Information Network and fusion centers. As discussed more fully in Chapter 9, this conflict has resulted in millions of dollars wasted, duplicative FBI and DHS programs, and confusion at the state and local levels.

Ultimately, three changes need to occur: first, DHS needs to cede control of state and local information and intelligence gathering, analysis, and dissemination to the FBI, which includes combining fusion centers with JTTFs; secondly, the FBI must do a better job of working with DHS given the amount of information and intelligence possessed by DHS's operational components and treat states and localities as true partners, not just conduits of information; and, finally, states and localities must restructure themselves to leverage fully the vast amount of untapped information possessed at the state and local level. With these changes, America can build a shared information and intelligence structure where neither federal nor state and local entities are the lead, but where all three levels of government work collaboratively to detect and prevent terrorist attacks.

By assigning government roles more equitably and more properly between the federal government and states and localities, the federal government can refocus on fixing what remains broken at DHS and the FBI, while states and localities can reassert themselves and take ownership of areas in which they stand a far better chance of succeeding. These revised assignments are more consistent with the historical civilian defense roles played by each level of government and the Constitution.

The unanswered questions are: will governors and mayors find their voices again, and will Washington loosen its grip on power so that the "laboratories of democracy" can solve our complex homeland security challenges?

PART II

Where We Should Go from Here

4

Where Are All of the Federalists?

> All that progressives ask or desire is permission ... to interpret the Constitution according to the Darwinian principle.
>
> President Woodrow Wilson[1]

> Good intentions will always be pleaded for every assumption of power.... It is hardly too strong to say, that the Constitution was made, to guard the people against the dangers of good intentions.... There are men, in all ages, who mean to exercise power usefully; but they mean to exercise it. They mean to govern well; but they mean to govern. They promise to be kind masters; but they mean to be masters.
>
> Daniel Webster[2]

Washington, not surprisingly, is not a popular place with Americans. A Democracy Corps poll in August 2007 found that 57 percent of Americans believe that government makes it harder for them to get ahead and 83 percent believe that if government has more money it will waste it.[3] From the size of Swiss cheese holes to the way we run our local schools, Washington's presence in our day-to-day lives is as pervasive as ever. Unfortunately, without a sustained national effort to get power out of Washington, its presence in and over our lives will only get bigger.

Over the last thirty-five years, several efforts were made to shrink the size of the federal government. All of those efforts—from Richard Nixon's New Federalism to Newt Gingrich's Republican Revolution—failed.[4] Even President Reagan, one of America's greatest presidents and opponents of big government, could not fundamentally reverse the movement of power to Washington. The discouraging reality is that many politicians who go to Washington eventually succumb to Potomac Fever. Washington just has a way of wearing down even the strongest person if they dare stay too long.

The best example of this toxicity is the transformation of the Republican Revolution in 1994 to the Republican Corruption in 2006. In 1994, the Republican Party offered voters the Contract with America. The Contract with America contained pledges to reform the Congress, practice fiscal responsibility, promote personal responsibility and reinforce family values, enact legal reform, and return the Congress to the "citizen legislature" it once was.[5] The voters accepted their offer by giving Republicans control of the House of Representatives for the first time in forty years.

In the first years, the Republicans waged a bitter fight with President Clinton on the federal budget, which eventually led to the government shutdown in 1995. Although President Clinton won the public relations battle, Republicans could take solace in the budget restraint showed by the Clinton Administration in 1996 that, along with a surging economy, resulted in a balanced budget. The Republicans also forced President Clinton to accept revolutionary welfare reform legislation that freed states from federal requirements, which led to massive declines in welfare rolls across the country.

Unfortunately, the Republicans became intoxicated by power and decided it was more important to stay in power than to stay principled. It was at that moment that the Republicans abandoned the fight over the size of the federal government in favor of advocating for its kind of big government. With the addiction to power, not surprisingly, came corruption.

In the twelve years after gaining control over the House of Representatives and winning the presidency, Republicans increased the size of the federal government by passing Medicare Part D, expanded the federal role in education with the No Child Left Behind Act, grew non-defense, non-homeland security spending substantially more than inflation, significantly accelerated the use of earmarks from 1,300 in 1994 to 14,000 in 2005, created a new federal department, and spawned the doubling of lobbyists in Washington to almost 35,000.[6] Disgusted with the massive growth in government and corruption, voters ended the Republican's hold on the House of Representatives in 2006.

Admittedly, unlike in 1981 when President Reagan so famously noted that government *was* the problem, many Americans today believe that government does have a role to play in making their lives better and safer. Because of this reality, it is vital to cast the debate on the role of government as a debate over which level of government Americans prefer to have involved in their lives. Given the disdain Americans have for the federal government, most Americans likely would prefer to deal with their state or local government because those governments are much closer to the people and, therefore, far more knowledgeable, responsive to their needs, and accountable.

To win the battle to get power out of Washington and return it to the states, it is important to know what has been lost and how the power in America shifted from the states to the federal government. Part of this knowledge includes understanding that today there simply is no check on the growth of Washington's power. That was not always the case.

FEDERALISM AND THE FEDERAL GOVERNMENT

The Constitution lists the various powers of the federal government. Because some state ratification convention attendees expressed concerns about the powers granted to the federal government, the Bill of Rights was added to the Constitution in 1791.[7] The Bill of Rights expressly states the rights the people possess vis-à-vis the federal government. Importantly, the Ninth and Tenth Amendments firmly established the importance of federalism to our system of government by first stating that the rights contained in the Bill of Rights should "not be construed to deny or disparage others retained by the people" and then adding the corollary limiting provision that "powers not delegated to the United States by the Constitution ... are reserved to the States respectively, or to the people."[8] As James Madison noted, "The powers reserved to the several States will extend to all the objects which, in the ordinary course of affairs, concern the lives, liberties, and properties of the people, and the internal order, improvement, and prosperity of the States."[9]

Another structural protection added by the Founding Fathers when they designed our system of government was the system of checks and balances they inserted both among the branches of the federal government and between the federal and state governments. Because America is a republic, not a direct democracy, the Founding Fathers sought to ensure that elected federal government officials represented the various interests outside of Washington. The system of checks and balances would make it harder for the federal government itself to accumulate too much power or abuse it. As Madison noted in *The Federalist* 51, "In the compound republic of America, the power surrendered by the people is first divided between two distinct governments ... [that] will control each other."[10]

By design, the House of Representatives, being popularly elected by the people, served to protect the interests of the people within their congressional districts, and districts were allotted to states by population totals. The Founding Fathers felt that the small house districts would serve as a check on the ability of local factions to gain control of the levers of the federal government to enact bad laws or oppress opponents. As Madison noted in *The Federalist* 10, "The influence of factious leaders may kindle a flame within their particular States but will be unable to spread a general conflagration through the other states."[11]

In contrast to the House of Representatives, the Senate was madeup of two senators from every state who were elected by the state legislatures. The senators' primary role was to represent the interests of their states, which might, at times, be in conflict with the majority of people of the states. The fundamental reason why senators were elected by state legislatures was because that process guaranteed that the senators would fight in Washington for the interests of the states. The equality of representation among the states served as a check so that larger states could not exert undue influence over the smaller states, which could be done in the House of Representatives due to the allocation of seats by population. With the House of Representatives and the Senate representing their differing interests, Madison believed that "no law or resolution can now be passed without the concurrence, first, of a majority of the people, and then of a majority of the States."[12]

Finally, the President was elected in a manner that gave both the people and the states a role in his election and he served to represent America writ large—both the people in America and the states that madeup America. Specifically, the people vote for electors who are then certified by the state to support the candidate who received the most votes in the Electoral College process, which is when the President technically gets elected.

For the first 126 years of American history, the system largely worked. During that period of time, America expanded from the original thirteen states to the forty-eight states making up the continental United States. It fought and won the War of 1812, the Mexican-American War, and the Spanish-American War. It fought the Civil War to end the institution of slavery. By the eve of World War I, it had developed economically and culturally in a manner that made it among the world's greatest powers.[13]

Yet, progressives like Woodrow Wilson felt constrained by the constitutional structure as it prevented him from using the power of a centralized government to shape society as he deemed. Wilson believed certain men were able to "embody the projected consciousness of their time and people" and that these men whose "thought[s] run forward apace into regions whither the race is advancing" would master progress.[14] Progressives sought to use government power to make society as their advanced minds saw fit.

With the passage of the Seventeenth Amendment in 1913 during the Progressive Era, senators were elected popularly by the people, which disconnected them from being accountable to state legislatures. That seemingly insignificant change launched the era of unfunded mandates, the massive expansion of the federal government, and the rise of the administrative state via the New Deal and the Great Society. The near simultaneous passage of the federal income tax under the Sixteenth Amendment in the same year provided the means to fund the activities of the expanding federal government.

Critically, when states lost their ability to rein in recalcitrant senators who voted for legislation that would grow federal power at the expense of state power or for legislation that would pose an unfunded mandate on the states, senators could support legislation despite the short- or long-term consequences of the legislation on the states. Once the Supreme Court gave in to President Roosevelt's threat to pack the court with justices more inclined to uphold federal laws that violated the Constitution's federalism principle, states and localities were left largely powerless.[15]

A recent example is the passage of the Real ID Act that requires states to add federal requirements to their driver's licenses without receiving sufficient federal funds to adopt those requirements. Estimates put the price tag of the Real ID Act for states at over $11 billion.[16] Despite this enormous unfunded mandate, Washington passed the Real ID Act by a vote of 386 to 58 in the House of Representatives and in the Senate by a 100 to 0 vote.[17] Some states and localities led by Governor Mark Sanford of South Carolina have attempted to oppose the Real ID Act, but have little support in Washington.

Given the many failed attempts at reducing the power in Washington, Americans must recognize that this structural change to our system of government may have dealt a deadly blow to federalism. We have made what happens in Washington and those in it far more important than our Founding Fathers envisioned. As a result, more Americans can probably name at least one of their three congressional members more easily than they can name their state house or senate members. It is as if the federal government leviathan has crushed federalism so thoroughly that most Americans cannot even contemplate what such a system looks like.

As this book outlines, federalism can once again strengthen America. The case studies included in Chapters 4 through 10 unequivocally demonstrate that states and localities continue to be innovators. We need more, not less, state and local action. To do that, we need leaders.

LEADERSHIP REQUIRES LEADERS

A day does not go by without a governor or mayor blaming Washington for some problem within his or her state or city. In many cases, Washington is to blame for the problem. In other cases, however, the blame is used to avoid responsibility for a problem and rarely is cast with a request for Washington to get out of the way. It is time governors and mayors stop using Washington as an excuse and start telling Washington to respect federalism. Two examples vividly demonstrate the difference between taking leave and taking charge.

The first example shows what a lack of leadership looks like. It involved Ohio Governor Ted Strickland and Ohio's budget shortfall. In announcing $700 million in budget cuts, Governor Strickland claimed "we are paying the price in Ohio for the debacle that is Washington, D.C."[18] Forget for a moment that Ohio government spending increased by over 70 percent over the last fifteen years, which outpaced inflation by 25%.[19] Forget also that Ohio ranks forty-seventh in economic competitiveness, has the third highest corporate income tax, and has the sixth highest personal income tax.[20] Finally, ignore the fact that Governor Strickland tried four times during the 1980s and 1990s to get elected to Washington before finally winning and spending twelve years inside the Beltway just before becoming governor of Ohio.[21] Do not blame him, though. In addition to casting blame, Governor Strickland unashamedly held out his hand and asked Washington for more money.

The second example shows leadership at its best. This example involved Florida Governor Jeb Bush and the role of the federal government in disaster management after Hurricane Katrina. Fair or not, the largest share of blame for the response to Hurricane Katrina fell on the federal government and the Bush Administration. As a result, policymakers and pundits started advocating for a further expansion of FEMA's powers and responsibilities.

In the face of this "consensus," Governor Bush defended the sovereignty of the states and told Washington (and his older brother) to back off. In his own words, Governor Bush wrote:

> As the governor of a state that has been hit by seven hurricanes and two tropical storms in the past 13 months, I can say with certainty that federalizing emergency response to catastrophic events would be a disaster as bad as Hurricane Katrina.
>
> Just as all politics are local, so are all disasters. The most effective response is one that starts at the local level and grows with the support of surrounding communities, the state and then the federal government. The bottom-up approach yields the best and quickest results—saving lives, protecting property and getting life back to normal as soon as possible. Furthermore, when local and state governments understand and follow emergency plans appropriately, less taxpayer money is needed from the federal government for relief....
>
> If the federal government removes control of preparation, relief and recovery from cities and states, those cities and states will lose the interest, innovation and zeal for emergency response that has made Florida's response system better than it was 10 years ago....
>
> But for this federalist system to work, all must understand, accept and be willing to fulfill their responsibilities.[22]

When Hurricane Wilma hit Florida just a few weeks later and the state response failed to meet Governor Bush's expectations, he did not run from his words; rather, he forcefully stated: "If anyone wants to blame anybody, blame me. I'm not going to criticize anybody and I'm not going to let anybody criticize FEMA for something we accept responsibility for."[23]

When it comes to pushing back on the federal government and taking control over homeland security issues within their states and cities, there is a glaring absence of federalists. Other than complaining each year about how much federal grant money DHS gave their jurisdiction or how the federal government has not solved the immigration crisis, state and local leaders are remarkably quiet. An increasing chorus of federal voices whose words come with a steep price meets this silence.

In its *Mayors 2004 Agenda* for homeland security, the U.S. Conference of Mayors mainly called for "continued support."[24] With all of the federal grant requirements to deal with, such a request makes sense. It does not, however, make for an increase in our security. The only way this process-centric system works is if al Qaeda decides to attack us with a paper shredder. If that happens, paraphrasing Khrushchev, we will bury them. Since it will not happen, we need to stop the madness and free states and localities so they can build critical capabilities.

In reviewing its *2005 National Action Plan on Safety and Security in America's Cities*, it is clear that mayors who contributed to the report believe that the federal government has primary responsibility to fix or fund every aspect of homeland security.[25] This silence and lack of leadership is surprising given that, as two leading homeland security experts have noted, "The people closest to the problem are the ones best equipped to find the best solution."[26] Part of this problem is that most of the big city mayors are liberal proponents of big government in Washington.

For example, of the sixty-seven named cities eligible for the Urban Areas Security Initiative (UASI) grant program, fifty-four cities are led by Democratic mayors, four cities are led by independent mayors, and only nine cities are led by Republican mayors. When 81 percent of the leadership in the jurisdictions where the risk of a terrorist attack is deemed the highest are aligned with an ideology that believes more power in Washington is good, is it really that surprising that few of those politicians are clamoring to take the lead on homeland security or other domestic issues? These are the same politicians who reflexively demand Washington's involvement whenever something happens in their cities.

With such a strong track record of success, one has to wonder why governors and mayors are so hesitant to take the lead on homeland security issues. As previously discussed, innovative solutions to America's most difficult problems have always come from outside of Washington. States and localities in the four key areas noted in Chapter 3 can lead the way.

In building capabilities, a prepared America is an America where the higher-risk jurisdictions possess the capabilities they will need to prevent, protect, respond to, and recover from a major event. A national effort to identify critical capabilities involving all levels of government, the private sector, and nongovernmental organizations resulted in the development of a capabilities-based approach—the TCL. Rather than waiting on Washington, states and localities should adopt this approach to transform their jurisdictions from tactical followers to strategic innovators. Specifically, states and localities should use the national template to identify capabilities they need based on their unique risk and need portfolio.

From the ability to share information both vertically and horizontally with key authorities to the public health system's surge capacity, governments now share a common framework on which to build a national preparedness system. Because each capability contains personnel, equipment, and training requirements, as well as performance measures and metrics, states and localities will be able to demonstrate gains made each year so that taxpayers get a more transparent view of homeland security efforts. This process also will serve as an incentive for other jurisdictions to move forward as failure to do so will create negative public scrutiny.

In disaster management, the federalization of disasters has had two interrelated effects. First, as FEMA paid for and took greater control over routine disasters, states and localities possessed few incentives to build strong disaster management capabilities that would allow them to handle all but the truly catastrophic disasters. Moreover, without clearly delineated roles and responsibilities, states and localities could default to a FEMA-driven model, thereby deftly passing accountability and costs without suffering any penalties. With constant budgetary pressures, elected officials could divert finite resources to other more pressing needs like education, health care, and transportation costs.

Secondly, as FEMA federalized more routine natural disasters, it spent all of its time and resources dealing with a new declaration—a new one every third day—and failing to build catastrophic disaster capabilities, which is a proper activity for FEMA. As a result of these two effects, most governments are not prepared to handle anything but the smallest disasters. Because disasters other than hurricanes fail to provide us notice before hitting, first responders will be on their own for the first twenty-four to seventy-two hours before federal resources can be marshaled. By taking the lead, state and local emergency management agencies will ensure that they build appropriate disaster management capabilities, thereby allowing them to handle noncatastrophic, or routine, natural disasters.

While section 287(g) of the Illegal Immigration Reform and Immigrant Responsibility Act of 1996 allowing state and local law enforcement agencies to enforce federal immigration laws is finally getting used after ten years of lying dormant, the entire premise that states and localities need the agreement of the federal government to control their jurisdictions is baseless. By crafting their own interior enforcement legislation, they can take the lead by dealing with illegal immigrants and those who employ, house, or otherwise aid them. These actions will create greater pressure on the federal government to allocate the detention and removal resources necessary to deport illegal immigrants apprehended by state and local law enforcement.

Finally, with so few resources, a counterterrorism strategy almost wholly dependent on federal entities is doomed for failure. Terrorists who make it to America will spend their time planning and organizing in cities across the country. The best chance we have at detecting and apprehending these terrorists will be at the hands of the million men and women in state and local law enforcement who patrol our streets, investigate complaints, and know enough about their communities to notice when something just is not right.

States and localities must create robust counterterrorism capabilities that include organizational changes, leveraging assets such as publicly-funded higher education institutions to develop much needed language and intelligence skills, developing information-sharing initiatives that meet state standards of privacy and coordination, and providing law enforcement entities with authorization to use investigative methods subject to judicial oversight that are desperately needed in this post-September 11 environment.

We face a crossroad. Today, we stand at the intersection of federalism and centralized government. The roads that led us to this intersection involved many twists and turns. We can choose one of two paths forward. The left path leads us further away from our constitutional underpinnings where the federal government takes still more power from states and localities under the guise of the latest emergency. Whether the war was spent fighting a depression, poverty, or the ills of society, the means are always the same. At the end of this path, we are sure to find what we have found each time we took this path: more government, less freedom, and few results.

We could, however, take the road less traveled. The right path may seem battered and poorly maintained, but it looks vaguely familiar. This path will lead us back toward our constitutional underpinnings where the federal government possessed limited and discrete powers and where states and localities possessed the bulk of the powers that impacted our lives. The last time we took this path was after spending thirty or so years on the left path where we fought a battle over how best to provide welfare to the least fortunate in our country. The results achieved once we took the right path were stunning. With our very way of life at stake, we do not have thirty years to fight this battle over where the power of homeland security should reside. If we take the right path, we can be sure that the results will be as stunning as they have been each time we have upheld our Constitution.

CASE STUDY 1

Don't Mess with Texas

From disaster response to immigration to counterterrorism, Texas has taken an approach steeped in federalism in its homeland security efforts. Although it appreciates the supplemental support it may get or need from the federal government for catastrophic hurricanes or border security, leaders such as Director of Homeland Security Steve McCraw fundamentally understand that it is Texans who will protect and secure the state, not federal employees sitting 1,527 miles away in Washington. With this realization, Texas has dedicated significant resources to ensure that it possesses the capabilities to meet its constitutional responsibilities to its citizens.

As part of its efforts to prepare for a disaster, Texas has taken many steps to assume responsibility. Texas's primary operating belief is that Texans must be prepared—regardless of federal action. Secondarily, Texas knows that it cannot create a risk-free state. Citizens should expect much from government, but also do much for themselves. Lastly, by an executive order from the governor, local governments are in charge during disasters. Having learned several lessons from previous disasters, Texas has identified four operational priorities: evacuation, search and rescue, shelter hub network, and community re-entry.

Texas expressly acknowledges that its private partners have an enormous stake in their communities and possess substantial resources and capabilities that make little sense to duplicate. With these realities in mind, Texas has incorporated over fifty-four private partners into the Texas Operational Team. These partners range from energy companies and grocery stores to big box retailers and telecommunication providers. Using the Emergency Management Council, Texas engages these private partners in pre-disaster coordination to build capacity and in post-disaster recovery to serve impacted communities.

For example, in evacuation operations, Texas leans on private partners to manage distribution, coordinate retailers and suppliers, and acquire fuel for its contingency tanker fleet. The same approach embodies its special needs evacuation activities, including putting in place a robust tracking system and supplies of busses. Related to these actions, Texas has executed firm fixed contracts for search and rescue aircraft and ambulances.

When it comes to communicating with affected jurisdictions, Texas has instituted a statewide teleconference capability to gain situational awareness. In one recent disaster, over 1,100 individuals participated in the teleconference, thereby providing Texas with existing gaps and needs across the state. When needed, Texas activates the Radio Amateur Civil Emergency Services network to provide operators for State Operations Center and emergency operations centers across the state.

On immigration, Texas took the position that, while securing the border is primarily a federal role, an insecure border puts Texas and its people at risk. Recognizing the weak federal effort to secure the border, the Texas legislature appropriated significant resources to put in place the capabilities necessary to secure the border starting in 2005. To secure the Texas border from all potential threats such as drugs, human smugglers, and terrorists, Texas began a series of operations that build on each other.

By unifying local, state, and federal assets, Texas centralized key intelligence-driven multi-jurisdictional patrol operations and investigation to have a maximum impact on criminal activities. Operation Rio Grande consisted of six border operations (Del Rio, Laredo, El Paso, Big Bend, Valley Star, and Corridor) that took place from June 2 to October 8, 2006. Each operation lasted from eight to twenty-four days and involved local law enforcement agencies, partnered with state and federal agencies, to target border areas. During Operation Rio Grande, crime along the border decreased from 25 percent to 85 percent in affected areas.

Next, Operation Wrangler consisted of five operations along the border, high-traffic corridors, and urban areas to deter, disrupt, and disorganize crime. Using land, air, and water assets of local, state, and federal law enforcement agencies, Operation Wrangler included 6,894 personnel, 2,200 land vehicles, seventy-eight aircraft, and thirty-five watercraft. Operation Wrangler resulted in a 25 percent to 40 percent reduction in Type I crime in Texas.

The latest operation—Operation Border Star—again focuses on the border and aims to "dominate" the border by preventing all crime in the areas of focus. Operation Border Star is a partnership with CBP that "overwhelms" the border with local, state, and federal personnel and capabilities. Operation Border Star has six operational sectors (El Paso, Big Bend, Del Rio, Laredo, Rio Grande Valley, and Coastal Bend) in twenty-five ports of entry. Operation Border Star is a continuous operation where resources and assets are rapidly redirected based on real-time needs.

Texas created a resource in March 2006 to assist in operations when it started the Border Security Operation Center along with six Joint Operations and Intelligence Centers to enhance unified command in the border security sectors. With those assets, local, state, and federal personnel jointly plan and conduct integrated patrols. These joint patrols have resulted in the seizure of over $50 million, 1.5 million pounds of marijuana, 29,000 pounds of cocaine, 1,400 pounds of methamphetamine, and 170 pounds of heroin. Using the referral of 32,361 suspected illegal immigrants from local and state law enforcement, 681 illegal immigrants have been apprehended trying to cross the border from countries posing a counterterrorism threat, including individuals from Afghanistan, Iran, North Korea, Pakistan, and Syria.

Because of its immigration efforts, Texas experienced a 65 percent decrease in serious crime along the entire border from October 2005 to December 2007. At the same time, CBP apprehensions decreased by 45 percent, indicating that illegal immigrants are getting the message that trying to enter Texas illegally does not pay and criminals will be caught.

On counterterrorism, Texas recognized early that the key to detecting and deterring terrorists is in leveraging the "crown jewels" of highly relevant data embedded in the legacy record management systems in the roughly 2,600 law enforcement agencies across the state, and making sure that the 70,000 local and state law enforcement personnel possessed the latest threat information and collection protocols. Texas fundamentally understands that the best way to stop terrorists is to detect suspicious activity through the "cop on the beat," to analyze the suspicious activity with other relevant data through data fusion, and to arrest the terrorists with solid evidence developed from the fused data.

Because Texas covers over 262,000 square miles and possesses so many law enforcement agencies, as well as other agencies with a need for data, it made little sense to "warehouse" people in one central location. Instead, Texas focused on putting data already legally sharable among law enforcement agencies into a shared virtual repository. Because the data resided in many disparate systems and in many disparate formats, Texas moved to upgrade all record management and jail management systems to the National Information Exchange Model standard.

Once a system is converted to the common standard, Texas connects the system to a central data location that allows law enforcement users to conduct powerful, predicated, and federated searches and links analyses within a secure environment constrained by appropriate internal controls such as audit trails and segregation of law enforcement data from publicly available data.

Instead of waiting for federal action, Texas developed its own concept of operations for a statewide intelligence capability. With the launch of the Texas Data Exchange System, Texas has connected seventy-five million local law enforcement records, including thirty-five million offender records from 1,400 jails in thirty states, five million offender photographs, and thirty-five million incident and citation records from 241 Texas agencies. Every month, Texas adds another 500,000 offender records, 115,000 offender photographs, and 1.2 million incident and citations records. Law enforcement users in Texas conduct roughly 35,000 queries every month.

The Texas Data Exchange system is a pointer-index system, which means that users are "pointed" to law enforcement agencies that have potentially relevant information about the subject of the query. Equally as important, the system includes an automated alert system that notifies users when a law enforcement agency has added new information on the subject of a past query. This function will decrease the chances that a potential terrorist will slip through the system.

In fact, JTTF agents and analysts use the Texas Data Exchange system every day, and it is viewed as an essential tool in their counterterrorism efforts. Although details cannot be disclosed by Texas law enforcement, it has aided the investigations of suspected terrorists in Texas.

Although the federal government has continued to grow over the last eight years, some state leaders know that the key to success in fighting Islamic jihadists rests in the innovation and flexibility of states and localities. Federalism may be on the ropes, but it is not dead yet—at least not in Texas.

5

The Role of Risk in Determining Where to Allocate Limited Resources

> Reports that say that something hasn't happened are always interesting to me, because as we know, there are known knowns; there are things we know we know. We also know there are known unknowns; that is to say we know there are some things we do not know. But there are also unknown unknowns—the ones we don't know we don't know.
>
> Defense Secretary Donald Rumsfeld[1]

> An Ant was spending a frosty winter's day drying grain he had collected during the summertime. A Grasshopper, dying of hunger, passed by and earnestly begged for a little food. The Ant inquired of him, "Why did you not stock up on food during the summer?" He replied, "I had no time. I passed my days singing." The Ant then said in derision, "If you are foolish enough to sing all summer, you'll dance supperless to bed in winter."
>
> The Ant and the Grasshopper[2]

The risk of a terrorist attack or catastrophic natural disaster is not the same everywhere in America. The resources we possess to build capabilities to deal with a terrorist attack or catastrophic natural disaster are not limitless. We must, therefore, make the difficult choice of allocating our limited resources to those places in America where we think the risk of either of those events is the greatest. Using risk is vital; we can make more informed decisions as to where preparedness capabilities need to be the strongest, where disaster management resources need to be focused, and where individuals are in our country and what they are doing that could harm us.

What exactly is risk? The *New Oxford American Dictionary* defines risk as the "possibility that something unpleasant or unwelcome will happen."[3] On a daily basis, we face numerous risks such as automobile accidents, workplace injuries, and mishaps that can occur when doing mundane tasks like cooking.

Yet, each of us makes the perfectly rational decision to get out of bed and get on with our lives knowing full well that living life is not a risk-free endeavor. The reality of risk does not paralyze us. In fact, as we gain experience, we prepare for known risks.

Risk is such a part of our everyday lives that an entire industry exists with the sole aim of calculating risk, using those calculations to place monetary sums on activities, and issuing policies to insure policyholders against those risks.[4] From homeowners' insurance to life insurance to injury insurance for star athletes, billions of dollars are spent every year on premiums and paid out on policies.

Functionally, the insurance industry charges a premium to assume the given risk for which insurance is offered. The insurance industry's profitability depends on its ability to understand risk and put in place models that ensure that, over the course of time, it pays out less in redeemed policies than it collects in premiums plus interest. To do this, the insurance industry uses actuarial data such as life expectancy tables, probability factors, and algorithms.

As the insurance industry has gained greater understanding of risk, secondary markets have sprung up that serve to further insure the primary insurance industry against risk. This reinsurance market serves to spread the risk from a single insurer to multiple insurers or from a single region to multiple regions. By spreading the risk more broadly, the insurance industry lessons the chances that a single event will financially overwhelm the market.

In most cases, the insurance industry and the reinsurance industry do an excellent job of forecasting risk. Where things fall apart is where large amounts of uncertainty exist. These are the unknown unknowns. Where there are large amounts of uncertainty, the focus must shift to the aspects of the uncertainty that can be defined.

Essentially, when the probabilistic aspect of risk is difficult to define, it makes eminent sense to focus on the vulnerabilities and consequences of the risk as those aspects can be defined. As risk expert Nassim Nicholas Taleb has noted, "This idea that in order to make a decision you need to focus on the consequences (which you can know) rather than the probabilities (which you can't know) is the central idea of uncertainty."[5]

The two areas where large amounts of uncertainty exist are terrorism and catastrophic natural disasters. In the former case, terrorism by its very nature is unpredictable. Although we may be able to identify terrorist groups and theorize about possible targets and methods of attack based on intelligence, terrorism involves the willful act of sentient beings; therefore, our ability to predict the time, place, and means of attack is inherently limited. Unfortunately, there is little evidence that our record in predicting big events like terrorist attacks will improve anytime soon. This reality means that, when it comes to terrorism, uncertainty is and will continue to be our bedfellow.

The insurance industry has refused to issue terrorism insurance without the protection of the government in the form of the Terrorism Risk Insurance Act,[6] which was set to expire on December 31, 2005, but Congress passed extension legislation keeping it in place until December 31, 2014.[7] This extension to 2014—over thirteen years after the September 11, 2001, attack—illustrates the difficulty the insurance industry is having developing models to predict the risk of terrorism.

Conversely, the Congress's extension of the Terrorism Risk Insurance Act also could reflect the power of the insurance industry to get government to subsidize its riskier activities. After all, if it can get the federal government to cap possible losses, why would the insurance industry not engage in social loafing by delaying the development of terrorism risk models? Most security experts would agree that, although the certainty of an attack in the future is high, the particular risk across the United States of that attack is infinitesimally small. Additionally, most security experts would agree that the list of targets is enormous. Thus, if the particular risk is very small and the list of targets is very large, the insurance industry should be able to make billions of dollars, as most insured targets will never be hit (lots of premiums minus few payouts equals lots of profits).

In the case of catastrophic natural disasters, the insurance industry has turned to the reinsurance market to help spread the costs of such events. In addition, the insurance industry has tightened insurance policies by excluding certain aspects of natural disasters such as flood damage. Finally, the insurance industry has pulled out of certain markets where it has judged the risk too great based on the limit on premiums it can charge individual policyholders due to state regulatory caps, on the predicated cost of payouts due to the density of policyholders in known risk areas, and on the frequency of events such as hurricanes in the Gulf Coast region.

For catastrophic disasters, as Hurricane Katrina demonstrated, the insurance industry—despite lawsuits by corrupt trial lawyers like Dickie Scruggs—handled the enormous losses without requiring government intervention. That being said, had the United States suffered a second catastrophic natural disaster in 2006 or 2007, chances are that the insurance industry would have faced severe financial pressures.

When it comes to natural disasters, FEMA has collected data for almost sixty years. Over those sixty years, FEMA has issued 2,773 declarations.[8] Of those, only 113 declarations, or 4%, involved the types of disasters that could be deemed catastrophic.[9] Specifically, FEMA has issued declarations for seventy-one hurricanes, twenty-four earthquakes, seven levee or damn ruptures, five volcanoes, four terrorist attacks, and two tsunamis.[10] Of those 113 potentially catastrophic types of disasters, the vast majority of them occurred in the areas where one would expect them to occur; namely, the Gulf Coast and eastern seaboard (hurricanes), the Pacific states (earthquakes), California (levees), Hawaii and Washington (volcanoes), New York City and the National Capital Region (terrorist attacks), and the Pacific territories (tsunamis).[11]

When it comes to the remaining 2,650 routine natural disasters, the insurance industry and government possess enormous amounts of data. These rich data allow the insurance industry to quantify risk in a manner that prevents financial crises. These data also should allow governments at the state and local level to adequately prepare for expected routine natural disasters so that federal involvement is unneeded.

For example, as Table 5.1 demonstrates, the data for each state indicates a fairly clear picture of how many routine natural disasters it will experience each year and the types of routine natural disasters most likely to occur.[12]

Roughly 60 percent of the disaster declarations occurred after January 19, 1993, which only represents 28 percent of the years in which the federal government issued disaster declarations.

From a risk standpoint, the data reveal that eleven states face less than one routine natural disaster each year; twenty-four states face less than two routine natural disasters each year; seven states face less than three routine natural disasters each year; and only eight states face more than three routine natural disasters each year.[13] Such predictability allows the insurance industry to adjust premiums in a manner that insures profitability.

These rich data also should drive states and localities to build capabilities to handle these routine natural disasters, especially given that the relative infrequency of those events each year in most states means that those states should be able to handle them without federal assistance. From a mitigation standpoint, the data should drive states and localities to discontinue the counterproductive policy of rebuilding in areas rife with systemic routine natural disasters.

The key point is that, with routine natural disasters, the private sector and government entities possess large amounts of data that should allow them to make sound decisions and be prepared for the known risks at all levels of government. To the contrary, the unpredictability of terrorism renders any predictive data largely meaningless. As a result, the private sector stays clear of such analyses and the federal government focuses on terrorism risk by looking at what it knows: credible threats, vulnerabilities, and consequences.

THE FEDERAL GOVERNMENT'S APPROACH TO RISK

The federal government has spent millions of dollars trying to determine risk. One approach to answering this question focuses on gathering as much data as possible and then creating a complex and classified algorithm to translate the data into risk scores for the largest jurisdictions in America. Another approach scoffs at the complexity approach by dismissing it as "bean counting" and opts for simplification that looks at smaller sets of data. The reality is that both approaches result in similar outcomes.

For the first few years, DHS developed a risk formula for the nation's largest urban areas that looked largely at population totals, population densities, presence of critical infrastructure, and threat data from intelligence sources.[14] Initially, an urban area was made up of the core city and the core counties.

TABLE 5.1 Disaster Declarations by State, Number, Type, and Per Capita[1]

State	All Declarations	Types of Routine Natural Disasters[2]	Percent after 1992	Disasters per Year after 1992	People per Disaster
Alabama	61	Severe storms, flooding, and tornadoes	61%	2.44	75,866
Alaska	44	Severe storms, flooding, and fires	50%	1.45	15,534
Arizona	60	Fires, severe storms, and flooding	75%	2.97	105,646
Arkansas	51	Severe storms, flooding, and tornadoes	35%	3.36	55,584
California	164	Fires, severe storms, and flooding	42%	4.55	222,885
Colorado	63	Fires	76%	3.16	77,167
Connecticut	20	Snow, severe storms, and flooding	50%	0.66	175,115
Delaware	15	Severe storms and flooding	80%	0.79	57,651
District of Columbia	10	Severe storms	90%	0.59	58,829
Florida	121	Fires, severe storms, and flooding	74%	5.93	150,836
Georgia	44	Severe storms, flooding, and tornadoes	52%	1.52	216,926
Hawaii	40	Fires, severe storms, and flooding	55%	1.45	32,085
Idaho	27	Floods, fires, and severe storms	37%	0.66	55,533
Illinois	51	Severe storms, flooding, and tornadoes	47%	1.58	252,010
Indiana	41	Severe storms, flooding, and tornadoes	54%	1.45	154,763
Iowa	42	Severe storms and flooding	40%	1.12	71,144
Kansas	41	Severe storms, flooding, and tornadoes	56%	1.52	67,707
Kentucky	55	Severe storms, flooding, and tornadoes	53%	1.91	77,118
Louisiana	60	Severe storms and flooding	38%	1.52	71,553
Maine	45	Snow, severe storms, and flooding	67%	1.98	29,271
Maryland	21	Severe storms and flooding	57%	0.79	267,540
Massachusetts	32	Severe storms and flooding	56%	1.19	201,555
Michigan	31	Severe storms, flooding, and tornadoes	42%	0.86	324,897

(*Continued*)

TABLE 5.1 (*Continued*)

State	All Declarations	Types of Routine Natural Disasters[2]	Percent after 1992	Disasters per Year after 1992	People per Disaster
Minnesota	52	Severe storms, flooding, and tornadoes	44%	1.52	99,954
Mississippi	50	Severe storms, flooding, and tornadoes	36%	1.19	58,376
Missouri	49	Severe storms, flooding, and tornadoes	57%	1.85	119,968
Montana	51	Fires, severe storms, and flooding	65%	2.18	18,782
Nebraska	41	Severe storms, flooding, and tornadoes	51%	1.38	43,282
Nevada	67	Fires and flooding	78%	3.43	38,289
New Hampshire	27	Severe storms, flooding, and snow	63%	1.12	48,734
New Jersey	36	Severe storms and flooding	58%	1.38	241,276
New Mexico	54	Fires, severe storms, and flooding	70%	2.50	42,887
New York	76	Severe storms and flooding	55%	2.77	253,917
North Carolina	43	Severe storms and flooding	53%	1.52	210,721
North Dakota	42	Severe storms and flooding	55%	1.52	15,231
Ohio	47	Severe storms, flooding, and tornadoes	49%	1.52	243,977
Oklahoma	106	Fires, severe storms, and tornadoes	70%	4.88	34,126
Oregon	73	Fires, severe storms, and flooding	53%	2.57	51,335
Pennsylvania	46	Severe storms and flooding	50%	1.52	270,278
Rhode Island	13	Snowstorms	46%	0.40	81,372
South Carolina	20	Severe storms	70%	0.92	220,385
South Dakota	48	Flooding, severe storms, and fires	63%	1.98	16,588
Tennessee	47	Severe storms, flooding, and tornadoes	62%	1.91	130,994
Texas	244	Fires	75%	12.06	97,969
Utah	20	Fires	70%	0.92	132,267
Vermont	26	Severe storms and flooding	62%	1.05	23,894

Virginia	49	Severe storms and flooding	65%	2.11	157,390
Washington	91	Fires, severe storms, and flooding	63%	3.76	71,082
West Virginia	47	Severe storms and flooding	51%	1.58	38,554
Wisconsin	38	Severe storms and flooding	39%	0.99	147,412
Wyoming	20	Fires	70%	0.92	26,142
Total	2,662	Severe storms, flooding, and fires	60%	105.07	113,306

[1]Federal Emergency Management Agency, "Disaster Search," accessed on March 31, 2008.

[2]For this chart, routine natural disasters will include all types of natural disasters except hurricanes, earthquakes, levee failures, volcanic eruptions, terrorist attacks, and tsunamis. Although floods, severe storms, fires, and tornadoes are catastrophic for those communities that experience them, in most cases, those types of disasters do not or should not overwhelm state and local government capabilities. Conversely, while some hurricanes, earthquakes, levee failures, volcanic eruptions, terrorist attacks, and tsunamis may not be catastrophic, those types of disasters pose threats that can overwhelm state and local government capabilities.

As part of its investigation into the September 11 attack, the 9/11 Commission reviewed DHS's risk approach and grant allocations in the first few years. After its review, the 9/11 Commission recommended:

> Homeland security assistance should be based strictly on an assessment of risks and vulnerabilities. Now, in 2004, Washington, D.C., and New York City are certainly at the top of any such list. We understand the contention that every state and city needs to have some minimum infrastructure for emergency response. But federal homeland security assistance should not remain a program for general revenue sharing. It should supplement state and local resources based on the risks or vulnerabilities that merit additional support. Congress should not use this money as a pork barrel.[15]

Shortly after joining DHS, Secretary Chertoff attempted to implement that recommendation. In July 2005, he announced that risk would be measured using three factors: threats, vulnerabilities, and consequences.[16] In this model, in a general sense, threats are those possible attacks where there is a "likelihood of activity against a particular individual, asset, location, or function [and where] the adversary's capabilities [to] accomplish" the attack are viable; vulnerabilities involve "identifying weaknesses in structures..., systems, or processes that could be exploited by a terrorist;" and consequences are those effects "that will be achieved if the adversary accomplishes his goals."[17]

In FY 2006, Secretary Chertoff's first full cycle managing the homeland security grants, DHS significantly changed its risk formula. Specifically, the "new approach to allocating the... funds required an assessment of risk using a formula that consider[ed] the threat to a target/area, multiplied by vulnerability (V) of the target/area, multiplied by consequence (C) of an attack on that target/area."[18] This approach analyzed threats to both assets and geographic areas.[19]

Substantively, as Secretary Chertoff noted, DHS got "more particular and granular" by analyzing data that "would occupy over 30 million Excel spreadsheet cells and would include 3.2 billion—with a B—calculations."[20] In FY 2005, the data only occupied 43,000 Excel spreadsheet cells with two million calculations.[21] This data-driven analysis typifies the complex approach.

Secretary Chertoff also changed the composition of the Urban Areas Security Initiative (UASI) jurisdictions by combining adjacent jurisdictions to form "super" UASI jurisdictions. For example, before FY 2006, Dallas, Fort Worth, and Arlington existed as separate UASI jurisdictions. In FY 2006, DHS combined those three jurisdictions along with several other jurisdictions to form the Greater Dallas jurisdiction and then analyzed the risk within the entire combined area. The basis for this change was an acknowledgment that an event in one of those jurisdictions would impact the other jurisdictions, so treating them as isolated jurisdictions made little sense. Additionally, as separate UASI jurisdictions, each would build critical capabilities at a level that, when combined, would result in large overinvestments.

In FY 2007, however, DHS made yet another change to the risk formula aimed at simplifying it. Specifically, DHS "is treating vulnerability (V) and consequence (C) as an amalgamated, single variable... due to difficulties associated with differentiating vulnerability values across areas and states."[22] As a result, DHS has "assigned a value of one to vulnerability."[23] The data analyzed in FY 2007 involved far fewer categories and details than the FY 2006 data.

A final change made by DHS to the risk formula in FY 2007 involved using a historical threat trend for each jurisdiction that analyzed intelligence and investigation data from the September 11 attack to the release of the grant guidance.[24] Previously, DHS had looked only at the previous year of threat data for each jurisdiction.

With all of these changes to the risk formula each year, consistency and transparency become real challenges. Even something as simple as maintaining the same number of eligible jurisdictions proved a Herculean task. In FY 2003, the two rounds of grant funding involved thirty jurisdictions. In FY 2004, DHS expanded the number of eligible jurisdictions to fifty. It remained at fifty in FY 2005. Although DHS made progress in FY 2006 to reduce the pork barrel aspect of the UASI program when it reduced the number of fully eligible jurisdictions to thirty-five, that progress was short-lived when the program was expanded to forty-six in FY 2007 and sixty in FY 2008.

Despite DHS's constant shifting of formulas and jurisdictions, we can use its work to better understand the risk portfolio of states and localities and allocate resources accordingly.

A SIMPLIFIED APPROACH TO RISK

We must acknowledge a fundamental fact. Namely, that the risk of a terrorist attack is not the same all across America. The risk of a terrorist attack in New York City because of the large number of people, the density of those people, the presence of key critical infrastructure, the iconic value of certain targets, and the consequences economically (to name a few reasons) is exponentially greater than the risk of a terrorist attack in Des Moines.

When the federal government inflates the risk everywhere, it does the American public a great disservice and creates either apathy (with so few resources, there is little that can be done, so doing nothing makes sense) or unnecessary fear (an attack is imminent and the likelihood of it happening here is high). After all, a review of terrorist attacks globally indicates that "even with the September 11 attacks included in the count, the number of Americans killed by international terrorism since the late 1960s (which is when the State Department began counting) is about the same as the number of Americans killed over the same period by lightning, accident-causing deer, or severe allergic reaction to peanuts."[25]

More critically, a review of terrorist attacks conducted by or attributed to al Qaeda reveals that other than five attacks, every al Qaeda attack outside of Iraq occurred in an urban area with a population of over 510,000 people. Of the five exceptions, two were in Saudi Arabia (Dhahran and Khobar), one was in Pakistan (Marden), one was on the Tunisian island of Djerba, and the last was the nightclub attack on the Indonesian island of Bali. In the United States, only thirty-three urban areas possess populations greater than 510,000 people.

An important lesson from the Cold War is that fear must not drive us as it leads to the same type of tyranny we have fought and defeated. As John Lewis Gaddis, quoting George Kennan, noted:

> "The fact of the matter is that there is a little bit of the totalitarian buried somewhere, way down deep, in each and every one of us," Kennan told students at the National War College in 1947. "It is only the cheerful light of confidence and security which keeps this evil genius down.... If confidence and security were to disappear, don't think that he would not be waiting to take their place." This warning from the founder of containment—that the enemy to be contained might as easily lie within the beneficiaries of freedom as among it enemies—showed how pervasive fear had become in a postwar international order for which there had been so much hope. It helps explain why Orwell's *1984*, when it appeared in 1949, became an instant literary triumph.[26]

The reality is that while the risk of a terrorist attack anywhere in America exists, the probability of a terrorist attack in most of America remains very low.

That said, the risk of a terrorist attack is higher in some jurisdictions in the United States. In order to determine where those higher-risk jurisdictions are so we can invest resources to build the critical capabilities needed to protect, prevent, respond to, and recover from a terrorist attack should one occur, we should use the millions of dollars and hours spent by the federal government and aggregate the data it produced for the UASI program from FY 2003 to FY 2008.

As noted above, the actual risk rankings developed by the federal government are classified due to the threat information contained in the risk formula. Because the federal government used only risk in FY 2003, FY 2004, and FY 2005, however, we can assume that the funding received by each jurisdiction reflected its risk ranking among the eligible jurisdictions. For FY 2006 to FY 2008, while the federal government used effectiveness in addition to risk to allocate funds, based on the two case studies discussed below, it would appear that the effectiveness factor had little impact on the final rankings. Thus, for purposes of this simplified model, we will assume that the level of funding received was based on the jurisdiction's risk ranking.

For our model, based on the amount of funding received each year, each jurisdiction is given points based on its relative standing. For example, in FY 2004, New York City received the most funding, so would receive fifty points, as there were fifty jurisdictions eligible that year. In contrast, San Antonio received the least funding, so it received one point. Based on this approach and awarding points to all jurisdictions that have ever been eligible for the UASI program, New York City, not surprisingly, received the most points (254) and Rochester received the fewest points (3).

This risk model uses the Metropolitan Statistical Area to define jurisdictions, which results in combining the Greater New York City area (New York City, Jersey City, and Newark), the Greater Los Angeles area (Los Angeles, Long Beach, Anaheim, and Santa Ana), the Bay area (San Francisco, Oakland, and San Jose), the Greater Miami area (Miami and Fort Lauderdale), and the Greater Dallas area (Dallas, Fort Worth, and Arlington) listed in the UASI program. Although not perfect, these aggregated data (as compared to a single-year snapshot when the risk formula may contain flaws) and combined Metropolitan Statistical Area approach demonstrate consistency as twenty-six jurisdictions made the eligibility list every year for the UASI program.

These jurisdictions based on points are: Greater New York City (254), Greater Los Angeles (246), National Capital Region (240), Chicago (238), Bay Area (229), Houston (216), Philadelphia (213), Greater Miami (204), Boston (201), Greater Dallas (194), Detroit (192), Seattle (178), Baltimore (175), San Diego (168), Kansas City (146), Phoenix (145), St. Louis (142), Portland (123), Pittsburgh (122), Tampa (121), Denver (118), Cincinnati (94), Cleveland (93), Buffalo (84), New Orleans (63), and Sacramento (60). The jurisdictions that did not make the UASI program list every year, but that received more points than Sacramento (the lowest that did) are: Atlanta (168), Las Vegas (129), Minneapolis-St. Paul (113), Jacksonville (88), Indianapolis (86), Orlando (84), Milwaukee (75), San Antonio (70), Honolulu (66), Charlotte (66), and Columbus (61).

In total, these thirty-seven jurisdictions consist of places where the federal government has deemed the risk to be the greatest, and where more than 142 million people live and work. Large populations imply higher population densities, a higher presence of critical infrastructure, and, critically, a diverse population where our enemies can go unnoticed. Approximately 48 percent of the population in the United States lives within these thirty-seven jurisdictions.

In looking at the list, one could argue that the cut-line imposed is arbitrary and should be dropped lower. Yet, when you step back and look at the broader picture, you must acknowledge that, using this simplified approach, the risk to the Greater New York City area (254) is over four times greater than the risk to Sacramento (60). In reality, the risk to the former is far in excess of that multiple. Adding only two more jurisdictions (Norfolk (58) and Memphis (45)) would mean that the risk to the lowest area (Memphis with forty-five "risk" points) is almost six times less than the risk to the Greater New York City area. By the time you expand the list to sixty as DHS did in FY 2008, the last jurisdiction (Rochester with three points) possesses a risk score that is almost 85 times smaller than the Greater New York City area. That type of imbalance just does not qualify as higher risk. At least it should not.

This group of thirty-seven higher-risk areas should become the focus of federal homeland security programs where our limited resources are utilized to build the critical capabilities. While other places may be able to present arguments in support of receiving federal funds, absent a truly compelling case, we must stop vacillating every year and get to work mitigating the vulnerabilities and consequences in these empirically higher-risk jurisdictions.

It goes without saying, of course, that any entity can use its own financial resources to build an appropriate level of capabilities. One would assume that any state or local leader who feels their particular jurisdiction needs to build critical capabilities would do so regardless of whether the federal government provides funds. That is leadership, after all.

As to the types of terrorist risks, we also must acknowledge that some risks are far more likely than other risks. For example, every foreign terrorist attack aimed at Americans over the last seventeen years has used explosives. As one policy expert noted:

> If, as some purported experts repeatedly claim, chemical and biological attacks are so easy and attractive to terrorists, it is impressive that none have so far been used in Israel (where four times as many people die from automobile accidents as from terrorism). Actually, it is somewhat strange that so much emphasis has been put on the dangers of high-tech weapons in the first place. Some of that anxiety may come from the post-September 11 anthrax scare, even though that event killed only a few people. The bombings of September 11, by contrast, were remarkably low-tech and could have happened long ago; both skyscrapers and airplanes have been around for a century now.[27]

As a result, our primary emphasis must remain on the use of explosives.[28] Secondarily, because of the large number of casualties, physical destruction, and economic harm that would occur if terrorists used a nuclear device on American soil, it makes sense to invest resources to prevent such an attack and to minimize the impact of such an event were one to occur.

When it comes to risk, we must separate what we know from what we do not know. With natural disasters, we know quite a lot. With terrorism, we know very little. By focusing finite federal funds on those higher-risk jurisdictions, we are simply making the tough choices expected by the American people.

By focusing our national resources on building critical capabilities in those thirty-seven higher-risk places and then layering lesser capabilities across the balance of the nation, we are not only securing the homeland in an efficient and effective manner, but we are sending a clear message to our adversary that the risk of failure is much higher than the risk of success.

Now that we have determined the jurisdictions where the risk of a terrorist attack is higher, we must explain how the decentralization of certain homeland security activities will reduce risk in these jurisdictions, and, therefore, in America.

CASE STUDY 2

A Tale of Two Cities

In FY 2005, DHS allocated UASI funds based purely on a risk formula. Using the risk formula, DHS ranked the eligible jurisdictions and then allocated funds accordingly. Although the risk rankings are classified, eligible jurisdictions could ascertain their relative risk ranking by simply looking at how much UASI funds they received as compared to the other eligible jurisdictions.

Based on the risk formula, New York City received roughly $207 million in UASI funds, which placed it at the top of the UASI list.[29] The National Capital Region received the second largest allocation of UASI funds, totaling just over $77 million, which was only 37 percent of the amount received by New York City.[30] Although the risk rankings and allocations likely were not linear perfect, it is clear from this significant difference that DHS concluded New York City possessed a substantially greater amount of risk than any other jurisdiction in the United States.

In FY 2006, DHS changed how it allocated UASI funds and for the first time used a grant allocation method that combined the relative risk of jurisdictions and the effectiveness of the solutions proposed in the investment justifications that each jurisdiction had to submit to DHS.[31] Originally, the formula was supposed to analyze risk and capability needs as listed in the TCL. As Secretary Chertoff stated at the press conference on January 3, 2006, when he announced the eligible jurisdictions and the use of the investment justifications, the TCL need element was added to "make... sure that not only are we allocating funding based on risk, but that the funding is being used to build the kinds of nationally critical capabilities that we've identified based on experience."[32]

At some point between January 4, 2006, and May 31, 2006, the need component was changed to "effectiveness" as Tracy Henke, the DHS official in charge of the grants, noted, "In the past, people might have said risk and need. It's actually, as the Under Secretary was pointing out, effectiveness of the proposed solutions that the states and the urban areas put forward."[33] Effectiveness, unlike the TCL needs assessment, is an extremely subjective basis on which to evaluate investment justifications.

For example, if a jurisdiction listed the absence of a specific TCL capability in its investment justification, then evaluating that investment justification is fairly straightforward. A reviewer simply asks and answers four iterative questions:

1. Would the funding request build a capability in the TCL?
2. Does the jurisdiction need that capability?
3. Would the request close an existing capability gap?
4. Is closing this gap in this jurisdiction important enough relative to other gaps in other jurisdictions to justify the investment?[34]

If the answer to any question is in the negative, then the funding request is denied.

In contrast, measuring effectiveness absent a common, objective standard is inherently difficult. The peer reviewers DHS used to evaluate the effectiveness of investment justifications scored each one using amorphous factors such as "relevance to the interim National Preparedness Goal, relevance to state and local homeland security plans, anticipated impact, sustainability, and regionalism."[35] Each factor depended largely on the subjective opinion of the reviewer, thereby undermining any claim to legitimacy.

In FY 2006, the risk scores were determined in December 2005 based on the risk ranking for each jurisdiction. On January 3, 2006, DHS announced the thirty-five jurisdictions that would be fully eligible for the UASI program and the eleven jurisdictions that would be eligible for sustainment funds only.[36] Those jurisdictions then had a defined period of time to determine their capability needs and submit investment justifications to DHS for review and scoring.

In New York City's case, even though the risk ranking remained classified, little changed from FY 2005 that would have moved it from the clear number-one risk target. In fact, Henke noted that there was no reason to state that the "risk in New York is any different or changed or any lower."[37] On its investment justification, New York City received one of the lowest scores because it had "done a poor job articulating its needs in its application."[38] Based on the combined risk and effectiveness scores, DHS allocated New York City only $124 million in FY 2006, which was an $83 million drop from FY 2005 despite fewer fully eligible jurisdictions (thirty-five versus fifty).[39] The National Capital Region, which occupied the second highest risk spot in FY 2005, also received a $31 million reduction in UASI funds.[40]

Interestingly, the decrease in appropriated funds for the UASI program in FY 2006 was roughly $72 million ($757 million versus $829 million) and the funds awarded to the eleven jurisdictions deemed eligible only for sustainment funds totaled approximately $70 million, or an average of over $6 million per jurisdiction, which was more than many higher-risk jurisdictions received.[41] Had DHS only awarded those eleven jurisdictions amounts reflective of sustainment levels of $3.7 million (the lowest amount awarded that year) rather than amounts in excess of their risk rankings, the combined decrease in appropriations and sustainment funds would have totaled $113 million, which closely tracked the $114 million decreases to New York City and the National Capital Region.

For FY 2007, DHS used a similar type of risk formula as it did in FY 2006. Even though DHS had expanded the list of fully eligible jurisdictions to forty-six jurisdictions and the Congress had appropriated $11 million less for the UASI program ($746 million), DHS increased New York City's allocation by $10 million to $134 million, which represented an 8 percent increase.[42]

Again, assuming that New York City's risk had not appreciably changed from FY 2006, the $10 million increase must have come from the quality of its investment application. In fact, New York City had the top investment justification in FY 2007. While applicants were told that the investment justification counted for one-third of the allocation formula, the reality is that DHS reduced the weight of the investment justification to less than 10 percent of the allocation formula. With that change, it makes sense that New York City only received a meager $10 million increase when its investment justification went from one of the worst to the best—the investment justification really did not matter.

As it turns out, DHS had done the same thing in FY 2006, which means that DHS's official explanation for the $83 million reduction in funding was baseless. This unexplained discrepancy not only undermines the credibility of DHS, but also fails to reward the work done by New York City to increase the quality of its investment justification, as well as every applicant that spent time and money doing the investment justification.[43]

Columbus is equally as perplexing, and indicates a flaw in the risk methodology. In FY 2004 and FY 2005 when DHS only used risk to make UASI allocations, Columbus came in as the eighteenth and twenty-eighth most at-risk jurisdiction, and averaged almost $8 million each year in UASI funds.[44] In FY 2006 and FY 2007, Columbus experienced a precipitous drop in homeland security funding. In those years, Columbus, despite being deemed a top thirty-five fully eligible jurisdiction, dropped to fortieth in FY 2006 and to forty-second out of forty-six jurisdictions in FY 2007.[45] As a result, Columbus averaged about half the UASI funds over the last two years.

In FY 2006, Columbus's investment justification was ranked thirty-sixth out of the forty-six jurisdictions. This low score could explain Columbus' allocation rank of fortieth. With prior risk scores in the teens and twenties, that likelihood seems small. In FY 2007, however, Columbus' investment justification improved substantially as DHS deemed it the seventeenth best out of the forty-six jurisdictions. Yet, Columbus lost ground in the allocation rankings and only received $300,000 more in UASI funds. With investment justification scores at both the high and low ends in successive years, something else had to be causing Columbus' drop.

In the allocation formula for FY 2006 and FY 2007, the risk score accounted for 90 percent or more of the total.[46] The risk score included the following elements (along with their weighting within the risk score): population (40 percent), economics (20 percent), threat (20 percent), infrastructure (15 percent), and national security (5 percent).[47]

In FY 2007, DHS ranked Columbus as the twenty-seventh largest jurisdiction in population (it is the fifteenth largest city according to the U.S. Census Bureau), the twenty-seventh largest in economics (it has the thirty-third biggest gross metropolitan product according to the U.S. Department of Labor), and a stunning eighty-third largest in critical infrastructure. Because the threat and national security factors are classified, it is impossible to know where DHS ranked Columbus. The very fact that Columbus was eligible for the UASI program, however, means that it had to be in the top forty-six jurisdictions under the total risk score.

The first probable error involved the incredibly low critical-infrastructure score. With all of the people who make Columbus the fifteenth largest city in America comes a significant amount of critical infrastructure, such as power sources, highways, entertainment venues, water systems, telecommunication systems, and other key critical infrastructure. A ranking of eighty-three would equate to a city with roughly 200,000 people, which is 1.5 million less than Columbus currently has.

The likely bigger error must have occurred in the classified threat and national security scores. Based on the facts that Columbus is one of the few jurisdictions in America that has had active terrorist activity, has secured convictions of terrorists, and historically averaged a risk score in the top twenty-three in FY 2004 and FY

2005, it is hard to believe that Columbus' threat score would have decreased so significantly.[48] DHS simply must have erred.

Because DHS can wrap itself in the cover of classified information, jurisdictions are left to wonder year-to-year what will occur behind the wizard's sheet. This just does not seem like a successful way to identify the higher-risk jurisdictions in a manner that does not lead to wild fluctuations in eligibility and funding. Stability is needed.

6

The Importance of Local Preparedness

We of the Republic sensed the truth that democratic government has innate capacity to protect its people against disasters once considered inevitable, to solve problems once considered unsolvable. We would not admit that we could not find a way to master economic epidemics just as, after centuries of fatalistic suffering, we had found a way to master epidemics of disease. We refused to leave the problems of our common welfare to be solved by the winds of chance and the hurricanes of disaster... [T]hey created a strong government with powers of united action sufficient then and now to solve problems utterly beyond individual or local solution... We are beginning to wipe out the line that divides the practical from the ideal; and in so doing we are fashioning an instrument of unimagined power for the establishment of a morally better world.

President Franklin D. Roosevelt[1]

This is the end of this business of centralization, and I want you to go back and tell the president that we're not going to let this government centralize everything. It's come to an end... As for your young men, you call them together and tell them to get out of Washington—tell them to go home, back to the states. That is where they must do their work.

Justice Louis Brandeis[2]

America's ability to withstand a catastrophic natural disaster or terrorist strike rests largely on the capabilities existing in its states and localities. Although actuarial data have provided us with a clear picture of where possible catastrophic natural disasters can strike, the very nature of the terrorist threat substantially undermines our ability to predict with a high degree of certainty where the next terrorist strike will occur.

This uncertainty, as discussed in Chapter 5, forces us to use risk formulas based on variables such as population, population density, and presence of critical infrastructure to identify higher-risk jurisdictions. Because there are not unlimited funds, targeting finite funds to these higher-risk jurisdictions allows us to mitigate the risk of a terrorist strike where the vulnerabilities and consequences are the greatest and, at the same time, accept some degree of risk in lower-risk jurisdictions. In a resource-constrained environment, risk management presents the only realistic option.

The bulk of preparedness activities must occur in those higher-risk jurisdictions. Historically, preparedness in the United States meant "preparing to respond." For the emergency management community, this definition made sense as it addressed their primary focus on natural disasters. For natural disasters, state and local personnel spent their nonresponse time preparing to respond and then, after an event occurred, responding.

The September 11 attack required a new approach. On December 17, 2003, President Bush issued Homeland Security Presidential Directive 8 (HSPD-8), "National Preparedness."[3] In HSPD-8, President Bush articulated a new definition of preparedness; namely, preparedness referred "to the existence of plans, procedures, policies, training, and equipment necessary at the Federal, State, and local level to maximize the ability to prevent, respond to, and recover from major events."[4] Unlike natural disasters, terrorist attacks could be prevented. With the addition of "prevent" to the definition, President Bush signaled a strong commitment not just to prepare to respond and respond, but also to prevent a terrorist attack from occurring in the first place.

Merely being prepared was not enough. In addition to being prepared, we had to ensure that capabilities possessed by federal, state, and local governments were resilient so that those capabilities could "withstand or recover quickly from difficult conditions."[5] With so many jurisdictions and possible threats, the task to build a prepared and resilient America would be monumental. It would require a truly collaborative approach across levels of government.

History provided a good guide. "Through the late nineteenth century, the national government confined itself mainly to military matters, foreign affairs, and international commerce. Most internal improvements (canals, roads, and railroads) were financed and organized by states, local governments, and private interests."[6] During the Cold War, the domestic role played by the federal government was to coordinate state and local efforts and to develop overarching policy. In response to the terrorist threat today, the federal government at times took a similar approach, but also too often engaged in noncollaborative approaches highlighted by the use of unfunded mandates and meaningless form-over-substance requirements and reports.

As discussed throughout this book, the federal government today feels more like the federal government of the New Deal Era when "in twelve months, the [National Recovery Administration] had generated more paper than the entire legislative output of the federal government since 1789."[7] Times have changed, but the federal approach to problem solving (read: throw more money at it and spread it around generously) has not evolved much beyond 1936. "It is no coincidence that the first peacetime year in American history in which federal spending outpaced the total spending of the states and towns was that election year of 1936."[8] We must move beyond generating paper and mandates—beyond just spending more money in more places.

State and local elected officials must stop spending all of their time and energy complaining about federal funding issues and put their own money where their mouths are. For example, the U.S. Conference of Mayors' "National Action Plan" consists of little more than demands for more federal funds as twenty of the thirty-three recommendations in the report involve money.[9]

Our challenge is to build a domestic set of capabilities that can thwart an adaptive enemy or minimize the harm it can do in our cities. This challenge requires the federal government to treat states and localities like the partners they are and make sure that the finite funds available go to the jurisdictions facing the gravest potential threats. At the same time, it requires states and localities to focus on more than how much money they can get from Washington, including a serious review of whether federal taxes should be reduced by the amount apportioned to homeland security activities so that states can increase their taxes accordingly. After all, raising state taxes to pay for an activity without reducing federal taxes that pay for the same activity makes little sense.

THE COLLABORATIVE DEVELOPMENT OF PREPAREDNESS POLICY

When facing the ever-present threat of a terrorist attack, policymakers are confronted by two competing approaches. The first approach aims to identify all of the possibilities of a terrorist attack and then build the various capabilities needed to prevent or minimize the impact of specific attacks.[10] This approach can be referred to as the 100 percent solution. The second approach aims to identify a representative set of possible terrorist attacks and then build the various common and more critical capabilities needed to prevent or minimize the impact of generalized attacks. This approach can be referred to as the 90 percent solution, and it most effectively mitigates against unforeseen events.

In a resource-constrained environment, it is critical to use resources (people, funding, and time) in a manner that increases effectiveness and decreases waste. Knowing that neither the Congress nor states and localities would appropriate funds to implement the 100 percent solution, it made logical sense to adopt the 90 percent solution approach, which was the approach contained in HSPD-8 and embodied in the TCL.

Among other items, HSPD-8 required the DHS Secretary "to develop a national domestic all-hazards preparedness goal."[11] Secretary Ridge assigned this responsibility to ODP. With the utmost respect for our federalism principles and consistent with the historical role of the federal government to develop broad policy and serve as a coordinator of the states, ODP undertook an enormous effort to collaborate with states and localities in the implementation of HSPD-8. Over the course of the next year, ODP, seeking not to repeat the mistake of those who drafted the National Response Plan (a plan that controlled the response to major events), spent significant amounts of time and resources reaching out to states and localities, first preventers, and first responders to ensure that the National Preparedness Goal (NPG) reflected a national consensus (as much as such a thing is possible).

In addition to the NPG, HSPD-8 contained the requirement to "establish measurable readiness priorities and targets that appropriately balance the potential threat and magnitude of terrorist attacks, major disasters, and other emergencies with the resources required to prevent, respond to, and recover from them."[12] In response, DHS created the TCL,[13] a catalog of critical capabilities needed at some level of government to prevent, protect, respond to, and recover from a natural disaster or terrorist attack.

Utilizing a capabilities-based planning process, ODP worked closely with hundreds of experts from across federal, state, and local governments; nongovernmental organizations; and the private sector to develop a list of tasks that would need to be performed to handle a natural disaster and terrorist attack. To create the task list, ODP developed and used fifteen National Planning Scenarios to compile a list of tasks that would need to be performed along the prevention to recovery spectrum for each of the fifteen scenarios.[14] The task list included roughly 1,600 separate tasks.[15]

As part of the developmental process, over 1,500 organizations received drafts and commented on the task list and TCL.[16] ODP posted the documents on numerous Web sites for review, and created a special electronic mail address to receive comments (hspd8@dhs.gov).[17] To ensure it respected the role of federalism and to assist in implementing HSPD-8, ODP created the HSPD-8 Senior Steering Committee, which was comprised of representatives from eight federal entities and seven state and local entities.[18] Some of the state and local representatives included Idaho Governor Dirk Kempthorne, District of Columbia Mayor Anthony Williams, Los Angeles County Fire Chief Michael Freeman, and Boone County, Missouri, Commissioner Karen Miller.[19]

For the development of the task list, ODP held its first task list workshop on June 23 to June 25, 2004, where teams worked through the National Planning Scenarios.[20] The National Planning Scenarios include fifteen scenarios along the chemical, biological, radiological, nuclear, and explosives spectrum, as well as an earthquake, a hurricane, and a pandemic flu outbreak.[21] The scenarios are listed in Table 6.1.

Each scenario tests response and recovery capabilities,[22] and comes with a scenario overview that describes the scenario generally, provides geographic considerations, includes a timeline/event dynamics section, and details any secondary hazards or events.[23] Each scenario also details the key implications of the scenario on the jurisdiction.[24] Finally, the scenario includes the mission areas that would be activated by the scenario.[25]

The first task list workshop included roughly 160 state and local representatives.[26] From July 12 to July 26, 2004, ODP sent the task list to states and

TABLE 6.1 National Planning Scenarios[1]

Scenario	Type	Threat
Nuclear Detonation	10-Kiloton Improvised Nuclear Device	Terrorist
Biological Attack	Aerosol Anthrax	Terrorist
Biological Disease Outbreak	Pandemic Influenza	Natural Disaster
Biological Attack	Plague	Terrorist
Chemical Attack	Blister Agent	Terrorist
Chemical Attack	Toxic Industrial Chemicals	Terrorist
Chemical Attack	Nerve Agent	Terrorist
Chemical Attack	Chlorine Tank Explosion	Terrorist
Natural Disaster	Major Earthquake	Natural Disaster
Natural Disaster	Major Hurricane	Natural Disaster
Radiological Attack	Radiological Dispersal Device	Terrorist
Explosives Attack	Bombing Using Improvised Explosive Device	Terrorist
Biological Attack	Food Contamination	Terrorist
Biological Attack	Foreign Animal Disease (Foot and Mouth Disease)	Terrorist
Cyber Attack	Computer Infiltration	Terrorist

[1]U.S. Department of Homeland Security, National Planning Scenarios, April 2005.

localities for a national review of the draft task list.[27] From August 13 to August 27, 2004, ODP posted the task list for a second national review.[28] The distribution list for both national reviews included all of the state homeland security advisors, all of the state emergency managers, forty-two law enforcement agencies, ninety-four fire stations, and seventy-six associations, as well as the thousands of individuals who received the draft documents from those groups.[29] On December 17, 2004, ODP released the second version of the task list.[30]

To create the TCL from the task list of roughly 1,600 tasks, the ODP-led national team identified the top 300 or so critical tasks common across the fifteen planning scenarios.[31] The group then determined the capabilities that would be needed to perform each task successfully.[32] This process resulted in the identification of thirty-six critical capabilities as listed in Table 6.2.

Because the capabilities were derived from both terrorist and natural disaster scenarios, the capabilities were considered an all-hazards tool.[33] Based on the failures in the response to Hurricane Katrina, many of the capabilities listed in the TCL proved to be highly accurate as to what was needed to handle a catastrophic event. After Hurricane Katrina and at the request of many who responded to it, the capabilities were revised and reorganized, which added one capability to the list.[34] Each capability contains a definition, outcome, major activities, critical tasks, preparedness measures and metrics, performance

TABLE 6.2 Target Capability List Capabilities[1]

Animal Health Emergency Support	CBRNE Detection
Citizen Preparedness and Participation	Citizen Protection: Evacuation and/or In-Place Protection
Critical Infrastructure Protection	Critical Resource Logistics and Distribution
Economic and Community Recovery	Emergency Operations Center Management
Emergency Public Information and Warning	Environmental Health and Vector Control
Explosive Device Response Operations	Fatality Management
Firefighting Operations/Support	Food and Agriculture Safety and Defense
Information Collection and Threat Recognition	Information Sharing and Collaboration
Intelligence Fusion and Analysis	Interoperable Communications
Isolation and Quarantine	Mass Care (Sheltering, Feeding, and Related Services)
Mass Prophylaxis	Medical Supplies Management and Distribution
Medical Surge	On-Site Incident Management
Planning	Public Health Epidemiological Investigation and Laboratory Testing
Public Safety and Security Response	Restoration of Lifelines
Risk Analysis	Search and Rescue
Structural Damage Assessment and Mitigation	Terrorism Investigation and Intervention
Triage and Prehospital Treatment	Volunteer Management and Donations
WMD/Hazardous Materials Response and Decontamination	Worker Health and Safety

[1] U.S. Department of Homeland Security, Interim National Preparedness Goal, March 31, 2005, 7.

measures and metrics, capability resource elements, planning assumptions and factors, national target levels, and assignments of responsibility.[35]

To develop the TCL, ODP held its first capabilities workshop for 350 state and local representatives on October 12 to October 14, 2004.[36] On December 8 to December 10, 2004, ODP oversaw capability working group meetings.[37] From December 17, 2004, to January 17, 2005, ODP distributed the draft of capabilities for a national review.[38] Concurrently, ODP oversaw a second capability working group meeting on January 6 to January 7, 2005.[39] After thousands of comments and numerous revisions from state and local representatives, ODP released the first version of the TCL on February 15, 2005.[40]

In drafting the NPG, ODP leveraged all of the groups and individuals who had participated in the development and review of the task list and TCL. ODP released a draft version of the NPG for its first national review on August 20, 2004.[41] On August 25, 2004, the HSPD-8 Senior Steering Committee convened to review the NPG.[42] On September 2, 2004, the State, Local, and Tribal Working Group convened to review the NPG.[43] The Homeland Security Advisory Council Emergency Response Senior Advisory Committee received two briefings on the NPG in September 2004 and November 2004.[44] The Homeland Security Advisory Council State and Local Senior Advisory Committee received a briefing on the NPG on September 21, 2004.[45] After a substantial number of comments and revisions, on February 12, 2005, ODP released the draft NPG for its second national review.[46]

Despite this national process involving thousands of experienced state and local officials, first preventers, and first responders, significant bureaucratic intransigence by the inexperienced Homeland Security Council almost derailed the publication of the NPG. To satisfy a handful of Homeland Security Council bureaucrats with a fraction of the experience of the thousands of individuals who reviewed the NPG, DHS agreed to call the NPG an "interim" NPG, and committed to issue the "final" NPG by the end of October 2005. On March 31, 2005, DHS released the Interim National Preparedness Goal (Interim).

Because the TCL is an evolving document—meaning, experience and additional work help further enhance the document—some capabilities and underlying components are more detailed than other capabilities. One of the key elements remaining to be developed is a tier structure that lets jurisdictions, based on their unique variables, determine the appropriate level of each capability needed.[47] After all, it would be an enormous waste of finite resources if we took a one-size-fits-all approach to building capabilities across the United States. The focus must be on building the right capabilities in the right places at the right level.

After additional work over the next seven months, a draft of the "final" NPG worked its way through the procedural federal review process and landed in the DHS front office in early November 2005. The final NPG remained in the DHS front office for roughly two years where it got lost in the stack of documents awaiting approval so that Secretary Chertoff could review it.

In the two years that transpired, very little substantively changed from the Interim to the "final" NPG, which was not released until September 2007. In fact, other than changing the name from the NPG to the National Preparedness Guidelines ("Guidelines"), shortening the "vision" statement, and adding "Strengthening Planning and Citizen Preparedness Capabilities" to the National Priorities, most of the Interim was repeated almost verbatim in the Guidelines.[48] An updated version of the TCL also faced this bureaucratic wasteland.

This inexcusable delay is not merely another example of why Washington is not best suited to lead America's homeland security efforts; rather, by sitting on the newest version of the TCL, the federal government implicitly communicated to states and localities that the capabilities-based planning document may not be the final policy guide on preparedness issues. As a result, precious time to build capabilities was lost.[49] At the federal level, efforts to refine the TCL, without the top-level support needed, lost momentum in early 2006, thereby compromising the support it had garnered and delaying the development of the tier structure and additional requirements granularity.[50]

The most significant aspect of the TCL is that it provides a solid foundation for the creation of a National Preparedness System (NPS). Specifically, the ever-evolving TCL provides federal, state, and local governments with a comprehensive list of the equipment, personnel, training, and exercise requirements needed to be prepared. If the ultimate goal is a nation prepared to protect, prevent, respond to, and recover from a natural disaster or terrorist attack, then nothing short of the NPS that allows us to determine capability expectations by jurisdiction, as-is capabilities by jurisdiction, and capability gaps by jurisdictions is required.

In addition to the NPG and TCL, HSPD-8 required DHS to "establish and maintain a comprehensive training program to meet the national preparedness goal" and to "establish a national program and a multi-year planning system to conduct homeland security preparedness-related exercises."[51] On training, the federal government created the Training and Data Exchange partnership to consolidate federal training courses for states and localities.[52]

DHS also created the Training Information System to help facilitate the training of first preventers and first responders using federal funds. In an effort to decentralize training efforts, DHS launched the Cooperative Training Outreach Program in October 2005 "to expand first responder preparedness training across the country by permitting the states to identify and approve institutions within their states, territories, or tribal entities that can adopt and deliver DHS standardized training courses." Finally, DHS worked with the National Domestic Preparedness Consortium to provide hands-on training to first responders along the weapons of mass destruction (WMD) spectrum at five training facilities across the United States.[53]

The National Planning Scenarios also became the foundation for the National Exercise Program so that any level of government could use a scenario to test its competency across the capabilities and, more importantly, establish an exercise program to continuously enhance its competencies and capabilities. As part of the exercise program, DHS developed the Homeland Security Exercise and Evaluation Program, which is "common exercise policy and program guidance that constitutes a national standard for exercises."[54] DHS also created the Corrective Action Program for "systematically developing, prioritizing, tracking, and analyzing corrective actions for improving exercises, and the planning, training, and equipment which drives the cycle of preparedness."[55]

With all of those tools, designing the NPS is possible. The NPS should have a resource element that focuses on the assets, equipment, and personnel that a jurisdiction needs under the TCL across the relevant capabilities. The second element of the NPS is the training needs of the jurisdiction in relation to both disciplines and asset or equipment training requirements. Finally, once a jurisdiction has acquired the needed resources and obtained the requisite discipline and equipment training, then testing competency via a robust and repeatable exercise program becomes the final key element of the NPS that would allow a jurisdiction to identify gaps in capabilities and constantly reduce those gaps over time. Together, these three elements allow each jurisdiction to gauge its overall preparedness and, in a mosaic with the other jurisdictions across the nation, allow DHS to report to the President, the Congress, and the taxpayers on the nation's overall preparedness.

The NPS also will allow federal, state, and local governments to fully account for what our financial investments have bought thus far, what remains to be done, and then what level, if any, of sustainability funds the Congress will need to provide in the future to keep the nation prepared. Although some work has been done that may lead to the NPS, the work is going too slowly and without the benefit of seeking much input from the private sector, which can bring to bear innovative technologies as well as develop new technologies to meet the challenges of building a robust NPS. With such transparency, taxpayers can exert pressure on their respective political leaders to ensure that their jurisdictions are doing all they can to be prepared.

To facilitate the development of capabilities across the country, HSPD-8 also called for the creation of "a system to collect, analyze, and disseminate lessons learned, best practices, and information from exercises, training events, research, and other sources, including actual incidents, and establish procedures to improve national preparedness to prevent, respond to, and recover from major events."[56] On April 19, 2004, DHS launched the Lessons Learned Information Sharing Web site (www.llis.gov) so that states and localities could learn from each other in an iterative and cost-efficient manner.

In light of the results of the Nationwide Plan Review conducted in 2006 that showed broad planning deficiencies across the United States, President Bush released Homeland Security Presidential Directive 8 Annex 1, "National Planning," on December 3, 2007.[57] The Annex required the development of "a standardized approach to national planning to integrate and effect policy and operational objectives to prevent, protect against, respond to, and recover from all hazards."[58]

These elements—the National Planning Scenarios, the task list, the TCL, the National Exercise Program, and eventually the NPS—form the foundational structure needed in the United States to secure the homeland. If the Federal Preparedness Coordinators in the FEMA regions focus on their responsibilities as defined, then significant progress can be made to advance the federal-state-local partnership and, in so doing, create a more cohesive homeland security enterprise.[59] Where to build those capabilities and how to fund their development are the much more difficult and more political questions.

BUILDING THE RIGHT CAPABILITIES IN THE RIGHT PLACES

At the end of FY 2008, DHS will have allocated nearly $23 billion to states and localities for building capabilities.[60] There are roughly 87,000 jurisdictions currently eligible for homeland security grants.[61] The vast majority of those funds have been spread like a thin layer of butter on toast across the United States, largely disconnected from actual levels of relative terrorism risk.

Because DHS has not conducted a national capabilities assessment to ascertain comprehensive capabilities since 2003—two years before the release of the TCL—no one really knows or has authenticated what capabilities states and localities have built, whether the capabilities built are needed, and whether the capabilities that are possessed are at the appropriate level given the specific attributes of each jurisdiction. As a result, it is highly likely that the federal government has underinvested in higher-risk jurisdictions and over-invested in lower-risk jurisdictions.

In textbook fashion, DHS has made the perfect the enemy of the good by failing to use the TCL to allocate limited federal resources to those jurisdictions facing the highest terrorism risk. The American taxpayers deserve a domestic security approach that minimizes waste. The only viable tool to accomplish that task is the TCL. Without the benefit of a national capabilities assessment and the NPS, DHS will continue to allocate resources in an inefficient and ineffective manner.[62]

We can ill afford to continue squandering our resources given the continued effort of terrorists to attack the United States. As the Congress wrestles with funding formulas and other grant-related issues, it fails to even analyze whether or even why additional funds are needed, where those funds are needed, and whether federal grants are the optimum method to deliver state and local assistance. On the first three issues, the TCL can help determine allocation decisions so that the Congress can discontinue formulaic minimums.

Specifically, with $23 billion out the door, lower-risk jurisdictions should have come a long way in building the lower-level capabilities they will need. If those lower-risk jurisdictions want to acquire more capabilities than the billions of dollars in federal funds already have built, then they can dedicate their own funding to those initiatives.

The larger issue is with the higher-risk jurisdictions. The Congress must minimize the continued widespread dilution of finite federal funds so that these higher-risk jurisdictions receive what they need to build critical capabilities. An excellent example of this dilution problem is the ever-swelling list of jurisdictions being declared fully eligible for the UASI program (Table 6.3). From FY 2003 to FY 2008, the number of fully eligible urban areas grew or remained the same—except in FY 2006, when it shrunk to thirty-five urban areas.

This continued swelling of fully eligible urban areas only guarantees that finite resources are spread too thinly to have the needed impact in the time desired. Rather than simply acknowledge that there are only thirty-seven urban

TABLE 6.3 Number of Fully Eligible Urban Areas[i]

Year	Number of Fully Eligible Urban Areas
2003	30
2004	50
2005	50
2006	35
2007	46
2008	60

[i]It appears that the sole reason that DHS expanded the list of fully eligible urban areas to sixty was because it did not want to exclude one urban area that had been fully eligible in FY 2007. Specifically, when the Congress changed the formula for determining urban areas, roughly fourteen new urban areas possessed higher-risk scores in FY 2008 than one or more of the fully eligible urban areas from FY 2007. Rather than expand the list of fully eligible urban areas—a move that would have a ratchet-up effect every year when one or more new urban areas achieved higher-risk scores than one fully eligible urban area from the prior year—in FY 2008, DHS could have taken the approach it established, but failed to implement, in FY 2006 when it allowed eleven urban areas that had been fully eligible in FY 2005 to apply for sustainment funds to finish building a capability where the risk and capability were deemed critical.

areas with a meaningful level of risk (explicit threats in places with large vulnerabilities that would result in heavy consequences), the federal government attempts to mollify elected officials who demand their pound of flesh.

Of the $23 billion appropriated by the Congress, a majority of those funds were allocated under two key programs: the State Homeland Security Program (SHSP) and the UASI program. For SHSP, the Congress has required that 80 percent of the funds given to the states get passed through to local governments across the states. For UASI, the funds have gone to the small number of urban areas deemed by the federal government to possess the greatest amount of risk from a terrorist attack. Given the dilution issue, it is time to reform both SHSP and UASI so that the aim of those programs can be achieved more effectively.

Under SHSP today, the 80 percent pass-though requirement presumes that the risk of a terrorist attack is largely the same across America. Because al Qaeda has focused virtually all attacks in large urban areas, the vast majority of the evidence would indicate that the risk of an attack is greater in large urban areas than in other parts of the country.

In fact, the UASI program itself historically made this distinction until FY 2008 when it decided to ignore reality and dictate that all urban areas were equally vulnerable to a terrorist attack. As the U.S. Government Accountability Office (GAO) concluded, "DHS's risk analysis model now considers the states and urban areas of the country equally vulnerable to a terrorist attack and assigns a constant value to vulnerability, which ignores geographic differences."[63] When a terrorist attack is being planned or occurs, the odds that it will happen in a large urban area *because*, unlike smaller urban areas, those jurisdictions possess the population densities and lots of vulnerable elements (for example, subway systems, heavily traveled bridges and tunnels, tall buildings, and large arenas and stadiums) that could produce significant consequences.

As a result, first preventers and first responders in large urban areas serve on the front line in disrupting or dealing with an attack. The next level of government most likely to assist in preventing or responding to a terrorist threat is the state. Because of the pass-through requirement, too many states have been unable to acquire the capabilities needed at that level to be prepared. That must change.

Through UASI, higher-risk urban areas have been able to acquire some of the capabilities needed to effectively prevent or respond to a terrorist threat. While the country will know more once DHS conducts a full capabilities assessment that identifies capabilities gaps, given the unmet requirements in areas such as WMD detection, information and intelligence gathering and sharing, medical surge, mass prophylaxis, and citizen evacuation, there is plenty of work left to do in the urban areas designated eligible for the UASI program.

These higher-risk urban areas need a greater level of federal funding to facilitate the acquisition of critical capabilities. Although we should take some comfort in the fact that a terrorist attack has not occurred in America in almost seven years, we must keep in mind that eight years lapsed between al Qaeda's second domestic attack on America and its first domestic attack on the WTC back in 1993. We can ill-afford to let many more years pass without putting in place the capabilities we think are necessary to prevent or minimize the impact of a terrorist attack.

With so much at stake, higher-risk urban areas and their political leaders are on the hot seat to get things done. If they are responsible, they should be able to control the entire process. Rather than slowing things down with bureaucratic processes and unnecessary chaperoning, it is time for the federal government to work directly with UASI-eligible urban areas by allowing them to apply for, receive, and administer their allocations with state officials serving only to check that the urban areas in their states are building the right level of capabilities and are coordinating with state activities and other urban areas to create a layered level of capabilities.

As required by HSPD-8, the federal government should be making "awards ... in a form that allows the recipients to apply the assistance to the highest priority preparedness requirements at the appropriate level of government."[64] Any allocation that fails to utilize the TCL (or a similar comprehensive, objective capabilities tool) as the benchmark for determining whether to fund a request is an allocation based on subjective opinions that can differ from opinion-maker to opinion-maker. DHS's current use of "effectiveness" fails the objective test as it suffers from human bias.[65] Subjective allocations are very difficult to defend because one expert can argue the merits of a request as another expert dismisses the request (or, as is typically the case, one Congressman can argue in support while one Congressman argues in opposition based on little more than opinion).

The Congress also should acknowledge that, while every community may possess a degree of risk, the risk of terrorism in most communities is fairly small. Because the UASI program already targets funds to the jurisdictions deemed to possess a greater degree of risk, the Congress should stop requiring the states to pass-through a large percentage of funds from the SHSP to other local governments where the risk of a terrorist attack is low. Otherwise, funds are wasted as evidenced by the small Ohio county that bought a $30,000 Hazmat truck that went unused for four years and now costs too much for the county to maintain so they are trying to sell it.[66]

Instead, the Congress should allow states to keep 100 percent of SHSP funding. Because the states represent the second line of offense and defense in dealing with a terrorist threat, it makes little sense to require states to pass 80 percent of the funds it receives to low-risk local governments. The states need to retain those funds and acquire the capabilities appropriate for their expected role and responsibilities.

In conjunction with this change, the Congress should decrease the funds to SHSP and increase funds to UASI. With states keeping 100 percent of SHSP funds, that program does not need the level of funding it currently receives. At the same time, because America's urban areas represent the first line of offense and defense in dealing with a terrorist threat, and are deemed to possess higher risk due to large, compacted populations and critical infrastructure, the urban areas need a higher level of funds to acquire the capabilities as quickly as possible.

Rather than expanding the number of eligible urban areas, the UASI program needs to focus on jurisdictions where the historical data indicate a higher level of risk. As discussed in Chapter 5, there are thirty-seven urban areas that year after year demonstrate a high degree of risk. The Congress should restrict UASI funding to those thirty-seven urban areas, so capabilities can be acquired in a timely fashion. For jurisdictions not on that list, if their political leaders believe that a measurable risk exists, then they should allocate funds from their own coffers to build the capabilities they believe are needed. The federal government cannot and should not be the check writer for every urban area in America.

Another means to fund state and local preparedness is to create special entities similar to port authorities that focus on homeland security issues. Such a new creation in the face of a global threat would not be historically out of step. For example, South Carolina created the South Carolina State Ports Authority during World War II "in furtherance of the war operations and needs of the United States."[67] Similar to port authorities, these homeland security authorities could be empowered to issue bonds, apply for federal funds, and levy charges where appropriate.

Although homeland security authorities might not be feasible for some jurisdictions, they likely would prove beneficial to the larger urban areas. This approach overcomes jurisdictional issues between cities, counties, and other government forms by creating a quasi-governmental, cross-jurisdictional entity that overlaps all of the relevant jurisdictions. As the GAO has concluded, even in the five-year-old National Capital Region, the various states and localities that make up that area "had not worked together to develop plans and coordinate expenditures for the use of federal funds."[68]

This approach also minimizes the dilemma faced by first preventers and first responders who want to work full-time on homeland security issues, but see no upward mobility in their current structures due to the focus on chronic day-to-day challenges. This approach provides for a dedicated funding stream for homeland security programs without the yearly budget fluctuations of donor agencies with competing priorities. Even more critical, a dedicated funding source will help urban areas unlatch themselves from the federal government teat.

One critical action for state legislatures is to codify the TCL so that states and localities focus on and are accountable for building the capabilities needed to defeat the terrorist threat. The codification of the TCL should include requirements that applications for federal funds focus on capability gaps. A secondary benefit to using the TCL is that it allows applicants to engage in meaningful, concrete strategic planning focused on building the right suite of capabilities rather then succumb to the whim of newly elected officials or directors who know better than the collective wisdom of thousands of state and local representatives.

Another critical reform is to streamline procurement processes so that unnecessary delays do not stand in the way of security. Finally, state legislatures must reform their homeland security-related academies and institutions so that professionals can broaden and deepen their competence and see a career path in homeland security.

Despite the positive steps the federal government has taken to serve as a coordinator, facilitator, and collaborative developer of broad preparedness policy, too often DHS has unnecessarily expanded its role by issuing unfunded mandates, instituting meaningless reporting requirements, and failing to coordinate on major issues. An internal study of requirements generated by preparedness programs at the federal level identified 314 different requirements.[69] Each one of these requirements imposes costs on states and localities and is tangentially related, at best, to the development of critical capabilities. As a result, states and localities spend millions of dollars on process requirements that do little to enhance security.

Applicants legitimately complain that these requirements result in lots of work and little value. As the internal comprehensive review found: "The overwhelming majority (95%) of States indicated the current Federal reporting requirements do not effectively assess or evaluate State/national preparedness. More than 75% of the States indicated existing Federal reporting requirements simply quantify or count 'things;' they do not measure preparedness capabilities and capacities."[70]

For example, the Categorical Assistance Progress Report and the Biannual Strategy Implementation Report are reports that DHS requires states and localities to submit every grant cycle. States and localities correctly complain that the former "provides no significant data," the latter "is not responsive to State needs," and "too much data is requested that does not appear to be used and shared."[71] As one senior DHS official who has reviewed thousands of pages of the reports has remarked, it is impossible to ascertain any consistent quantitative and qualitative pattern or result within and across jurisdictions.

On top of reporting requirements, much of the grant guidance issued by DHS has sown confusion and hindered progress in failing to contain meaningful preparedness specifics that states and localities could use for long-term strategic planning. As the GAO found prior to the release of the TCL: "The lack of such guidance has in the past been identified as hindering state and local efforts to prioritize their needs and plan how best to allocate their homeland security funding."[72] With the TCL, states now have the structural basis for future investments.

Although DHS did spend significant resources to coordinate and collaborate with states and localities in the development of key preparedness policies, in many other areas the federal government has failed to reach that same pinnacle of achievement. For example, in the development and implementation of the National Incident Management System, which is a common template for incident management, FEMA failed to seek sufficient state and local input and employed a "'one size fits all' methodology, which diminishes [its] credibility."[73] The program mandates sixty-three different requirements on states and localities, which is three times as many program requirements as the next largest preparedness program.[74] As a result, states view their relationship with DHS unfavorably and feel strongly that DHS needs to do a much better job of coordinating policies before implementing them.[75]

One of the most critical issues expressed by states and localities related to federal homeland security programs focused on the "overall preparedness/grant system and processes [that] lack partnership and collaboration."[76] Specifically, states and localities stated: "The Federal to State relationship is primarily one of compliance measured by counting dollars, exercises, training courses, and/or equipment. Processes are inconsistent and uncoordinated with no substantive feedback given to the States. State and local expertise is not being effectively utilized. A national framework in which States can prioritize, apply, and fill capability gaps is missing."[77] There is a better way to protect America that will honor our federalist tradition and focus on building capabilities where they are needed most.

Following September 11, 2001, DHS operated in an environment that hampered significant reengineering and imperiled general effectiveness. Programs were administered by a new, confused, and entangled department and caught in the scramble at all levels of government to establish new homeland security and grant administrative functions. They flooded an ill-prepared system with guidance, and distributed funding at a volume and velocity that overran and outpaced the system's capacity to absorb it. Most importantly, programs were the subject of intense bureaucratic struggles for primacy over billions of dollars in new funding.

The two agencies contesting for control within DHS—FEMA and ODP— had historically relied on, respectively, cooperative agreements and grants for their assistance programs. Cooperative agreements are used when substantial involvement of the federal government is expected; grants are used when substantial involvement of the federal government is not expected. Once the skirmishing ended, the programs were consolidated under ODP, and precisely the wrong instrument—grants—became the preferred tool for assistance. The results were predictable: little meaningful engagement between the federal government and states and localities over desired or realized outcomes, consistently exaggerated risk and unmet needs by applicants, and underreporting of capabilities.

Rather than address the root cause—the nature of the relationship—the Congress and DHS reacted by encumbering the process with additional steps, and levying increasing reporting requirements on states and localities. State and local officials repeatedly advised that grant administration was excessively burdensome; that they did not have sufficient time, expertise, or tools to prepare adequate strategies or applications; and that inadequate guidance was contributing to the problem.

Emblematic of the problem is the addition of a peer review process to determine the effectiveness of grant applications after submission of investment justifications. Determinations of effectiveness that should be a result of substantial involvement at the beginning of the process (an "engaged partnership") have been relegated to surrogates. In 2006, GAO noted: "What is remarkable about the whole area of emergency preparedness and homeland security is how little we know about how states and localities (1) finance their efforts in this area, (2) have used their federal funds, and (3) are assessing the effectiveness with which they spend those funds."[78]

If national strategic aims as well as those of states and localities are at stake, then our current reliance on grants and broadly stated conditions is akin to driving nails with a cannon—the effects are imprecise, indiscriminate, and hard to measure. We need to discard grants as the primary instrument for building our security arrangement.

The focus should be on multiyear capability building through the use of performance-based cooperative agreements. The cooperative agreements would be used to define and negotiate both an initial (or current) and full operational capability level drawn from the TCL and tailored to risk profile and needs. Rather than single-year grants, to achieve full capabilities, a series of annual increments adjusted to annual available resources could be executed that provide an increase in performance and capacity. This approach would allow us to achieve a level of full operational capabilities and then transition from capability building to maintenance and sustainment. It also would allow us to negotiate risk reduction and capability targets and readiness levels. By tying the agreement's scope to a jurisdiction's risk, the multiyear agreement would establish the type and extent of required capabilities and level of desired preparedness.

The advantages with cooperative agreements are many. With a combined perspective and shared "ownership" of goals and outcomes, planning and programming horizons can be extended to predict roughly the resources needed to achieve desired outcomes and risk reduction. It also substantially reduces administrative and applicant fatigue by dispensing with cumbersome annual applications and investment justifications in favor of a multiyear capability program. Allocation decisions would be more effective and efficient as progress in building capabilities could be considered. Rather than focusing on loosely affiliated grant projects, resources could be aimed at delivering demonstrable all-hazards operational capabilities, which would establish the means to conduct systematic preparedness assessments.

Whether it is the IG or GAO, audit after audit of states and localities reveal that grant management capabilities are weak.[79] As a result, grant funds are spent improperly, delays in allocating or spending funds occur, and other effectiveness and efficiency issues arise.[80] Most of the time, these issues happen because states and localities facing budget shortages and staffing issues simply double or triple task existing personnel to do the grants management work. This is penny-wise and pound-foolish, and, more importantly, unfair to those state and local workers trying to get things done.

To facilitate grant management capabilities, DHS should have done a far better job in developing a grants management system and support structure to assist states and localities. As the IG concluded:

> Our reports also pointed out the need for DHS to monitor the preparedness of state and local governments, grant expenditures, and grantee adherence to the financial terms and conditions of the awards. Given the billions of dollars appropriated annually for disaster and nondisaster grant programs, DHS needs to ensure that internal controls are in place and adhered to, and grants are sufficiently monitored to achieve successful outcomes.[81]

Attempts were made to reform the DHS grants management component so it would be more customer-service oriented, but bureaucratic opposition and egos got in the way. Perhaps DHS can get it right with cooperative agreements.

During the Cold War, some civil defense critics suggested, "It just is not possible to provide an effective civil defense organization that can maintain a high degree of operational readiness over what may be a protracted period of many years... Perhaps the main obstacle has been the sense of futility stemming from the realization that the task is too big and too complex to tackle."[82] Failure was not an option then nor is it now. The dense thicket of terrorism and catastrophic natural disasters warrant a more tightly coupled security relationship among levels of government. The stakes are simply too high to accept the dominant, failing paradigm.

CASE STUDY 3

Lessons Learned from SARS Elevates Seattle/King County Preparedness Efforts

Sensing it could significantly improve on its preparedness capabilities and lessons learned from the Severe Acute Respiratory Syndrome (SARS) scare in 2002 to 2003, the Seattle/King County public health community went to work committed to establishing an innovative approach to a possible pandemic flu outbreak or other catastrophic event. Over the course of the next five years, the list of preparedness accomplishments is long as Carina Elsenboss and her colleagues instituted innovative changes. Even more critical is that Seattle/King County has shared their transformative preparedness work with other states and localities.

The Seattle/King County area is home to more than 1.8 million people who speak over forty-six different languages.[83] It encompasses thirty-nine cities, over 130 special-purpose districts, and roughly 540 elected officials.[84] The public health community itself includes eighteen hospitals with emergency rooms, twenty-seven safety net clinics, and over 1,100 long-term residential care facilities.[85]

In 2006, Seattle/King County created the Vulnerable Populations Action Team "to reach individuals who may not or cannot access information from traditional sources that serve the general public."[86] The team focuses on several population segments, including the disabled, seniors, individuals with limited English proficiency, the homeless, and children.[87] As part of the initiative, the team created the Community Communication Network for public health, community-based organizations, and community leaders to reach those vulnerable populations through familiar contacts.[88] By keeping updated emergency contact information of these community entities, the team is able to provide real-time health and safety information to the area's most vulnerable populations, and work with the communities to ensure basic levels of preparedness.[89]

Because the program proved so successful, DHS featured it as a "Good Story" on the Lessons Learned Information Sharing Web site.[90] Specifically, after severe windstorms hit the area in December 2006, the public health team noticed an increase in East African immigrants seeking treatment at local hospitals for carbon monoxide poisoning.[91] These immigrants were burning charcoal indoors to stay warm, which drastically increased the levels of carbon monoxide in their homes.[92] By activating the team, the public health team was able to work through the Horn of Africa, which is a community organization focused on East Africans, to warn other immigrants about the danger of burning charcoal inside their homes.[93] This notice undoubtedly saved lives.

As a sign of their commitment to state and locally led innovation, Seattle/King County routinely scours the country looking for good ideas. After adopting these new ideas, they work to systematically share the innovation with other entities. For example, Seattle/King County has utilized several documents from the Oakland, California-based Collaborative Agencies Responding to Disasters such as "Partnering for Strength: MOUs Getting Your Relationship in Print" and "Agency Emergency Plan: A Simplified Version for Community-Based Organizations." It also conducted a two-day conference for public and private agencies focused on the lessons learned from Hurricane Katrina. With over 130 participants, the conference identified ways to ensure that local agencies that serve the most vulnerable populations are prepared and resilient.[94]

The Seattle/King County Public Health team and the Vulnerable Populations System Coordination Steering Committee jointly developed Community Based Organizations standards and indicators for emergency preparedness and response. Specifically, to assist community-based organizations "in the development of their emergency preparedness programs and activities," the group designed "measurable indicators... for emergency responders and communities to evaluate the status of their capacity/capability to respond in an emergency."[95] The tool has six outcomes, sixteen standards, and thirty-four indicators.[96]

For example, in the expected outcome, "Plans and protocols are shared, exercised, and tested," the standard is that "all staff and key stakeholders have been trained on the AEP (Agency Emergency Plan). Key partners have been provided a copy."[97] The three indicators for the outcome are: (1) "The AEP is accessible to all staff and volunteers." (2) "The language used in the AEP is understandable and devoid of jargon or technical slang," and (3) "AEP procedures are regularly exercised and tested."[98] This planning document is available to all relevant entities in the jurisdiction.

To improve communication and coordination, Seattle/King County created the King County Healthcare Coalition. The Coalition is "a network of healthcare organizations and providers that are committed to coordinating their emergency preparedness and response activities... [through] coordination, effective communications, and optimal use of available health resources in response to emergencies and disaster for all hazards."[99] The Coalition includes over sixty members and partners that form an Executive Council, a Staff Coordinating Group that works with two Special Advisory Groups, four Operational Planning Committees, four Regional Surge Capacity Projects, and six Clinical Planning Groups, as well as a Regional Medical Resource Center.[100]

Because of the SARS and pandemic flu concern in the Pacific Northwest, the Special Advisory Group on legal issues created a protocol for isolating or quarantining individuals, which is posted on the Seattle/King County Web site for other communities to use.[101] The Regional Medical Resource Center "provides situational awareness for the healthcare system [and] anticipates the needs, monitors available resources and coordinates deployment where needed during emergencies."[102]

Each year, the Coalition issues an annual report so that the communities it covers can keep up to speed on its activities. In 2008, the Coalition conducted a two-day seminar for healthcare providers on business resiliency issues, which covered issues such as regional hazards, essential services and critical functions, surge capacity, evacuation, and financial resiliency.[103] With its commitment to communicate with the community, Seattle/King County also continually provides information to residents via its monthly "Region 6 Healthcare Preparedness" publication and such unique tools as its "Incident Command System: A Tool for Responding to Emergencies."

King County also created an electronic mail alert system that allows individuals to sign up to receive electronic mail alerts on a variety of topics (bioterrorism, disaster response, isolation and quarantine, and pandemic flu) if something were to occur. To communicate with citizens most effectively, King County has translated key documents such as biohazard and disaster response fact sheets and preparedness check lists into many languages, including Spanish, Chinese, Vietnamese, Korean, Russian, Somali, and Cambodian.

Unlike many jurisdictions, in its drive to improve on its preparedness capabilities, Seattle/King County subjected themselves to an After Action Report process following severe windstorms in December 2006. The windstorms caused much of the area to lose power for several days due to 50- to 70-mile per hour winds that downed trees and power lines.[104] The disaster allowed Seattle/King County to test the innovations it had made and find additional capability gaps. The After Action Report noted several areas for improvement: add rapid translation capabilities, learn positive communication techniques, develop restaurant food waste plans; implement agreements for back-up storage sites and generators; improve situation updates and health order distribution lists and methods; and improve logistics support.[105] Roughly a year and a half later, Seattle/King County has implemented thirty-five (59 percent) of the recommendations.

Because of these initiatives, Seattle/King County serves as an Advance Practice Center where it develops and distributes innovative tools and guides to communities across the United States. For example, as part of its duties, it created an Advanced Training Practice kit on public health risk communication titled, "Speak First: Communicating Effectively in Times of Crisis and Uncertainty." Although not done initially under its Advance Practice Center role, Seattle/King County created a video for businesses, government, and community-based organizations titled, "Business Not as Usual: Preparing for Pandemic Flu," which it distributed to over 2,000 entities all over America. The video contains strong testimonials from citizens and business owners on the importance of preparedness. It also contains twenty-two recommendations every entity should follow to achieve a proper level of preparedness.[106]

From government agencies to community-based organizations, Seattle/King County has made great strides in preparing for the next catastrophic natural disaster or terrorist attack. By embracing a culture of preparedness, it ensures that lessons learned from past events and exercises are applied and disseminated, thereby making Seattle/King County an innovator that gets results.

7

Decentralizing Disaster Management

> We need to curb our casual use of government—especially, the federal government—as the problem solver of last resort. It has clearly failed in this role, and unless we narrow its responsibilities, we can expect the failure to continue and worsen.... A clearer split of responsibility among the federal, state, and local governments would encourage better government at all levels, because voters would know who to blame for failures.
>
> Robert J. Samuelson[1]

> Nagin Re-elected as New Orleans Mayor
>
> *New York Times* Headline[2]

After Hurricane Katrina, the Bush Administration and the Congress spent much time and energy developing plans to "fix" FEMA.[3] In a speech in February 2006 to the National Emergency Management Association's Mid-Year Conference, Secretary Chertoff highlighted four broad areas that would be fixed at FEMA in response to its performance during and after Hurricane Katrina.[4] Those areas were logistics management, claims management, debris removal, and communications.[5]

In October 2006, the Congress added its weight to strengthen FEMA. The legislation, among other reforms, placed most preparedness functions within FEMA, made the FEMA Administrator an equivalent to the DHS Deputy Secretary, and made the FEMA Administrator the primary advisor to the President during a disaster.[6] The legislation also required that the FEMA Administrator possess certain experience thresholds.[7]

Lost in all of the fixes was any real analysis or discussion on the historical role of FEMA and whether the role it performs today makes sense. As any emergency manager will tell you, all disasters are local. When a disaster happens, it is the local emergency response personnel who respond, not state or federal personnel. In support of federalism, Florida Governor Jeb Bush warned after Hurricane Katrina, "Before Congress considers a larger, direct federal role, it needs to hold communities and states accountable for properly preparing for the inevitable storms to come."[8]

Our system of government honors the sovereignty of state and local jurisdictions, which is why governors and mayors take offense to federal intrusion into their traditional spheres of power. In a poll in 2005, *USA Today* found that at least thirty-six governors disagreed with a significantly greater federal role in disaster responses.[9] Yet, the system that has arisen in the last two decades with its focus on getting federal disaster funds undermines state and local sovereignty. In short, it creates dependency.

Hurricane Katrina provides a casebook example of how the system is broken.

Based on public reports, only one federal, state, or local government employee lost his job because of the inept response to Hurricane Katrina—FEMA Administrator Michael Brown. One person, while certainly culpable for a chunk of the federal government's weak response, cannot possibly represent the pool of individuals who deserved reprobation. Because the media focused on the federal response deficiencies, state and local government employees slipped under the radar.

As for Brown, he deserved to go, but he was not alone. During the initial three days of the disaster, the ability of Secretary Chertoff and his team to deploy forces was severely compromised because Brown and his team largely refused to provide Secretary Chertoff or other DHS leaders with any real-time information.[10] Instead, Brown ignored the National Response Plan's organizational requirements and operated as if he was still a direct report to President Bush.

I personally recall spending most of one day trying every communication method available to get Brown to call the Secretary for a critical update. Despite being on television throughout the day and routinely communicating to staff "about restaurant reservations and his Nordstrom wardrobe" and to his White House allies, Brown ignored our requests until well into the night.[11] Ironically, despite this fact, critics of DHS assert that it was because Brown was not a direct report that FEMA performed so poorly. For those critics, being a direct report to the President again became the holy grail of the emergency management community.[12]

Other than Brown, no other federal employees, including those individuals at the White House who encouraged and enabled Brown to circumvent Secretaries Ridge and Chertoff over the previous two years, were disciplined. Not one. In fact, some received promotions. The White House investigation into the response to Hurricane Katrina conveniently ignored the role senior White House officials had in encouraging Brown's evasion of and fights with DHS.

Although Brown and other revisionists frequently claimed that FEMA was a tragic victim of DHS ineptitude, budgetary thievery, and micromanagement, the facts do not support this version of history. The familiar refrain is that, during the halcyon days before FEMA became part of DHS, it was fully capable of dealing with catastrophic disasters. This view is best represented by testimony given by emergency management leader Albert Ashwood on July 31, 2007.[13]

In his testimony, Ashwood reflected on the "success stories of the 1990s" in comparison to "the disassembling of FEMA under the Department of Homeland Security (DHS) structure and the total de-emphasis of natural disasters from September 11, 2001 through July 2005."[14] It goes without saying that the nation can be forgiven for focusing on the threat of terrorist attacks following the events of September 11, 2001, when almost 3,000 individuals died. In his rush to indict DHS, Ashwood ignored the fact that FEMA remained an independent agency for almost 40 percent of the time between the September 11, 2001, attack and Hurricane Katrina. Are Americans supposed to believe that what FEMA had become from 1993 to 2003 was so easily destroyed from 2003 to 2005 by a simple movement on an organizational chart?

In addition to the direct report canard, the revisionists blame FEMA's woes on three specific events: first, the loss of $270 million in FY 2004 and FY 2005—a mere 3 percent of FEMA's roughly $9 billion budget—that DHS used for shared services such as printing costs over the two years before Hurricane Katrina that FEMA was part of DHS; secondly, the movement of two grants programs out of FEMA in 2004; and, lastly, the attempted unification of preparedness programs outside of FEMA in late 2005.[15]

Given the sheer scope of FEMA's deficiencies and ineptness in catastrophic events, FEMA needed far more money and, more critically, needed the leadership, foresight, and initiative to start building the catastrophic capabilities in the 1990s due to the size and complexity of changes required. Hurricane Katrina demonstrated how acute the deficiencies were.

During the first few days, it became clear to DHS that FEMA had done little to prepare for a catastrophic event. Whether it was the lack of a disaster mortuary plan, a long-term housing plan, call center and victim registration capacity, or gaining real-time visibility into its commodities inventory and distribution, FEMA was in bad shape. These deficiencies went unnoticed as FEMA had dealt well with the routine natural disasters across the country and because the biggest disasters occurred where the states were fully capable to handle things (Florida in 2004). The routine, however, simply would not work for the catastrophic.

Although DHS moved two of the grants programs in mid-2004, little substantively or financially changed about those programs. The grants were administrated by the exact same people using the same policies as FEMA used. Because both grant programs distributed funds to thousands of recipients across the United States and were not retained by FEMA, there simply is no evidence that moving these grant programs contributed to FEMA's alleged decline starting in March 2003.

Finally, the consolidation of preparedness programs outside FEMA did not begin until October 2005—two months *after* Hurricane Katrina. Specifically, as part of the Second Stage Review launched by Secretary Chertoff in March

2005, he did not announce the unification of preparedness programs under a new directorate until July 13, 2005.[16] Between that speech and August 29, 2005, little to nothing occurred to move preparedness functions out of FEMA.

As to the alleged perfection of FEMA in the 1990s under James Lee Witt, the impact of Hurricane Floyd—a vastly smaller hurricane than Hurricane Katrina—demonstrated the same types of deficiencies that plagued FEMA during Hurricane Katrina six years later.[17] Instead of New Orleans, the city FEMA left in dire straits was Princeville, North Carolina. FEMA was heavily criticized for the poor evacuation of impacted residents, its slow response, and its failure to meet the needs of victims for many weeks after the hurricane hit.[18] Even Jesse Jackson—a loyal supporter of the Clinton Administration—criticized FEMA when he noted, in remarks equally applicable to Hurricane Katrina, "It seemed there was preparation for Hurricane Floyd, but then came Flood Floyd."[19]

It is time for the FEMA as DHS victim ruse to die. Whether it was Hurricane Andrew in 1992, Hurricane Floyd in 1999, or Hurricane Katrina in 2005, FEMA has a long and painful history of failing to prepare for catastrophic disasters. FEMA has spent too much time since 1993 responding to routine natural disasters. With this distraction, FEMA has little institutional capacity left to prepare for catastrophic disasters.

When FEMA federalizes routine natural disasters, states and localities lose the incentive to prepare for those events. As a result, FEMA will inherit the load. At the same time as changes were happening in Washington that caused substantial complaints from the emergency management community, states, responding to the federalization of disasters, were cutting emergency management budgets by an average of almost 25 percent.[20] As the National Emergency Management Agency correctly pointed out:

> Like anyone else, emergency managers can't accomplish their tasks if they lack essential funding, personnel and equipment. Mission capabilities become degraded and staff become demoralized. Retiring emergency management professionals are not being adequately replaced by a new generation because it appears to be a career path fraught with instability. Yet, as our nation continues to experience an increasing number of disasters, the federal government is undercutting our future ability to cope with them.[21]

It is correct on the problem. It is, however, blaming the wrong entity. Federal funds were always meant to supplement, not supplant "essential funding, personnel and equipment." Those basics are inherent state and local government responsibilities.

This acquiescence to federalizing disasters allows states and localities to blame FEMA when things go wrong, and undermines accountability. When the federal government attempts to inject accountability, governors and mayors, unaccustomed to such actions, become offended. For example, after Hurricane

Katrina, DHS launched a project to review the emergency plans of the states and higher-risk urban areas, and found that the plans were inept.[22]

We must, therefore, reverse the current trend of federalizing more and more disasters and get back to a decentralized model of leadership and accountability for routine disaster response. This shift would allow FEMA to focus more intensely on preparing for its *raison d'etre*—catastrophic natural disasters.

THE HISTORICAL ROLE OF THE FEDERAL GOVERNMENT DURING DISASTERS

Disasters of all kinds have occurred throughout our nation's history. For much of that history, disasters were dealt with at the local level given the physical inability of other government actors to assist.

The first recognized instance where the federal government provided disaster relief to state government occurred in 1803 in response to a fire in Portsmouth, New Hampshire.[23] Another example of federal disaster support followed the Chicago fire in 1871.[24] This piecemeal approach would guide federal disaster activity until World War I.

The tension between proponents of centralization and proponents of decentralization is not new. One early example is the failed attempt by the federal government to provide disaster relief in 1887 for a drought in Texas. The Congress passed the Texas Seed Act in 1887 that would have given seeds to farmers.[25] In response, President Grover Cleveland vetoed the legislation and noted:

> I can find no warrant for such an appropriation in the Constitution; and I do not believe that the power and duty of the General Government ought to be extended to the relief of individual suffering which is in no manner properly related to the public service or benefit. A prevalent tendency to disregard the limited mission of this power and duty should, I think, be steadily resisted, to the end that the lesson should be constantly enforced that, though the people support the Government, the Government should not support the people.[26]

President Cleveland believed that federal action "encourages the expectation of paternal care... and weakens the sturdiness of our national character," and he appealed to the charity of fellow Americans to aid their neighbors in need, which in fact occurred.[27]

Two years later, the federal government provided disaster relief in response to the Johnstown flood of 1889.[28] At the turn of the century, the federal government provided help following the destruction of Galveston, Texas, by a hurricane that killed over 6,000 Americans.[29] Other than those catastrophic events, states and localities mostly dealt with disasters without federal support.

The federal government's intervention seemed inconsistent from 1900 to 1932. For example, following the San Francisco earthquake and fire in 1906, the federal government provided disaster assistance.[30] In 1926, a hurricane hit

Miami, Florida, causing over $40 billion in inflation-adjusted damages.[31] The federal government declined to provide disaster assistance.[32]

During the height of the New Deal, the Roosevelt administration and the Congress greatly expanded the role of the federal government following disasters by expanding three entities. The Reconstruction Finance Corporation was permitted to provide loans following earthquakes.[33] The Bureau of Public Roads was allowed to provide funds to repair roads and bridges after a hurricane.[34] The U.S. Army Corps of Engineers received greater authority to implement flood measures.[35]

Despite these additional powers, states and localities still handled most disasters. This fact is borne out by the low number of federal declarations issued up to 1972. Until 1972, the highest number of declarations issued in a year was twenty-nine.[36] From 1972 to 1979, however, the number of declarations per year doubled from the yearly average of the preceding twenty years.[37]

In 1974, state emergency managers created the National Emergency Management Agency, which served as their own interest group to represent and advocate for them inside the Beltway.[38] It also helped emergency managers "exchange information on common emergency management issues that threatened their constituencies."[39] As the federal government's role increased, the trade group became a powerful player inside the Beltway and encouraged centralization.

Mainly in response to hurricanes and earthquakes, the federal government added other federal powers to be used during disasters.[40] Perhaps in response to this more active role and further expansion of federal entities involved in responding to a disaster, states and localities requested President Carter to create a single entity for them to deal with during a disaster.[41] In 1979, President Carter created FEMA, which merged multiple agencies and programs.[42]

In 1988, the Congress passed the Robert T. Stafford Disaster Relief and Emergency Assistance Act ("Stafford Act"), which is the key federal authority under which FEMA acts.[43] The Stafford Act authorized the federal government to provide "not less than 75 percent of the eligible cost" of declared disasters.[44] Such a generous cost-sharing requirement laid the foundation for the rapid federalization of disasters.

From 1980 to 1992, the number of declarations ranged from a low of sixteen to a high of fifty-three.[45] On average, FEMA was involved in thirty-three declarations per year.[46] During those years, FEMA dealt with nineteen disasters with damages in excess of $1 billion with each disaster estimated to average $10.6 billion and causing 948 deaths.[47] Of those, almost half were hurricanes and an earthquake—the rest were storms, floods, and droughts.[48]

During President Clinton's two terms, FEMA's involvement in disasters greatly increased. From 1993 to 2001, FEMA was involved in an average of 89 declarations per year—almost triple the previous twelve years.[49] In fact, from 1953 to 1992, the total number of declarations issued totaled 1,137.[50] In only eight years, FEMA issued 707 declarations.[51]

Under Clinton, FEMA dealt with thirty-three disasters with damages in excess of $1 billion, with each disaster estimated to average $4.3 billion (41 percent of the previous twelve-year average) and causing sixty-one deaths (6 percent of the previous twelve-year average).[52] Of those, only six were hurricanes and one was an earthquake—the other twenty-six disasters were storms, floods, and droughts.[53] It is easy to look good when the challenges are small.

Remarkably, FEMA would get even busier during the Bush presidency. From January 20, 2001, to January 19, 2009, FEMA was involved in an average of 130 declarations each year and issued 1036 declarations,[54] almost equal to the total output of FEMA over its first thirty-nine years.[55]

In March 2003, FEMA became part of the newly created DHS. From 2001 to 2006, FEMA dealt with twenty disasters with damages in excess of $1 billion, with each disaster estimated to average $244.5 billion (over half from Hurricane Katrina alone) and causing approximately 2,360 deaths (again, most from Hurricane Katrina).[56] Of those, almost half were hurricanes—the rest were storms, floods, and droughts.[57] It should be noted that few criticized FEMA under President Bush prior to the Hurricane Katrina debacle.

In fact, less than one year earlier, FEMA earned praise when, in partnership with the well-oiled Florida response team, it performed well dealing with four successive hurricanes in Florida in September 2004. With the 2004 Presidential election a little over a month away, flashbacks to August 1992 and Hurricane Andrew caused high levels of anxiety. Had FEMA erred in Florida, President Bush's reelection victory (286 to 251) could have become a defeat (259 to 278).

As Figure 7.1 indicates, the move toward greater federalization of routine natural disasters continues at an increasing pace each presidential term regardless of party affiliation.[58] Other than during a slight decrease during Lyndon B. Johnson's administration and a significant reduction during the Reagan

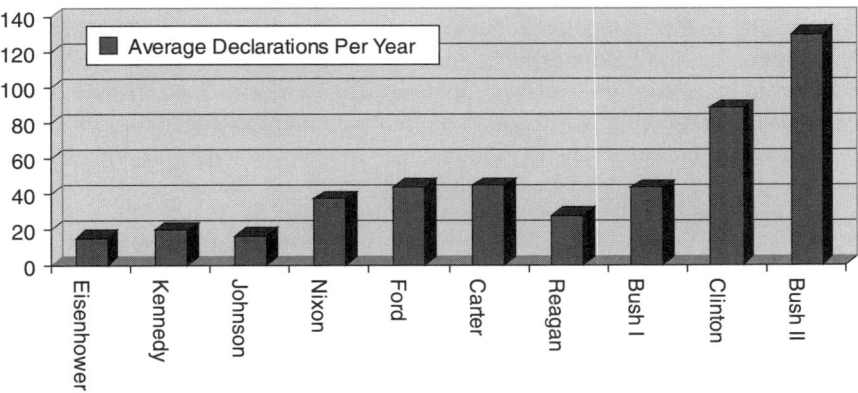

FIGURE 7.1 Disaster Declarations by Presidential Administration

administration, each president since Dwight D. Eisenhower has increased the number of declarations. As noted in Figure 7.1, things accelerated substantially under Presidents Clinton and Bush.

Given the tripling of declarations from 1992 to 2006, one would have expected a substantial increase to FEMA's budget. After all, in FY 1992, FEMA had roughly 2,500 employees and a nominal appropriation of $4.8 billion.[59] In FY 2006, FEMA had roughly the same number of employees and a slightly larger budget.[60] Hence, after fourteen years and three times as much activity, it simply is not a surprise that FEMA was unprepared for the most catastrophic event to hit America in recorded history.

While some place the dramatic increase in FEMA activity starting in 1993 on global warming, two more likely explanations come to mind. The first reason is that some political operatives attributed the re-election loss by President George H.W. Bush to FEMA's poor response to Hurricane Andrew in Florida during the 1992 general election.[61] With such a vivid reminder of how FEMA's execution can impact electoral politics, it came as no surprise that both Presidents Clinton and Bush actively increased FEMA's activity during their tenures.

In fact, in the election year of 1996, FEMA issued 157 declarations—a record that still stands today.[62] The years before and after the 1996 election, FEMA only dealt with thirty-eight declarations and forty-seven declarations, respectively—the two lowest numbers of declarations during the Clinton presidency.[63] Weather does not explain the anomaly.

The second reason is that, for the first time, the leadership of FEMA came from political circles. For most of FEMA's history, the director was a Washington bureaucrat or former military person.[64] In 1993, under President Clinton, Witt became the first state emergency manager to head FEMA.[65] President Clinton elevated FEMA to a cabinet-level position.[66] Witt came from Arkansas where he had worked for Governor Clinton as an emergency manager for four years.[67] Prior to his four years of experience as an emergency manager, Witt had been an elected politician in Arkansas where he won seven elections.[68]

In 2001, President Bush brought Allbaugh with him from Texas.[69] Allbaugh had served as a long-time political operative for President Bush. His last position prior to coming to Washington was serving in a high position in President Bush's campaign during the 2000 election.[70] When Allbaugh left after FEMA was merged into DHS, the much-maligned Brown took over the reins.[71] Brown also came from a political background, but had spent the bulk of his career as the head of an international horse association.[72] Brown lacked any meaningful emergency management experience other than the time he worked at FEMA under his longtime friend Allbaugh.[73]

Witt, Allbaugh, and Brown all acutely understood the political importance of a vibrant response—no matter how small the event. Certainly their willingness to send federal funds to states did not hurt the re-election efforts of their bosses. During Witt's term, declarations covered over 6,500 counties in all fifty states.[74] Witt even acknowledged the political benefit of his 1996 largess when he noted that "disasters are very political events."[75] Given the staggering rate of declarations from 1992 to today, it is hard not to tie that rate to the political nature of the individuals being appointed to FEMA.

By involving FEMA in an average of 130 declarations per year, or one every three days, FEMA spends all of its time and resources responding to a continuous flood of routine natural disasters. Little time or attention is spent building an organization capable of effectively handling a catastrophic event, especially in a post-September 11 world. Hence, rather then protecting against another Hurricane Andrew problem, FEMA has morphed into an agency of the routine over the last fifteen years, ensuring that it was not prepared when a truly catastrophic event like Hurricane Katrina struck.

Unfortunately, after Hurricane Katrina and its impact on the 2006 election, no president is going to put FEMA in a position where it can be faulted for an anemic response effort. Unless the Congress takes action to rein in FEMA or governors and mayors find their voices, it will continue to be an agency of the routine.[76] Rather than continued federalization, decentralizing routine natural disasters would secure America in a broader and more strategic manner.

LOCAL CONTROL IS KEY

Even after the September 11 attack, the federal government expressly acknowledged the primary role of states and localities in disaster response efforts. Specifically, Homeland Security Presidential Directive 5 (HSPD-5) titled, "Management of Domestic Issues," published the day before DHS officially became a department, notes that:

> The Federal Government recognizes the roles and responsibilities of State and local authorities in domestic incident management. Initial responsibility for managing domestic incidents generally falls on State and local authorities. The Federal Government will assist State and local authorities *when their resources are overwhelmed*, or when Federal interests are involved (emphasis added).[77]

Despite this express acknowledgement, HSPD-5 then encouraged a centralized approach in the creation of the National Response Plan, stating DHS must develop the plan "in consultation with other Federal departments and agencies,"[78] but not necessarily with states and localities. As a result, the National Response Plan, sold as a national rather than a federal plan, gave little expression to state and local primacy. This federal bias is reflected on the signature page, which contains the signatures of only federal officials.[79]

Nonetheless, HSPD-5 does provide a solid conceptual framework for disaster response, and it articulates a response partnership between the federal government and states and localities similar to roles developed during the Cold

War. HSPD-5 outlines a coordination and support role for the federal government. It reads:

> The Secretary will coordinate with State and local governments to ensure adequate planning, equipment, training, and exercise activities. The Secretary will also provide assistance to State and local governments to develop all-hazards plans and capabilities, including those of greatest importance to the security of the United States, and will ensure that State, local, and Federal plans are compatible.[80]

The coordination role is one ideally suited for the federal government as it can ensure interoperability and common standards among the fifty states.

Similar to the requirement in the Stafford Act, under HSPD-5, "the Secretary shall coordinate the Federal Government's resources utilized in response to or recovery from terrorist attacks, major disasters, or other emergencies if and when any one of the following four conditions applies: (2) the resources of State and local authorities *are overwhelmed* and Federal assistance has been requested by the appropriate State and local authorities (emphasis added)."[81] Neither the Stafford Act language nor the language in HSPD-5 is given any consideration when deciding on issuing federal declarations today.

For example, one emergency manager from Oklahoma recounted that his state had "experienced wildfires, ice storms, tornadoes and floods which... resulted in six major disaster declarations, one emergency declaration, and 26 fire management assistance grants."[82] How many of these declarations—or any declarations issued over the last sixteen years—truly were "of such severity and magnitude that effective response *was beyond the capabilities of the State and the affected local governments*" to respond?[83] The truth: not many.

The fundamental reality is that the current federalization of disasters is about nothing more than money and politics. If a state can get the federal government to pay for a disaster so that the costs are transferred from the state's taxpayers to taxpayers spread across the country, then it will. Does anyone seriously think that federal declarations would be sought if the declarations came without federal money? When trade groups voice concerns over disaster management in America, the concerns focus mostly on money.

Again, Albert Ashwood best demonstrated this centralization mindset. Ashwood testified, "It seems the Katrina federal legacy is one of minimizing exposure for the next event and ensuring future focus is centered on state and local preparedness efforts."[84] If Ashwood and the emergency management community believe their own motto, that is exactly how it should be. This federalization of disasters is turning the axiom that all disasters are local on its head so that all disasters become federal issues. Although it is indeed financially tempting to keep FEMA involved in all of the routine disasters that befall America, such constant activity creates several operational problems.

After Hurricane Katrina, many in Washington argued for a significantly enhanced federal response capability. Such an approach sounds good; however, there is little proof that a beefed-up federal response effort can accomplish much more than it has done previously in those critical twenty-four to forty-eight hours after a disaster strikes. Fundamentally, moving response assets into a disaster area still involves a logistics lag-time between event, especially a no-notice event, and in-theater arrival. Hence, it is still vital that response capabilities exist at the state and local level to respond during this lag-time.

Even if such an enhanced federal response is a good idea that can actually be implemented in a timely manner, we must preserve such responses for catastrophic disasters, not routine ones. For example, because of political pressure, FEMA spent roughly $50 million on a cloudy day in Houston in August 2007 when Hurricane Dean posed the *possibility* of hitting Texas.[85] Hurricane Dean did not come close to Texas, never moving north of 20.6 degrees latitude. If FEMA spends $50 million every time a hurricane *could* hit the United States, billions of taxpayer funds will be wasted.

As was demonstrated by Hurricane Katrina, when FEMA spends all of its time dealing with routine disaster declarations every three days, little is being done to build an entity that can handle a catastrophic event. A 2008 audit concluded, "FEMA continues to perform well responding to non-catastrophic or 'garden variety' disasters; however, it still has much to do to become a cohesive, efficient, and effective organization to prepare for and respond to the next catastrophic event."[86] In the nine critical areas reviewed in the audit, in the almost three years since Hurricane Katrina, FEMA had "made moderate progress in five of the nine areas, modest progress in three areas, and limited progress in one area."[87] With constant activity, FEMA staff and systems are simply overworked.

Next, if the federal government is going to deploy its response assets for every fire, drought, freeze, snowstorm, tornado, landslide, or tropical storm that occurs in America, then expect state and local leaders to divert their finite resources away from disaster response preparedness to other, more chronic needs. After all, if the federal government is going to provide the resources, then state and local leaders will react to such an incentive exactly as they have to date; namely, by requesting declarations for even the smallest events regardless of whether those events reach the "severity and magnitude" threshold and cutting state emergency management budgets.[88]

In order for FEMA to have been prepared for Hurricane Katrina and to be prepared for a future catastrophic event, it needs to be transformed into a twenty-first century agency with twenty-first century tools and technologies. The reforms begun by Secretary Chertoff are exactly the right reforms—just ten years too late.

Even with these reforms, the Congress must ensure that FEMA is constructed, staffed, and empowered as a catastrophic response agency, rather than as an agency of the routine, which is what it became over the last sixteen years. To do this, FEMA must evaluate and align its regions in accordance with the actuarial data that it has amassed over the last sixty years.[89] This realignment means that staffing levels and disaster assets should differ greatly so that regions (Regions VI and IV) with a far higher volume of catastrophic events (Category 1 or higher hurricanes) have far greater capabilities than those regions with less catastrophic activity (Regions VIII and V). This action would reduce costs and accelerate disaster response.

The reality is that most catastrophic disasters occur in the twelve states that straddle the Gulf Coast and the lower Atlantic Ocean. At some point, it becomes unfair that taxpayers in the rest of the United States must continue to subsidize the federal activity of those few states that possess higher risks from natural disasters. We must reverse course and place the burden of routine natural disasters back where it belongs; namely, with state and local governments. This reallocation of risk will allow lower-risk states and localities to address their needs more properly, and concomitantly, allow higher-risk states and localities to invest in greater response capabilities. FEMA then can focus its finite resources on a regional basis, with greater resources in those regions with greater disaster activity.

A FEMA prepared for a catastrophic event will not exist if the agency continues to spend finite time, money, resources, and personnel on every disaster that happens somewhere in America. Landslides, severe storms, and tornados may be disastrous for those people impacted by them, but, in most cases, the resources at the state and local level are more than adequate to deal with such events. The longer the Congress supports the federalization of routine natural disasters or governors and mayors game the system, the harder it will be for FEMA and its dedicated staff to perform the mission for which they are needed in the twenty-first century—catastrophic disaster response and recovery.

As noted recently, with the federal government providing funds to states and localities for homeland security, governors and mayors are pulling back on disaster response funding.[90] Is it any surprise that the results of DHS's Nationwide Plan Review were overwhelmingly poor for most states and cities? They have heard the message from FEMA that all disasters—no matter the size—are federal.

It does not have to be this way. States and localities possess all the assets they need to handle all but the truly catastrophic disasters. Most first preventers and first responders are under the control of states and localities. As discussed in Chapter 6, if equipment, training, or planning gaps exist, funding efforts can be focused on filling those gaps. States also have control over the National Guard. As the 9/11 Commission noted:

> Pursuant to the Nunn-Lugar-Domenici Domestic Preparedness Program, the Defense Department began in 1997 to train first responders in 120 of the nation's largest cities. As a key part of its efforts, Defense created National Guard WMD Civil Support Teams to respond in the event of a WMD terrorist incident. A total of 32 such National Guard teams were authorized by fiscal year 2001. Under the command of state governors, they provided support to civilian agencies to assess the nature of the attack, offer medical and technical advice, and coordinate state and local response.[91]

With such power, one would think governors and mayors would keep the federal government at bay. The lure of easy money, however, is simply too much.

The Congress must put in place clear requirements that constrain when declarations can be issued. One way to accomplish this task is to align declarations to the various scales used for disasters (The Saffir-Simpson Scale, The Richter Scale, The Fujita Scale, etc.). For example, nothing below a Category 1 hurricane is eligible for a declaration. That would eliminate all tropical storms that cause some damage, but are not "of such severity and magnitude that effective response is beyond the capabilities of the State and the affected local governments and that Federal assistance is necessary."[92]

Another way to accomplish this task is to eliminate certain types of disasters from FEMA's portfolio entirely. For example, there are more efficient ways to deal with a freeze that destroys agriculture crops and little else than to burden FEMA with administering disaster relief. Similarly, droughts are tragic, but largely impact the agricultural community. The insurance market can deal more efficiently with both types of disasters. Finally, severe storms and tornadoes tend to be localized events that cause property damage and cost lives, but are rarely if ever of a scale that outstrips the abilities of states and localities per the Stafford Act requirement.

By shifting the risk of the routine natural disaster back to the states and localities where those disasters occur, the federal response can be enhanced as recommended by the post-Hurricane Katrina reports—focused on those catastrophic events where state and local assets are truly overwhelmed, not just where the costs are high.

In a post-September 11 and Hurricane Katrina environment, we can ill afford to maintain incentives or disincentives that place the burden of expectation for over 130 declarations per year on FEMA. At the current pace, by 2016, FEMA will be issuing roughly 200 declarations per year, or one every 1.8 days. Such a pace will only serve to degrade the federal response as assets are mobilized and used, staff are overworked, and reform efforts are sacrificed to the operational tempo of a perpetual response agency, which creates or reinforces an "aftermath ethos" and inhibits the ability to perform steady state preparedness.[93]

If the Congress wants to continue to provide funds for routine disasters, then it should provide states and localities with funds via cooperative agreements that allow them to build response assets for routine disasters where state and federal governments jointly negotiate outcomes. These funds should include strong financial management and oversight requirements to minimize any waste, fraud, or abuse. Any funds provided by the federal government should include a matching requirement so that states and localities stop supplanting state and local funds with federal funds.

When states and localities once again bear the burden of most disasters, they will find a renewed interest in protecting their citizens' tax payments. For example, based on a population per disaster ratio, Michigan, which is the eighth largest state, but has had only thirty-one disaster declarations over the years, is certainly paying more in federal taxes that go toward federal disaster assistance than they should. In contrast, Oklahoma, which is the twenty-eighth largest state, but has had over three times as many disaster declarations as Michigan, pays less in federal taxes that go toward federal disaster assistance than they receive.[94]

As with many other areas where federal taxes create inequities among the states, inequity in federal disaster funds creates an opportunity for state and local elected officials to argue for a radical realignment in taxes. Specifically, in exchange for taking back responsibility for routine natural disasters, states should demand a specific federal tax reduction so that they can raise their own taxes to fund this purely state activity. Ironically, the federalization of disasters resulted in the compilation of years of actuarial data that should allow economists to accurately estimate the amount of federal taxes that went to routine disasters and, therefore, could be cut.

Additionally, the Congress and states should provide insurance companies with the flexibility to charge homeowners rates reflective of the actual risks they face based on geographic and historical data. Such a move would discontinue the counterproductive policy that creates incentives for people to build or rebuild in disaster-prone locations, which tend to be highly dense, costly places to live. Again, homeowners in places less prone to disasters and less densely populated should not have to subsidize the risk assumed by those who chose to live in more scenic, but more dangerous places to live. This principle applies with greater force when those who have assumed the risk decide to rebuild in those higher-risk areas.

As they say, facts are stubborn things. The facts show an unprecedented federalization of disasters, regardless of magnitude and severity. The facts also show that such an approach undermines FEMA's ability to build catastrophic capabilities and creates incentives for states and localities to divert their resources to more pressing voter needs. The solution is to decentralize routine natural disasters back to states and localities so that those most able to respond effectively do and so FEMA can make itself into the world-class preparedness and response organization needed given today's potential threats, both manmade and natural.

CASE STUDY 4

An Honest Approach to Disasters in Ohio

Ohio is the seventh largest state in America, but has had less than 2 percent of the disaster declarations from FEMA since 1950.[95] That means Ohio taxpayers are paying into a federal disaster system that is being disproportionately used in other states. Many states see FEMA disaster declarations as opportunities to shift the costs of routine natural disasters from their state to other states through the federal government. Ohio is an exception to the case. The Ohio Emergency Management Agency (OEMA), led by Nancy Dragani and her top-notch team, pushes decision-making down to local governments as much as possible.

On public assistance disaster relief, OEMA starts at the local level and works to the state level.[96] For example, procedurally, the governor of Ohio will not issue a disaster proclamation unless the local governments have first declared disasters. This grassroots approach ensures that all local assets are first deployed before injecting state assets. OEMA provides local governments with its *Public Assistance Handbook* so that they know what to do should they need public assistance.[97]

For individual assistance, the process requires a local disaster declaration followed by both the governor's proclamation and a declaration from the Small Business Administration.[98] This eliminates duplication of FEMA programs and ensures that the Small Business Administration loan route is not available. OEMA's approach also ensures that state funds are not going to individuals who possess insurance, individuals who receive funds from volunteer groups, and individuals able to secure loans from the Small Business Administration.

In deciding whether to request a declaration disaster from FEMA, OEMA strictly adheres to the requirement that a minimum of twenty-five homes and/or businesses with 40 percent uninsured damages must have occurred in a county.[99] To assist in this assessment, OEMA developed the *EMA Preliminary Damage Assessment Field Guide*, which contains detailed pictures and descriptions of single-family dwellings and mobile homes.[100] For both wind and flood damage, the *Field Guide* categorizes the level of damage as affected, minor, major, and destroyed.[101] The *Field Guide* allows field assessors to quickly and accurately estimate the damage from a natural disaster so that OEMA can decide whether to seek a federal declaration.

Another innovative tool created by OEMA is the *Assistance Toolbox*. Created in 2006, the *Assistance Toolbox* provides "information for County EMA Directors, local governments and OH EMA personnel to effectively accomplish response and recovery activities."[102] The *Assistance Toolbox* details the sequence of events, damage assessment process, assistance requests, and "what to expect" should a federal declaration be issued.[103] OEMA has sent the *Assistance Toolbox* to other states such as Illinois, Wisconsin, Minnesota, Iowa, and Louisiana.

OEMA offers training programs on both the *Assistance Toolbox* and the *Field Guide*. In one year, OEME conducted twenty-seven courses on response and recovery. Due to the volume of requests, OEMA now conducts training five times per year regionally.

Because many village and township trustees serve part-time, OEMA developed a "Cost Documentation Course" and "Damage Assessment Workshop" to teach them how to administer public assistance and other grant funds.[104] OEMA also tweaked FEMA guidance to create an Ohio version of "Recovery from Disaster: Role of Local Officials," which it offers as part of a professional development series online.[105] These courses are offered throughout the year in the various districts.

Because FEMA has not provided guidance to the states on how to best identify potential Disaster Relief Centers, OEMA decentralized this decision to local governments who sit in the best position to make such decisions. After all, a local government official is more familiar with the area, so can best decide where a Disaster Relief Center will best serve the people and remain out of harms way. OEMA aggressively partners with community-based organizations to provide mass care, including leveraging senior volunteer programs.

Based on lessons learned, OEMA reorganized its Emergency Operations Center to focus on greater information sharing with local governments. The reorganization included a technical upgrade to its Video Telecommunication Conference capabilities so that over fifty Ohio counties now meet the required standards. With its new system, FEMA Region V personnel can access OEMA's system to gauge resource needs and run reports. Not surprisingly, OEMA cannot access FEMA's system to see what resources it has.

To ensure interoperable communication, OEMA partnered with the Buckeye Sheriffs Association to acquire eleven communication vehicles. The vehicles are strategically positioned in eleven counties across Ohio. When deployed, the vehicles link local and state radio systems so that all disciplines and jurisdictions have real-time communication capabilities.

OEMA also adopted a forward-looking approach to build capabilities by tailoring the TCL to Ohio and its unique risks. Because the TCL currently lacks a tier structure, OEMA created its own by using risk to determine which jurisdictions in Ohio should have capabilities at the highest, middle, and lowest levels. Specifically, OEMA developed the Ohio Response System, which is made up of roughly nineteen Technical Advisory Committees that are responsible for the applicable capabilities that correspond to their subject areas.[106] Each team is staffed by subject matter experts from around the state and from all levels of government and the private sector.

More critically, each committee determines the resources needed for the three tier types (I, II, or III) for capabilities based on the unique issues in Ohio.[107] For example, the Hazmat Response Committee is responsible for the capability "WMD/Hazardous Materials Response and Decontamination" capability. The Hazmat Response Committee made adjustments to response times based on Ohio's geography and population. As a result, the Hazmat Response Committee determined that Cincinnati, Cleveland, Columbus, Toledo, Akron, Dayton, and Lima should have Tier Type I capabilities, while the remaining urban/suburban and rural jurisdictions should have Tier Type II and Tier Type III capabilities, respectively. The committees also conduct site verifications to ensure preparedness and readiness levels.

For any county that receives homeland security funds, OEMA requires the county to form a multidisciplinary committee that decides how the funds are spent. This approach started in 2002, which was four years before DHS adopted a similar approach for the UASI program. This approach ensures that one dominant discipline doesn't use all of the funds for their capabilities while other disciplines live on the crumbs.

OEMA also divided Ohio into eight districts. Each district is required to have a planner and field liaison to ensure that plans possess a minimum level of components and meet established planning requirements. OEMA requires all plans to be updated, revised, and repromulgated every four years to ensure that the plans meet current needs. To assist local governments, OEMA distributes two videos titled, "Plan Development and Review Guidance for Local Emergency Operations Plans" and "Continuity of Operations Plan (All Hazards) Overview and Guidance for Local Government."[108] FEMA Region V also uses OEMA's "Emergency Operations Procedure Guidance Document for Local Emergency Managers" as a best practice tool across the region. Since 1985, all eighty-eight Ohio counties conduct exercises every year.

As part of its efforts to decentralize disaster response efforts, OEMA created the "Ohio Family Preparedness Wheel" so that citizens understood their roles, too. On one side of the wheel, information details what citizens should do to prepare for an event; on the other side of the wheel, information details what citizens should do during an event. Each side covers nine disasters: excessive heat, floods, winter storms, fires, lightning, hazardous material incidents, tornados, earthquakes, and terrorism. The wheel also contains recommended preparedness kits for home and for cars, as well as links to other resources. OEMA has distributed over 10,000 wheels across Ohio.

In many cases, states manipulate the FEMA disaster relief program to shift costs from their states to other states. Ohio is an exception to the rule. Because of this honest approach to disaster management, Ohio and its citizens are better off.

8

Illegal Immigration and the Laboratories of Democracy

If states like Arizona could pass their own immigration laws, workers and employers alike would face a patchwork of conflicting and incompatible requirements based on local politics and conditions, and it would be impossible to have a meaningful policy.

Omar Jadwat[1]

The state governments have a full superintendence and control over the immense mass of local interests of their respective states, which connect themselves with the feelings, the affections, the municipal institutions, and the internal arrangements of the whole population. They possess, too, the immediate administration of justice in all cases, civil and criminal, which concern the property, personal rights, and peaceful pursuits of their own citizens.

Justice Joseph Story[2]

No issue generates more passion in voters today than the issue of illegal immigration. Because of the focus on the economic aspect of illegal immigration, the security aspect of it gets lost in the debate. It is axiomatic, however, that if twelve million illegal immigrants looking for work can cross America's porous borders or overstay visas, then a handful of terrorists certainly can, too. This reality, therefore, requires us to determine who is here, who is coming, and who is going. While key aspects of that activity are properly the role of the federal government, other equally critical aspects are properly the role of states and localities pursuant to the Tenth Amendment.

As with most complex issues, it simply has become too easy to demagogue the opposition by focusing narrowly on one aspect of the illegal immigration problem.[3] With 24-hour news channels desperate to fill dead air time and advocates searching out the latest "evidence" of how our system is broken, we should acknowledge that illegal immigration results in both vicious crimes being committed by illegal immigrants and innocent children being caught up in their parents' decision to illegally enter America.

These examples and others like them do not mean we should throw our hands up and launch a mass deportation program or provide amnesty "one last time." Heretofore, the federal government has acted without giving proper thought to the incentives or disincentives related to illegal immigration. This history makes it all the more important that we fix the problem by enforcing existing laws, providing additional authorities where needed, reforming our counterproductive visa and naturalization system, and encouraging states and localities to act. Once our borders are secure, foreign visitors can not overstay their visas, employers can fill their hiring needs with legal rather than illegal workers, and we can deal with the remaining problem of those illegal immigrants still in America by creating a permanent solution that Americans will support.

In all of the heated rhetoric on immigration, we have lost sight of the progress made thus far and of both the ultimate goals and the ultimate customer. First, we must use all legal means to secure America. Next, in our effort to secure America, we must make sure that our security efforts do not undermine our ability to build a robust economy that attracts the world's best and brightest to where those who want to work can. Finally, efforts to secure America and create prosperity must keep in mind that it is the American taxpayer who pays the bill and on whose behalf our government serves. Sometimes, our elected leaders forget that it is "we the people" who provide them powers, not the other way around.

THE HISTORY OF IMMIGRATION ENFORCEMENT IN THE UNITED STATES

The American story is an immigrant's story. Founded by those fleeing religious persecution and built on the backs of those who came to America unwillingly and those who believed the "streets were paved with gold," wave after wave of immigrants brought with them the dreams of a better tomorrow and the work ethic to realize those dreams. Those immigrants introduced new foods, new cultural traditions, and new approaches to complex problems that over time became distinctly American.

With each immigration wave, however, the newly arrived immigrants faced the "economic stresses of working-class Americans, ethnic and racial animosities, and national security jitters."[4] One of the strongest anti-immigrant movements occurred in reaction to the arrival of Chinese workers who came to fill labor jobs in the mining and railroad industries in the 1870s.[5] These immigrants were viewed as "a race of godless opium addicts, prostitutes and gamblers."[6] In reaction to these immigrants, states enacted laws against Chinese immigrants and the Congress passed the Chinese Exclusion Act of 1882, which stopped additional Chinese immigration for ten years.[7]

The next large-scale movement against immigration occurred with the arrival of Southern and Eastern European immigrants.[8] These immigrants came during the rise of the Progressive Era and its adherence to social Darwinism and eugenics, and they were deemed "hereditarily inferior" to the Northern Europeans already in the United States.[9] At the height of the Progressive Era, Margaret Sanger, the founder of Planned Parenthood and a leader of the eugenics movement, advocated a "stern and rigid policy of sterilization and segregation to that grade of population whose progeny is already tainted or whose inheritance is such that objectionable traits may be transmitted to offspring."[10] As evidence of the broad influence the eugenics movement had in America, even the Supreme Court engaged in this abhorrent behavior when it upheld a law permitting forced sterilization where the great Oliver Wendell Holmes proclaimed: "Three generations of imbeciles are enough."[11]

In 1917, the Congress passed a law requiring passage of a literacy test and payment of a head tax for admission into the United States.[12] Due to political pressure for cheap labor, Mexican migrant workers received a waiver from the literacy test and head tax.[13] As proponents of cheap labor pointed out, "We do not want to see the condition arise again when white men who are reared and educated in our schools have got to bend their backs and skin their fingers."[14] Clearly, the notion that Americans would not do certain types of work has a rich (and erroneous) history.

The Congress then added national origin quotas in 1921 and 1924 that largely stopped the influx of Southern and Eastern Europeans, as well as Asians.[15] Again, Sanger summed up the Progressive Movement's support of the 1924 legislation because it kept "the doors of immigration closed to the entrance of certain aliens whose condition is known to be detrimental to the stamina of the race, such as [those that are] feebleminded, idiots, morons, insane, syphilitic, epileptic, criminal, [and] professional prostitutes."[16] These quotas remained in place for several decades and prevented the larger rescue of Jews during the Holocaust.[17] Once again, the federal government treated the cheap Mexican migrant laborers differently so that industry could continue to use them.[18] The unions tried to change this favored status in the mid-1930s, but failed.[19]

In 1942, with an increased demand for Mexican migrant labor, the federal government launched the *Bracero* Program.[20] Under the *Bracero* Program, the Mexican government would recruit temporary workers for the United States, and the U.S. government would guarantee that their "wages, living conditions, workplace safety, and medical services would be comparable to those of native workers."[21] Although Mexico met its obligations, the United States failed to meet its obligations and the Mexican temporary workers received less pay and fewer protections.[22] This inequity planted the seeds for today's illegal immigration problem because it created the foundation for a black market for cheap labor.

With the growing clout of organized labor in the 1950s and 1960s, the Congress ended the *Bracero* Program in 1963.[23] In 1965, the Congress amended the nation's most significant immigration law—the Immigration and Nationality Act of 1952 (INA)—by eliminating the national origins quotas and moving to a family-based preference system for immigration.[24] The law also contained a limit on the number of visas that could be issued to Canada and Mexico.[25] Border enforcement remained weak.

With the end of the *Bracero* Program and the visa restrictions in place, industry lost legal access to its supply of cheap labor. Not surprisingly, workers from Central and South America came pouring across the largely unprotected border to meet the demands of American companies. The mass migration of illegal immigrants was underway. From 1961 to 1979, the number of illegal immigrants apprehended and deported rose from just under 89,000 to over 1 million per year.[26]

After many years of vigorous debate and inaction by the federal government, the Congress finally passed the Immigration Reform and Control Act of 1986 (IRCA), which included weak employer sanctions and amnesty for illegal immigrants who had arrived in the United States by 1982 in exchange for promises of tougher border security and employer crackdowns.[27] Those promises were never delivered. Roughly three million illegal immigrants qualified for amnesty under the IRCA.[28] Not surprisingly, the IRCA did not stop or slow the massive influx of illegal immigrants into the United States.

In 2007, in response to a national outcry, the federal government attempted to pass a comprehensive immigration reform package that would have provided amnesty to the roughly twelve million illegal immigrants in the United States.[29] In a report that focused on the costs of the proposed legislation, the Congressional Budget Office (CBO)—the congressional entity charged with providing the Congress with "[o]bjective, nonpartisan, and timely analyses to aid in economic and budgetary decisions"—made an astonishing admission. CBO reviewed all of the measures the reform package would have instituted and concluded that "those measures would reduce the net annual flow of unauthorized immigrants by one-quarter."[30]

As a result of reports like the one from CBO, the reform package failed to pass. After all, a paltry reduction of only one of every four illegal immigrants every year made it virtually impossible for proponents to get the support of Americans. Such a result would mean that in another twenty years, instead of twelve million illegal immigrants, "only" nine million illegal immigrants would be in the United States. That does not sound like comprehensive reform.

For many Americans, the systemic failure of the federal government to enforce existing laws and secure the borders made any amnesty or amnesty-like proposal a bitter pill to swallow. As a result, and entirely consistent with other complex issues, states and localities have begun to assert themselves, especially on interior enforcement and employment issues where they have constitutional room to maneuver.

THE THREE-LEGGED STOOL OF IMMIGRATION

To identify a way forward, it is useful to view immigration as a stool built on three legs and recognize that a weakness in one leg creates structural pressure on the other legs, thereby risking the collapse of the stool itself. Because immigration is largely a classic supply and demand problem, we must acknowledge that there is a readily available supply of labor for employers and, given our traditionally low unemployment figures, a demand for that labor. To create a long-term solution to our mass illegal immigration challenge, we must ensure that our solution incorporates transactional costs—both direct and indirect— within each leg that provides the right incentives and disincentives for all parties involved in the debate.

The first leg is the security of our borders. Although the federal government has involved itself in many elements involving immigrants once here, under our Constitution, the two core functions specifically assigned to the federal government are protecting our borders and determining who is (and is not) an American citizen.[31] As another entry into the Restatement of the Obvious, if America cannot secure its border and by so doing significantly slow or stop the flow of illegal immigrants, it certainly will make it a Sisyphean task to locate, detain, and remove illegal immigrants once inside the country. In an environment where terrorists seek to enter our country to do us harm, not knowing who is in our country is unacceptable. This leg involves increasing the number of border patrol agents and building infrastructure (permanent walls or other detection capabilities) to stop or slow the flow of illegal immigration. Strengthening our ports of entry also is a priority.[32] These elements focus on reducing the supply of illegal immigration by significantly increasing the transactional cost for illegal immigrants and the people who aid their attempts to cross the border.

The next leg is the efficacy of our interior enforcement actions. By substantially reducing the number of illegal border crossings, we can focus the efforts of our interior enforcement personnel to first ensure that those visitors working or studying here on a visa leave when that visa expires, and secondly, crack down on businesses who hire illegal immigrants. These elements focus on the demand for illegal immigrants by increasing the transactional costs for employers, as well as on the supply of illegal immigrants by adding more transactional costs (harder to find a job) to illegal immigrants.

With increased worksite enforcement, more aggressive detention and removal activities, and stepped-up prosecutions of both immigrants and employers, we can send a strong message that our jobs are reserved for those individuals who come to America legally. Employers and other groups with a vested interest in cheap labor will use every legal means possible to stall or stop employment measures, so proponents should be ready for the fight.[33]

The third leg is an efficient and vibrant visa and naturalization system. Given our low unemployment, we must recognize that there are not enough Americans to fully meet the demands of labor—at both the high and low end of the economy.[34] In the annual battle for H-1B visas for immigrants in specialized fields, employers used the 65,000 allotment in under a day in 2007, which left tens of thousands of high technology jobs unfilled.[35] As Microsoft founder Bill Gates has noted: "We are very concerned that the U.S. will lose its competitive position."[36] This leg largely is made-up of visa transformation in which we substantially increase the number of visas that foreigners use to work in America so that employers can legally bring in labor where their needs remain unmet by the existing population. A concomitant action is to shorten the time it takes for foreigners to become American citizens. Transforming CIS is a must.[37]

These elements focus on the supply and the demand as such changes would substantially reduce the incentives to illegally enter the United States because an efficient, low-cost legal process exists for employers to satisfy the demand they have for low-skill, low-cost workers. Similarly, increasing the number of high-skill workers will ensure that the world's best, brightest, and greatest risk-takers compete for America, not against it.[38] In today's competitive global economy, America must retain its position as the global technology leader.

Once we have effectively made it easier for a legal supply and demand system to exist in America and our stool is sturdy, then we can turn our attention to the retrospective problem of those illegal immigrants who remain once the legal supply and demand system is in place. As we work to secure our border, leverage our interior enforcement activities, and reform our visa and naturalization process, many of the illegal immigrants here today will have either gone home because they could not find a job or figured out how to come to America legally.

Because no one can state with any certainty how many illegal immigrants will choose either of these paths, it makes little sense for us to act now by granting them amnesty or creating a special process for them that undermines our credibility with the countless immigrants who waited their turn and followed the rules. Let's first fix what is already broken. Then, we can ascertain the size of the remaining illegal immigration problem. Depending on the size of the remaining problem, our solution can be narrowly tailored in a manner that does not weaken the three-legged stool and, critically, once and for all ends *mass* illegal immigration and gains the support of a majority of Americans.

THE FEDERAL ROLE ON ILLEGAL IMMIGRATION

Most of the actions discussed under the three-legged stool are actions permissible under existing law. In fact, when he joined DHS, Secretary Chertoff quickly zeroed in on those existing authorities to gain more control over our illegal immigration problem. Unfortunately, he inherited an environment dating from the Clinton administration in which very little was done to deal with the illegal immigration problem.[39] For example, in 2004, ICE only arrested 685 employees who had violated immigration law, whereas in 2007, ICE arrested over 4,077 employees.[40] As a result of this neglect, the problem only got bigger and harder to solve.

Under Secretary Chertoff's leadership, the federal government has taken many positive steps in the last three years across the three legs to tackle this problem. These actions included changing the policy from "capture and release," where illegal immigrants simply disappeared to other parts of the country once released, to "detention and remove," where illegal immigrants are given the choice between being detained until their removal hearing or voluntarily agreeing to be removed without a hearing. Other actions taken by the federal government include completing more than 76 miles of a physical fence, doubling the number of border patrol agents to roughly 18,000 by 2009, arresting more than 7,655 gang members, identifying for removal 164,296 incarcerated illegal immigrants, arresting 4,940 employment violators, and obtaining more than $30 million in fines and penalties.[41]

As for the issue of children caught-up in the illegality of their parents, ICE does allow for humanitarian release in the case of sole caregivers.[42] In anticipation of family detentions, in May 2006, ICE opened the T. Don Hutto Residential Detention Center so families can remain together throughout the deportation process.[43]

We must keep in mind that the illegal immigrant parents of children born here can always go home. Any policy that rewards illegal immigrant parents who give birth to children in the United States only will incentivize a race to the border by such illegal immigrants. With a special interest lobby and television cameras eagerly awaiting those illegal border crossers, we cannot allow them to encourage such crossing and then justify those "humanitarian" cases *ex post facto*. In the extreme minority of cases (a handful out of 12 million) where the child of illegal immigrants is the high school class valedictorian (and other "feel good" cases), the Congress always has the power to act by passing private legislation granting those families citizenship.[44] We certainly should not, however, create policy based on the exception to the rule rather than the rule itself.

The federal government can do more.

First, the Congress needs to pass legislation permitting DHS to act on the Social Security Administration's No Match Letters. By regulatory action, DHS "clarifie[d] that employers may be held liable if they ignore the 'No Match' problems by failing to take specified steps within 90 days of receiving the letter."[45] As part of the regulation, DHS created a process by which employers could resolve a No Match finding, including giving employers a safe harbor for following the process and exercising due diligence.[46] The American Civil Liberties Union and the U.S. Chamber of Commerce filed lawsuits over the regulation, which has stalled the reform.[47]

Next, the Congress needs to fully fund programs within the three legs. These programs include the border fence (physical and virtual), detention facilities, more resources for attorneys to try illegal immigration cases, and identification programs like the Real ID Act and the Western Hemisphere Travel Initiative.

Funds also should be provided so that the FBI can increase the speed by which it performs background checks on visa applicants.

Importantly, the hurdles put in place by the *Orantes* permanent injunction that prohibits expedited removal of Salvadorans and significantly slows down their deportation must be eliminated.[48] This legislation should include stiffer penalties for illegal immigration offenses so U.S. Attorneys have greater incentives to try such cases (as these cases compete with other cases for finite judicial resources).

The Congress should reauthorize and require use of the E-Verify system for all employers. The E-Verify system is a free electronic system that allows employers to rapidly verify the employment data of potential workers.[49] E-Verify allows employers to electronically compare Form I-9 employee information against the 485 million Social Security Administration and DHS records in just a few seconds.[50]

The Congress must acknowledge the importance of keeping America competitive and substantially expand current visa programs and create new visa programs for low-wage, low-skill workers. Part of the reform must move America away from determining visa and citizenship eligibility based on chain migration factors and to factors like education levels and work skills. Many European countries are reforming their visa and citizenship policies in this manner, so America's competitive edge is at stake.[51]

Under a reformed visa system, we should do as some European countries are now doing and negotiate "readmission accords" that require countries in exchange for aid or participation in our visa or travel programs to agree in advance to accept back their countrymen illegally in the United States without burdensome bureaucratic hurdles to slow the process down.[52] Given the recalcitrance of some countries, we should consider putting diplomatic presence in the United States on the table so we can get these agreements in place. These readmission accords will expedite the deportation of illegal immigrants and reduce our need for more detention facilities and judicial resources.

For all visa programs, we must create an enforceable exit process. Part of this process should include incentives for visa holders to go home such as a requirement that a percent of the wages of workers here on visas be withheld pending their return to their home country on expiration of their visas. Similarly, individuals who come to the United States to study should have to provide a bond that would be lost should they fail to leave when their student visas expired. An individual's eligibility for future visas or naturalization should be contingent on the individual returning to his home country on expiration of the visa.

STATES AND LOCALITIES HAVE A VITAL ROLE, TOO

One of the strengths of America is the role federalism plays in our system. While allowing state and local law enforcement to aid in interior enforcement activities is a good start, more should be done to get the unjustifiable legal barriers off the backs of states and localities that decide to take a tougher stance on illegal immigration than the federal government or other states or localities.

We must distinguish the preemptive federal role on border security and visa policy from the shared role on interior enforcement, as well as employment, housing, and identification issues. As noted above, so long as action does not cover citizenship status issues, there is simply no reason why states and localities should not be able to enact laws against renting to or employing illegal immigrants.[53] Increased state and local action will create additional supply and demand pressures on illegal immigrants and their employers.[54]

As has been the case in reforming welfare, education, and health care, states and localities are the trailblazers that bring innovation and creativity to complex problems. It should not be any different in how America deals with illegal immigrants once they have crossed the border or overstayed their visas.

At the federal level, once an illegal immigrant crosses the border or overstays his visa, the task of apprehending, detaining, and removal of the illegal immigrant falls on ICE. ICE currently employs 6,000 agents to perform all of its missions, "which include enforcing immigration law in the interior of the United States, stemming the flow of illicit drugs, and deterring money laundering, among other things."[55] As with most elements of the federal government following the September 11 attack, "the majority of ICE's resources have been directed at stemming terrorist-related activities and activities that have a national security interest."[56]

With only 6,000 ICE agents—or one agent for every 2,000 illegal immigrants—focused on detention and removal activities in the United States, it simply makes little sense not to tap the full power of the one million state and local law enforcement personnel for our interior enforcement actions. These men and women serve as enormous force multipliers, and, given their familiarity with their communities, are far better at navigating the difficult issues involved with the detection, detention, and removal of illegal immigrants.

Although section 287(g) of the INA that allows ICE to deputize state and local law enforcement personnel to help enforce federal immigration law is finally getting used after ten years of lying dormant, the entire premise that states and localities need the agreement of the federal government to control their jurisdictions is simply baseless. By passing interior enforcement legislation, states will be empowered to enforce their own laws dealing with illegal immigrants and those who employ, house, or otherwise aid them and, thereby, drive down the demand for illegal immigrants. This action also will place greater pressure on the federal government to allocate the detention and removal resources necessary to deport illegal immigrants apprehended by states and localities.

Whether good policy or not, the reality is that "mere illegal presence in the U.S. is a *civil*, not criminal, violation of the INA, and subsequent deportation and associated administrative processes are civil proceedings."[57] This distinction is important and has become the focal point on which pro-illegal immigration groups are attacking state and local law enforcement action.

The highest hurdle that states and localities must overcome in dealing with illegal immigration issues within their jurisdictions is the Supremacy Clause of the Constitution. The Supremacy Clause states: "This Constitution, and the Laws of the United States which shall be made in Pursuance thereof; and all Treaties made, or which shall be made, under the authority of the United States, shall be the supreme Law of the land; and the Judges in every State shall be bound thereby, any Thing in the Constitution or Laws of any State to the Contrary notwithstanding."[58] The Supremacy Clause gives the Congress the authority to preempt state and local laws "where concurrent jurisdiction exists."[59] Congressional preemption can occur explicitly via statutory language stating as much or implicitly via an intention to regulate an entire field or when state or local law conflicts with federal law.[60]

Specifically, in express preemption cases, for the federal law to preempt state law, the federal law must contain explicit language that such preemption was "the clear and manifest purpose of Congress."[61] On immigration issues, because the Congress provided exceptions for state and local laws dealing with "licensing or similar laws" concerning the employment of illegal immigrants, the Congress failed to occupy the entire field of immigration law.[62] It goes without saying, of course, that the Congress could simply amend the statutory language that prohibits states and localities from doing even more to combat the employment of illegal immigrants. It is, after all, not a constitutional prohibition.

In implied preemption cases, the Supreme Court noted three situations where implied preemption negates state or local laws: first, if the state or local law attempts to regulate immigration; secondly, if the federal law "occupies the field;" and, thirdly, if the state or local law conflicts with federal law.[63] When evaluating a preemption claim, the courts are required to "start... with the assumption that the historic police powers of the States [are] not to be superseded by.... Federal Act unless that [is] the clear and manifest purpose of Congress."[64]

Nonetheless, states and localities did not cede their inherent police powers when the Constitution was ratified. As a result, states and localities retain inherent authority to enforce federal criminal law. Many experts believe states and localities also retain inherent authority to enforce federal civil law. After all, it would make little sense if states and localities were left powerless to deal with the influx of illegal immigrants into their jurisdictions. Absent a criminal violation, illegal immigrants could flout their presence in cities and states across America.

Certainly, the Founding Fathers did not intend such an outcome when they drafted the Constitution and included the Ninth and Tenth Amendments. As the Supreme Court has found, state and local police power is "an exercise of the sovereign right of the Government to protect the lives, health, morals, comfort and general welfare of the people."[65] Those sovereign powers "proceed, not from the people of America, but from the people of the several states; and remain, after the adoption of the constitution, what they were before."[66] As the Fifth Circuit Court of Appeals concluded: "No statute precludes other federal, state, or local law enforcement agencies from taking other action to enforce this nation's immigration laws."[67]

Obviously, this inherent authority becomes critical given that an illegal immigrant's presence in the United States is only a civil violation.[68] In 2002, Attorney General John Ashcroft announced that the federal government's position was that states and localities could enforce federal civil law. Specifically, Attorney General Ashcroft stated:

> When federal, state and local law enforcement officers encounter an alien of national security concern who has been listed on the NCIC (National Crime Information Center) for violating immigration law, federal law permits them to arrest that person and transfer him to the custody of the INS. The Justice Department's Office of Legal Counsel has concluded that this narrow, limited mission that we are asking state and local police to undertake voluntarily—arresting aliens who have violated criminal provisions of the Immigration and Nationality Act or civil provisions that render an alien deportable, and who are listed on the NCIC—is within the inherent authority of states.[69]

Importantly, "the authority of state and local law enforcement officers to investigate and arrest for violations of federal law is determined by reference to state law."[70]

This issue of whether states and localities possess the inherent authority to enforce federal civil law is not a theoretical one. To wit, "four of the nineteen 9/11 hijackers had law enforcement encounters with local police in the six months preceding September 11, 2001."[71] The four included ringleaders (and pilot) Mohammed Atta and Nawaf al Hazmi, as well as pilots Hani Hanjour and Ziad Jarrah.[72] Each one of these terrorists had violated civil provisions of federal immigration law.[73] Had there been a tighter partnership between the federal government and state and local governments and aggressive enforcement of our immigration laws, it is possible that at least one of the four—if not more—would have been caught, thereby thwarting the September 11 attack.

The use of section 287(g) started in 2002. As of April 1, 2008, in six years, ICE has entered into forty-one agreements, and trained and deputized 660 state and local law enforcement officers, or less than ten officers per month.[74] This represents a positive step, but it also demonstrates that section 287(g) on its own is not a panacea.

For states and localities to truly tackle their illegal immigration problems, they must take a more aggressive approach then simply relying on ICE to do its duty and to federalize a handful of state or local officers each year. There are many additional actions that states and localities can take. Some states such as Arizona and Oklahoma and some localities such as Valley Park, Missouri, have taken aggressive action. Thus far, most federal courts, as noted below, are finding these actions constitutional.

As the Supreme Court held in *De Canas v. Bica*: "States possess broad authority under their police powers to regulate the employment relationship and protect workers within the State."[75] As such, state and local actions "to prohibit the knowing employment by... employers of persons not entitled to lawful residence in the United States, let alone to work here, [are] certainly within the mainstream of such police power regulation."[76] In what is the strongest statement on this issue, the Supreme Court noted:

> Although the State has no direct interest in controlling entry into this country, that interest being one reserved by the Constitution to the Federal Government, unchecked unlawful migration might impair the State's economy generally, or the State's ability to provide some important service. Despite the exclusive federal control of this Nation's borders, we cannot conclude that the States are without power to deter the influx of persons entering the United States against federal law, and whose numbers might have a discernible impact on traditional state concerns.[77]

States and localities have wide latitude to enact laws concerning traditional issues within their jurisdictions.

In February 2007, the City of Valley Park, Missouri, enacted an ordinance that prohibited the employment of illegal immigrants.[78] A business found violating the ordinance would have its license suspended.[79] In January 2008, the United States District Court for the Eastern District of Missouri (Eastern Division) found in favor of the city that "the Ordinance is a regulation on business licenses, an area historically occupied by the states."[80]

In a major victory for federalism, the U.S. Court of Appeals for the Ninth Circuit—the most liberal appellate court in America—upheld Arizona's illegal immigration employment law in September 2008. As discussed in the case study below, the Ninth Circuit made three key findings. First, it found Arizona's law to punish employers who hire illegal immigrants by revoking their licenses to operate constitutional.[81] Next, it found Arizona's requirement for employers that they use the E-Verify system proper.[82] Finally, and, equally as significant, the Ninth Circuit concluded that the Supreme Court's holdings in *De Canas* were not superseded by the IRCA.[83]

Critically, it is not for the courts to decide whether a particular state or local law is good public policy or not. As the Supreme Court found, "debatable questions as to its reasonableness, wisdom and propriety are not for the determination of courts, but for the legislative body, on which rests the duty and responsibility of decision."[84] Nonetheless, state and local action should be aimed at "remov[ing] or reduc[ing] the economic incentives for unlawful presence."[85]

States and localities have many options they can adopt to stem the tide of illegal immigration. For businesses, they can urge the Congress to permit the use of the E-Verify system for all businesses for employment, financial, and housing transactions. They can suspend business licenses for the employment of unauthorized aliens, require business filings and business tax returns to include an attestation from the employer that they did not employ unauthorized aliens in the last twelve months and make it a felony to file a false attestation, and prohibit tax deductions for business expenses related to unauthorized aliens. They also can make it a crime to rent, lease, or sublease living space for use by unauthorized aliens. Finally, they can institute a withholding tax for all wire transfers to foreign parties or on negotiable bank drafts and international money orders without a valid social security number.

For individuals, states and localities can require state income tax returns to include an attestation from the filers that they did not employ unauthorized aliens in the last twelve months and make it a felony to file a false attestation, make it a felony for unauthorized aliens to work punishable by imprisonment and a fine, make it a felony to falsely claim legal presence in the United States, and make it a felony and a predicate racketeering crime to smuggle aliens.

For law enforcement, states and localities can expand law enforcement arrest power to include misdemeanor violations of the INA, and permit the temporary detention of individuals charged with misdemeanors such as traffic violations where probable cause exists that they are unauthorized aliens so that federal entities can retrieve them.

For other government entities, states can prohibit sanctuary cities, including day-labor sites, mandate the use of the Systemic Alien Verification for Entitlements system to verify entitlement to all state and local benefits, deny enrollment to or financial aid for state-licensed higher education institutions to unauthorized aliens, including in-state tuition qualification, restrict unauthorized aliens' access to non-essential public benefits and services, ban the use of foreign identification documents to establish identity or to obtain state identification cards unless accompanied by a U.S. document that demonstrates legal presence in the United States, and restrict the use of taxpayer identification numbers for purposes not authorized by the Internal Revenue Service, including identification, unless accompanied by a U.S. document that demonstrates legal presence in the United States.[86]

Some of these measures will increase the short-term costs of reducing illegal immigration, but the long-term costs should drop as illegal immigrants decide to remain in their own countries due to the lack of economic opportunities here or choose another state with more accommodating laws and regulations.

Although the costs of both legal and illegal immigrants are difficult to determine, The Heritage Foundation determined that for low-skill immigrants lacking a high school degree, immigrants receive "three dollars in government benefits and services for each dollar of taxes they pay."[87] Of the illegal immigration population, roughly "61 percent of illegal immigrant adults lack a high school diploma [while another] 25 percent have only a high school diploma."[88] The poverty rate for illegal immigrants is double the rate of Americans.[89] "Over a lifetime, the typical low-skill immigrant household will cost taxpayers $1.2 million dollars."[90]

For states and localities, the economic costs of illegal immigrants can be crushing. For example, "up to 3 million people who illegally crossed the border" are living in Texas.[91] Depending on the education levels and familial status of those 3 million illegal immigrants, Texans could be paying over $6 million per year in nonreimbursed government benefits and services.

In addition to the economic costs, as anyone who has spent time on the southern border knows, illegal immigrants cause significant environmental and property damage. Whether it is the tons of trash such as water jugs, clothes, or empty food cans discarded by illegal immigrants or the destruction of fences and trampling of plants and grasses as they make their way to pick-up destinations, illegal immigrants are doing untold harm to large swaths of land.

By creating a mosaic of interior enforcement regimes across America, illegal immigrants will find it harder and harder to find work. Those here will either go home or find a way to become citizens. Those thinking about coming, hopefully, will decide not to come in the first place or choose a legal pathway.

If a governor or mayor, however, wants to create safe havens in a state or city for illegal immigrants, then they should be free to do so subject to federal enforcement of federal immigration law. As with cities that welcomed the homeless and states that created generous welfare benefits for the poor, illegal immigrants will flock to those places and other jurisdictions seen as pro-illegal immigrant. The voters in those states and cities will deal with these politicians.[92] Just the same, if Hazleton, Pennsylvania, which was one of the first localities to place restrictions on illegal immigrants, wants to send a clear message to illegal immigrants and those who incentivize them that it is not a safe haven, then we should do what we can to permit that action.

Our nation is indeed a nation of immigrants. It is also a nation founded, built on, and wholly dependent on the sanctity we give to the rule of law. It is what distinguishes us from those countries run by dictators and democrats in name only. Americans understand that we should not cast aside that sanctity too lightly. All too often we hear politicians in Washington say the words, but then they vote for legislation that gives lip service to the rule of law. We cannot afford to continue sacrificing sound public policy at the altar of political expediency and cheap labor. It is the way of Washington, but not the way in all of those places outside the Beltway, where the people live, work, and dream.

Those people seek the freedom to act. It's time Washington gets out of their way so they can. As they say, if you are not part of the solution, you are part of the problem.

CASE STUDY 5

Arizonians Say "Enough!"

As a border state, Arizona sits on the front line in America's fight against illegal immigration. After years of neglect by the federal government, the citizens of Arizona took matters into their own hands. In 2000, Arizonians passed Proposition 203 with over 62 percent of the vote, requiring public schools to teach in English only and begin an English immersion program for non-English speaking people. Four years later, they passed Proposition 200 with 56 percent of the vote, requiring proof of citizenship to register to vote and to cast a ballot.

The most significant activity occurred in 2006 when Arizonians overwhelming passed three amendments to their Constitution and one referendum. The first amendment denies bail to individuals living illegally in the United States who are charged with a serious felony. The second amendment denies punitive damage awards to individuals living illegally in the United States in civil cases. The third amendment made English the official language of the state. The referendum made citizenship a requirement to receive subsidized services like in-state college tuition. These proposed amendments and referendum passed with 78 percent, 74 percent, 74 percent, and 72 percent of the vote, respectively.

The Arizona legislature also enacted several key provisions to gain control over illegal immigrants. In 2005, it passed the Human Smuggling Act, known as the "Coyote Act," that made knowingly smuggling an undocumented alien a class four or normal felony.[93] The Coyote Act covers those who transport undocumented aliens, those who receive money from undocumented aliens, those who launder money from undocumented aliens, and those who guard the houses where the undocumented aliens are held after crossing into the United States.[94] In June 2008, Maricopa County Sheriff Joseph Arpaio announced that his team had made the 1,000th arrest under the statute.[95]

The most important legislation passed by the Arizona legislature focused on the employment of illegal immigrants. In 2006, the legislature passed an employer sanction bill, but Governor Janet Napolitano engaged in a game of chicken by vetoing the bill and noting that the bill was not tough enough.[96] The legislature did not blink.

Instead, in 2007, it passed House Bill 2779, the Legal Arizona Workers Act ("LAWA"), which prohibited employers from hiring illegal immigrants and required them to use the E-Verify system to check all new hires' worker status. LAWA gave "the Superior Court of Arizona... the power to suspend or revoke the business licenses of employers who intentionally or knowingly employ unauthorized aliens."[97]

As expected, pro-illegal immigration and employer groups filed legal challenges to LAWA. On February 7, 2008, U.S. District Judge Neil V. Wake dismissed the lawsuit by concluding that the LAWA and the requirement to use the E-Verify system were constitutional.[98] Without missing a beat, in less than twenty-four hours, the losers filed an appeal to the liberal Ninth Circuit,[99] which heard oral arguments on June 12, 2008, with two of the three judges expressing support for LAWA.[100]

Specifically, one judge noted that Arizona has "the right to do what they need to do with unauthorized aliens in their state," and cited a total lack of any intent otherwise in the IRCA's legislative history. The other judge rhetorically asked what the problem was with Arizona, facing a different problem than the federal government faced, deciding to take a more effective approach by requiring the use of E-Verify due to the rampant fraud in the I-9 program.

On September 17, 2008, the Ninth Circuit issued its long-awaited decision on LAWA. Much to the surprise of pro-illegal immigrant groups, the Ninth Circuit found LAWA constitutional and breathed new life into the Supreme Court's *De Canas* decision.[101] With the federal appellate court's blessing, states that have been on the fence should move forward with laws identical to LAWA. During oral arguments, the losing coalition, in one last desperate gasp, warned the judges that if LAWA was not declared unconstitutional, "then every state is going to do this." That is a good thing. It is called federalism.

In 2008, the legislature passed House Bill 2745 to clarify parts of LAWA. House Bill 2745 also made knowingly accepting false identification a class four felony and required all state and local government contractors and subcontractors to comply with federal immigration laws and E-Verify requirements. The legislature also passed a bill requiring local law enforcement to work with federal immigration authorities, but Governor Napolitano vetoed the measure. The legislature is considering other bills aimed at reducing illegal immigration, including bills prohibiting sanctuary cities and curtailing selling or renting a home to illegal immigrants.

Meanwhile, Sheriff Arpaio—himself a child of immigrants—continues his crackdown on illegal immigrants in Maricopa County. Of the 77,000 inmates in his jails, roughly 17% are illegal immigrants.[102] Many critics question whether such an approach is getting results. As Sheriff Arpaio notes, "They're heading south, or they're going to California, but they're sure getting out of Arizona. If you can get them out of Arizona, you can get them out of the United States of America little by little. I'm not saying line up the buses, but put the pressure on them. Little by little they're going to leave because it's going to be hard to find a job and they're going to go to jail."[103]

Although obtaining hard data on how Arizona's actions have impacted its illegal immigration problem, especially in light of the economic downturn, one telling anecdote occurred during my cab ride from meetings with Representative Russell Pearce and former Senator, now Treasurer Dean Martin, the legislators who led the charge in Arizona. The cabdriver was a legal resident in the United States. He stated without hesitation that the laws were driving illegal immigrants from Arizona to other, more accommodating states. When asked if he wanted to become a citizen, he quickly stated that he did. When asked why, he said that the primary reason he wanted to become a citizen was so he could vote against the illegal immigration measures and politicians who support them.

Because Arizona is willing to exert its powers under the Tenth Amendment, other states and localities now have a bright path to follow in taking control of their jurisdictions. It is time more states and localities took a stand for their taxpayers and the Constitution. Hell hath no fury like scorned voters.

9

Counterterrorism from the Bottom Up

Since World War II, the U.S. intelligence community has failed to predict the North Korean invasion of the South, the Chinese intervention in Korea, Khrushchev's plan to place missiles in Cuba, the fact that U.S. strategy in Vietnam would fail, the fall of the Shah of Iran, the collapse of communism, or the breakup of the Soviet Union. Therefore, the general shock at the fact that the U.S. intelligence community failed to predict September 11 is rather surprising. U.S. intelligence has never been very good at forecasting the big things.

George Friedman[1]

If you looked at Enron from the perspective of the tax code, that is, you would have seen a very different picture of the company than if you had looked through the more traditional lens of the accounting profession. But in order to do that you would have to be trained in the tax code and be familiar with its particular conventions and intricacies, and know what questions to ask. "The fact of the gap between [Enron's] accounting income and taxable income was easily observable," Fleischer notes, but not the source of the gap. "The tax code requires special training."

Malcolm Gladwell[2]

In conjunction with the rise of information on the Internet, governments and the private sector have adopted data-driven models for all aspects of their operations. These data models have resulted in the creation of thousands of databases that contain information such as court records, business filings, and consumer records. Although end-users leverage these databases to increase productivity and conduct business more efficiently, these databases also provide law enforcement entities with rich sources for counterterrorism investigations. Because of the global reach of the Internet, al Qaeda and other terrorist organizations have relied heavily on the Internet to foment terrorism, recruit radicals, publish written and oral communications, and trigger attacks.[3]

When it comes to our domestic counterterrorism efforts, the focus on mining data for possible indications of terrorist activity and fusing that data has reached a deafening pitch. The federal government has tried numerous times to create massive data mining and analysis tools using foreboding names like Total Information Awareness and the Analysis, Dissemination, Visualization, Insight, and Semantic Enhancement system.[4] Privacy concerns forced the government to end the projects.

Even if such projects survived, given the track record of the Intelligence Community (IC) to detect significant events, serious doubts arise as to whether these tools would increase our ability to solve the mystery of the next terrorist attack. Frankly, the problem for the IC is not that it possesses too little data; instead, the problem is that it possesses too much data. With the growth of information sharing and intelligence programs all aimed at feeding information and intelligence to the IC, the risk of information overload becomes very real.

A useful analogy makes this problem clear. Assume pieces of data are like straws of hay. As the IC tries to gather more and more hay, the haystack gets bigger and bigger. Much of the hay added is meaningless hay. As the haystack grows, finding the proverbial needle in the haystack becomes harder and harder as more meaningless hay conceals the relevant hay. The key to managing the haystack and finding the needle is not to just add more hay; rather, it is to separate the meaningless hay from the relevant hay so that only relevant hay gets added to the haystack, which makes it easier to connect the dots and find the needle.

Today's data-driven model places a heavy emphasis on sending more state and local data (hay or background noise) to the federal government so the IC can use its tools to find the terrorist. As history has shown, such an approach is fundamentally flawed as it places an overreliance on the ability of the federal government to remove background noise and concentrate its resources on the actionable data.

A more effective and efficient model would place greater focus on building true counterterrorism capabilities in states and localities. Virtually all of the dialogue inside the Beltway on state and local counterterrorism has focused almost exclusively on information and intelligence sharing. Missing from the discussion is the importance of how data is collected and then used for operations and investigations. With only 15,000 FBI agents across the country, the federal counterterrorism capability is, at best, an inch deep and a mile wide. The FBI's counterterrorism unit is also grossly understaffed.[5]

In contrast, there are roughly one million state and local law enforcement personnel in the United States. Unlike most FBI agents who focus their efforts at investigating active cases, these men and women spend virtually every day on the streets or in prisons and jails keeping the peace. They are the eyes and ears of our communities. That daily exposure to communities and criminal elements allows these law enforcement officers to develop a robust sixth sense—a gut instinct—that enhances their ability to detect criminal activity.

In a terrorism context, that instinct allows local law enforcement to ignore useless data that will only clog the intelligence pipelines and focus on more relevant data. These local cops will not only feed relevant data into analysts, but also will take the actionable intelligence and conduct follow-up actions or surveillance.

Under this model, each jurisdiction would gather its own data, analyze it, remove the irrelevant data, and then focus additional investigative efforts on the actionable intelligence. Once the useful intelligence is identified and investigated, it can be shared with other states and localities, as well as the federal government. Collectively, the intelligence from federal, state, and local governments could be analyzed for trends and other suspicious activity—such as the increase of flight school students from the Middle East in Arizona, Minnesota, and Florida who make odd requests as happened in the lead-up to the September 11 attack.

One of the biggest advantages to a state and local counterterrorism capability is that it places those individuals closest to their communities on the front line. Whether it is the cop on the beat who notices something out of the ordinary or the cyber security officer who observes an increase (or calm-before-the-storm decrease) in Internet activity focused on his jurisdiction, those most familiar with their jurisdictions possess the greatest chance of detecting terrorism activities.

As one expert noted, "much of the information necessary to understand the dynamics of a threat—indeed, even to recognize that a threat exists—is developed from the bottom-up, as well as through horizontal (as opposed to top-down) structures."[6] In the strongest statement on the critical role of local law enforcement, the International Association of Chiefs of Police noted that "agencies have a need and obligation to participate in the process of intelligence gathering and sharing that is at least equal to that of national law enforcement and security agencies—as poignantly demonstrated by the fact that the September 11 perpetrators lived and trained in cities and towns across the U.S. long before their actions drew national and international attention."[7]

Equally as critical, those local experts are most likely to ask the right questions or look in the right places that will lead to possible terrorist activity. As Gladwell correctly noted:

> The national-security expert Gregory Treverton has famously made a distinction between puzzles and mysteries. Osama bin Laden's whereabouts are a puzzle. We can't find him because we don't have enough information. The key to the puzzle will probably come from someone close to bin Laden, and until we can find that source bin Laden will remain at large…
>
> Mysteries require judgments and the assessment of uncertainty, and the hard part is not that we have too little information but that we have too much…
>
> The distinction is not trivial. If you consider the motivation and methods behind the attacks of September 11th to be mainly a puzzle, for instance, then the logical response is to increase the collection of intelligence, recruit more spies, add to the

volume of information we have about Al Qaeda. If you consider September 11th a mystery, though, you'd have to wonder whether adding to the volume of information will only make things worse.[8]

To solve the mystery of the next terrorist attack, rather than looking at it from a traditional IC perspective, we might look at it from a local law enforcement perspective.

Paraphrasing Gladwell's conclusion on Enron as a mystery that could have been solved by looking at the tax code, to look at terrorism from a local law enforcement perspective, "you would have to be trained in [local law enforcement] and be familiar with its particular [rules and communities of interest], and know what questions to ask."[9] Rather than just focus on gathering more data, "mysteries demand experience and insight" to interpret the data and offer possible answers.[10]

Local law enforcement did not just become community experts in the twenty-first century. Its traditions date back thousands of years, and its methods evolved to meet local challenges. The challenge of Islamic jihadists, once they arrive in our cities, should be no different.

HISTORY OF DECENTRALIZED LAW ENFORCEMENT

As with many aspects of western civilization, it was the Romans who first developed an effective decentralized system to enforce the laws. Under Emperor Augustus around 4 A.D., as Rome became densely populated, it was divided into fourteen sections called wards. Each of the wards contained groups of *Vigiles Urbani*, or Watchmen of the City. The Vigiles Urbani served as both a police presence and as firefighters. This decentralized model took root across the Roman Empire as local chiefs oversaw maintaining the public order.

The later Anglo-Saxon model of law enforcement also employed a decentralized model. It consisted of a constable employed by the local ruling nobility. The constable made sure that lands overseen by the noble were safe and that the people living underneath the noble complied with the law and paid their "taxes."

Eventually, under the French King Louis XIV, the first police force was established in 1667 to police Paris. The Paris police arose from a royal edict establishing the Lieutenant General of Police to guarantee peace and quiet. The Lieutenant General oversaw sixteen districts led by Commissioners. In 1699, a second royal edict created similar systems across France. The first formal law enforcement doctrine titled, *Treatise on the Police*, was published in 1705 by Nicolas Delamare.

Although many law enforcement developments occurred in Western Europe in the 1700s, it was the United Kingdom's Parliament in 1829 that passed the Metropolitan Police Act establishing the London Metropolitan Police. Under the Metropolitan Police Act, the local constable had the power to arrest "all loose, idle and disorderly Persons whom he shall find disturbing the public Peace, or whom he shall have just Cause to suspect of any evil Designs." The London Metropolitan Police served as a model for the then-developing United States.

In the United States, the city of Boston possesses many of the firsts concerning law enforcement development. It was the first to establish a night watch in 1631. It was the first to employ full-time, paid police officers in 1712. The first modern police department started in Boston in 1838. Later, in 1858, Boston, along with Chicago, gave uniforms to its police officers. Finally, in 1863, Boston became the first police department to issue guns to its police officers as standard equipment.

With the development of police departments in cities across the United States, in 1891, police chiefs formed the first national police group, the National Chiefs of Police Union, in 1891. The group allowed police chiefs to regularly meet to share ideas about effective law enforcement techniques and strategies.

In terms of policing techniques to aid in catching perpetrators, the use of fingerprinting started in 1902. The first widespread use of police cars to patrol its jurisdiction occurred in 1914 by the Berkeley Police Department in California. In 1933, the Bayonne Police Department in New Jersey successfully used a two-way radio system to respond to an emergency. Due to the rise of handgun violence, police begin wearing body armor as a routine practice starting in 1974. In 1988, the FBI became the first law enforcement entity to use DNA to identify criminals.

Throughout the 1980s and 1990s, police departments across the United States adopted community-policing strategies, as well as problem-oriented policing strategies. These strategies include James Q. Wilson's and George L. Kelling's famous "Broken Windows" policing strategy deployed in New York City by New York Police Department (NYPD) Commissioner William Bratton. Community policing consisted of high-levels of interactions with community members aimed at developing strong bonds so that citizens would proactively work with police to identify criminals and deter potential criminals from acting. Many believe community policing is a "tremendous resource that allow[s] local law enforcement to gather information."[11]

Problem-oriented policing "is an approach to policing in which discrete pieces of police business... are subject to microscopic examination... in hopes that what is freshly learned about each problem will lead to discovering a new and more effective strategy for dealing with it."[12] The Broken Windows theory holds that addressing small issues such as fixing a broken window in a building deters criminals from breaking more windows in the building or using the building to engage in larger crimes because they interpret the police's attention to the building as a message that they will not let crime slide in that community.

Today, large urban police departments have adopted intelligence-led policing strategies to help them more effectively develop operational strategies.

Intelligence-led policing involves "a strategic, future-oriented and targeted approach to crime control, focusing upon the identification, analysis and 'management' of persisting and developing 'problems' or 'risks.'"[13]

This more recent use of information or intelligence is not the first time state or local law enforcement adopted policing methods to identify possible criminals. As early as the 1920s, law enforcement "borrowed an old method from the military known as 'the dossier system.'"[14] Under the dossier system, files would contain information on individuals who were suspected of criminal activity. With the rise of Communism, local law enforcement created files on individuals suspected of being communists.[15]

Later, during the upheaval of the 1960s, authorities—in parallel with the FBI—created files on individuals they viewed as anti-American or countercultural.[16] As word spread of the existence of such files, many Americans argued that such activities violated their constitutional rights. Citizens used 42 U.S.C. section 1983 to sue local law enforcement agencies for violating their civil rights.[17] Without proof of any criminality, courts found against law enforcement's use of such practices and "ordered intelligence files to be purged from police records."[18] Due to such negative publicity and financial costs, many states and localities disbanded their intelligence units or deferred to federal authorities.[19]

This pendulum swing to the protection of civil liberties, although understandable, created an enormous capability gap, which significantly increased America's vulnerability during the 1990s and into the new millennium as al Qaeda launched its war against us. With the September 11 attack, this vulnerability came to light, thereby reigniting the need for state and local intelligence capabilities focused on preventing a terrorist attack. All, however, was not lost in the struggle between law enforcement and civil liberties.

Some local law enforcement agencies retained their intelligence capabilities after the 1970s, and typically used them to target organized crime.[20] For those entities, the Commission on the Accreditation of Law Enforcement Agencies provided recommendations for intelligence capabilities that primarily advocated for the creation of collection procedures "limited to criminal conduct that relates to activities that present a threat to the community" and for policies aimed at the destruction of information once it was no longer tied to a present threat.[21] This important lesson—that information and intelligence efforts should be tied to a present threat—provides state and local law enforcement with a foundation from which to build a robust intelligence capability.

Given the lack of frequent terrorist attacks within the United States, prior to the September 11 attack, "very little of the sprawling U.S. law enforcement community was engaged in countering terrorism."[22] The counterterrorism capability at the federal level did not possess a great deal of robustness.[23] As the 9/11 Commission noted, "Counterterrorism and counterintelligence work, often involving lengthy intelligence investigations that might never have positive or quantifiable results, was not career-enhancing."[24]

Additionally, as these lengthy cases developed, the targets of investigations continued to conduct criminal activities. In some cases, that activity included raising funds for terrorists. As these federal cases spanned years, the funding reached into the millions.

Of the federal efforts underway at that time, very little interaction occurred with state and local law enforcement agencies.[25] In fact, because the federal entities took jurisdiction away from the local law enforcement, local law enforcement officers were forced to sit on their hands while criminals operated in their communities. Many experts believe that "there is a growing role for state and local law enforcement agencies" that "can cooperate more effectively with those federal authorities in identifying terrorist suspects."[26] Before September 11, 2001, there was historical support for greater involvement in counterterrorism efforts by state and local law enforcement.

Unfortunately, at the federal level, turf battles between entities and lack of real progress from the Information Sharing Environment have become the norm, so states and localities face a confusing set of priorities and demands from the federal government. With the federal obsession with gathering data, local law enforcement's superior community instincts remain grossly underutilized.

There is a better way.

ONE-STOP FEDERAL SHOP FOR STATE AND LOCAL COUNTERTERRORISM EFFORTS

As early as 1980, the FBI had established a JTTF at the state and local level to work cooperatively with law enforcement.[27] JTTFs are "small cells of highly trained, locally based, passionately committed investigators, analysts, linguists, SWAT experts, and other specialists from dozens of U.S. law enforcement and intelligence agencies."[28] In a collaborative manner, JTTF members investigate possible terrorist activities and then serve as the primary responders should an incident occur.

As the *9/11 Commission Report* noted, a JTTF was "first tried out in New York City in 1980 in response to a spate of incidents involving domestic terrorist organizations."[29] It was the New York City JTTF that brought together federal, state, and local law enforcement personnel after the first World Trade Center bombing in 1993.[30] In implicit recognition of the joint aspect of the JTTF, it had an equal representation of personnel from the NYPD and the FBI.[31]

Over the next eight years, the FBI established more JTTFs. On September 11, 2001, there were thirty-four JTTFs in operation across the United States.[32] The JTTFs suffered from a lack of full-time staff and national guidance, and, as a result, "many state and local entities believed they had little to gain from having a full-time representative on a JTTF."[33]

Currently, with over 100 JTTFs around the United States, "the JTTFs have substantially contributed to improved information sharing and operational capabilities at the State and municipal levels."[34] Roughly 5,085 members from federal, state, and local law enforcement belong to the JTTFs.[35] With the exception of Columbus, there are JTTFs in all thirty-seven of the higher-risk urban areas listed in Chapter 5.[36] With such a high-level of connections between the FBI and state and local law enforcement, a strong argument exists that the FBI should be the federal lead on counterterrorism efforts. In fact, under federal law, the FBI is the "lead agency in domestic intelligence collection."[37]

In New York City, the NYPD has assigned over 100 detectives to the JTTF, which is in itself more manpower than most, if not all other, intelligence units in the United States.[38] As the NYPD Deputy Commissioner for Counterterrorism, noted: "The only established information-sharing mechanism with real coherence and consistent value is the sharing of usually case-specific, classified information with the Joint Terrorism Task Force."[39]

With the creation of DHS, however, another entity with equity in state and local information sharing and intelligence arrived on the scene. As would be expected, DHS moved aggressively to assert itself into the debate over which federal entity "owned" state and local information sharing and intelligence. Based on expert opinion, however, the DHS effort is weak at best.

Specifically, the NYPD Deputy Commissioner stated: "The utility of the Department of Homeland Security's information-sharing initiatives is severely limited by DHS's apparent inability to treat various state and local agencies differently according to their role, their sophistication, their potential contribution to the national mission of combating terrorism, and their size and power. Consequently, NYPD's collaboration with other members of the Intelligence Community and with foreign law enforcement and intelligence agencies is substantially more valuable than is our collaboration with DHS."[40]

The primary tool used by DHS to inject itself into state and local information-sharing and intelligence efforts was the creation of "fusion centers." Prior to the creation of the first DHS fusion center, a group of federal, local, and state experts warned: "Information needs to rest in a single place, and the JTTF provides that forum. They are concerned that a different or complementary forum might undermine the JTTFs, provide confusion and redundancy, and further drain limited resources."[41] DHS ignored this prophetic warning.

Because it controlled the billions of state and local terrorism grants, it initially inserted language into the grant guidance in 2005 promoting the "hiring of contractors/consultants... for participation in information/intelligence sharing groups or intelligence fusion centers."[42] While some inside DHS argued against an interagency fight with DOJ and the FBI over state and local information and intelligence activities due to the existence and prevalence of JTTFs, common sense lost out to Potomac Fever. By 2007, DHS promoted the full "establishment of a network of fusion centers to facilitate effective nationwide homeland security information sharing."[43]

DHS's aggressive move seems to have paid off. As the *National Strategy for Information Sharing* noted, "Many State and major urban areas have established information fusion centers to coordinate the gathering, analysis, and dissemination of law enforcement, homeland security, public safety, and terrorism information."[44] As audits have discovered, however, many of the fusion centers get little specific or actionable information from DHS.[45] Moreover, DHS has been slow to provide fusion centers with useful guidance and training support.[46]

Despite the push for DHS fusion centers, the FBI continued to strengthen its ties to state and local law enforcement through the far greater presence of FBI agents in key jurisdictions, the JTTFs, Field Intelligence Groups, and the enhancement of multiple information sharing systems like Law Enforcement Online, the Regional Information Sharing System, National Data Exchange, FBINet (classified information), and Sensitive Compartmental Information Operational Network (top secret) networks.[47]

This federal scrum over controlling state and local information sharing and intelligence has led to redundant efforts from DHS and the FBI, as well as other resource-wasting initiatives such as DHS's much-maligned unclassified Homeland Security Information Network and classified Homeland Security Data Network. Many state and local law enforcement agencies, already understaffed and under-budgeted, are forced to make difficult choices in allocating resources (personnel and money) to these duplicative federal initiatives.

In fact, the 9/11 Commission acknowledged this conflict between federal entities. Specifically, the 9/11 Commission proposed three deputies—one for foreign intelligence, one for defense intelligence, and one for homeland intelligence—who would report to the National Intelligence Director.[48] For the homeland intelligence deputy, the 9/11 Commission recommended it be filled by "the FBI's executive assistant director for intelligence or the under secretary of homeland security for information analysis and infrastructure protection."[49] This interagency schizophrenia needs to stop.

The *National Strategy for Information Sharing* mandated that "a common framework be developed governing the roles and responsibilities of Federal departments and agencies relating to the sharing of terrorism information, homeland security information, and law enforcement information among Federal departments and agencies, State, local, and tribal governments, and private sector entities."[50] The federal government must continue to develop the Information Sharing Environment, especially the common framework for sharing information.

As important, it must eliminate the multiheaded federal lead on state and local counterterrorism by designating the FBI as the lead agency for state and local counterterrorism efforts. Under the FBI lead, the DHS fusion centers should be consolidated into the more established and numerous JTTFs.[51] In fact, roughly sixteen fusion centers are already collocated with the FBI.[52] The FBI has linked its secure computer system to over two-thirds of the fusion centers.[53]

From a resource allocation standpoint, because many JTTFs lack the trained analysts they need to do their work, rather then increase the demand for analysts by establishing somewhat redundant fusion centers (especially in places where little to no terrorist activities occur or are likely to occur), a combined entity will ensure that precious resources are allocated more efficiently.[54] State and local participants reported difficulties in staffing fusion centers.[55] Federal entities also face personnel constraints in assigning staff to both JTTFs and fusion centers. When asked, states commented that they wanted the FBI to take a greater role in the fusion centers.[56]

The JTTFs are by no means perfect. The FBI must develop the JTTFs into truly joint ventures where state and local law enforcement sit as partners with their federal counterparts. Ideally, the JTTF should be a place where representatives from federal, state, and local law enforcement sit down, evaluate leads, share and review all intelligence, debate pros and cons of proposed courses of action, and agree on a plan of action. An integral part of the discussion must center on which level of authority makes the most sense to assume leadership—local law enforcement sometimes possesses greater flexibility and power.

Today, most leads are federalized, thereby cutting out local law enforcement. This approach makes little sense. More problematic, federalizing leads and cutting out local law enforcement can undermine years of community policing efforts.[57] When so much of America's ability to stop a terrorist attack rests on its ability to penetrate murky and nebulous community-based entities, we can ill afford to ignore the strides made thus far.

To further conserve finite resources and reduce duplicative tools, DHS's networks should be eliminated or merged into the FBI's networks. State and local officials "found the multiple systems or heavy volume of often redundant information a challenge to manage."[58] The bottom line is that the federal government must remove roadblocks and improve its support of state and local counterterrorism efforts.

STATE AND LOCAL COUNTERTERRORISM CAPABILITIES

When it comes to the threat from terrorism, "the burden shifts instead almost entirely to local law enforcement."[59] Yet, thus far, we have focused on federal efforts. Due to the inherent bureaucratic nature of the federal government, as well as its lack of resources other than money, it simply fails as an incubator of innovation. After all, a decentralized approach "may help to overcome what Friedrich Hayek identified as the 'knowledge problem' where specialized, localized knowledge is lost the further up the chain of command decisions are made."[60]

We need to stop giving federalism lip service, and let states and localities lead the way. State and local law enforcement must be more than "adjuncts to a national strategy for improved intelligence communication."[61] They must be "founding partners of and driving participants in any organization that helps coordinate the collection, analysis, dissemination and use of criminal intelligence data in the [United States]."[62]

As many experts have concluded, terrorist threats "are most likely to be detected by dedicated investigators with both intimate knowledge of the population in question and mastery of human intelligence tradecraft who are backed by the full power and resources of a major law enforcement agency."[63] No one knows a particular population better than those men and women who spend every day of their lives in that population.

As the International Association of Chiefs of Police concluded, "Over the past decade, simultaneous to federally led initiatives to improve intelligence gathering, thousands of community policing officers have been building close and personal relationships with the citizens they serve."[64] The benefits of these activities are that local law enforcement gets "immediate and unfettered access to local, neighborhood information as it develops" as community members find them "to provide them with new information."[65] Because the terrorists "are living among us, watching and waiting to act, we can not rely solely on bits of information (often dated) provided by federal agencies that do not have the ability to determine the timely value of the information at the local or regional level."[66] It is time we provide local officers with all of the resources they need to leverage these relationships as much as possible.

Of growing urgency is the small, but ever-increasing, threat from citizens who become radicalized at home. Prisons and jails are the primary breeding ground for these homegrown converts to Islamic jihadism.[67] As of June 30, 2007, state prisons and local jails held roughly 1,395,916 prisoners (58.5 percent) and 780,581 inmates (32.9 percent), respectively; in comparison, federal prisons only held approximately 199,118 prisoners (8.6 percent).[68] California alone has more prisoners and inmates than the entire federal prison system.[69]

With responsibility for over 90 percent of all prisoners and inmates in the United States, state and local law enforcement are already deeply integrated into this burgeoning, radicalized population. The most famous public case occurred in July 2005 when authorities in California discovered that the radical group *Jam'iyyat Ul-Islam Is-Sheeh* had penetrated Folsom State Prison and started planning an attack.[70]

While the research on homegrown terrorists is in the early phases of development, experts have identified four steps in the radicalization process. The four steps are pre-radicalization, self-identification, indoctrination, and jihadization.[71] Many individuals who undergo the radicalization process are "looking for an identity and a cause."[72] The path through the radicalization process typically leads through mosques, the Internet, "cafes, cab driver hangouts, flophouses, prisons, student associations, nongovernmental organizations, hookah (water pipe) bars, butcher shops and book stores."[73] Because the radicalization process can occur subtly, local law enforcement entities, due to their strong community knowledge, likely possess the greatest chance to detect and disrupt it.

Related to the radicalization in prisons and jails is the increasing association of street gangs with radical Islamic groups. Both groups possess an antigovernment sentiment that bridges the religious differences between them. With the need to fund terrorist activities domestically and internationally, a strong economic incentive exists for Islamic jihadists to engage in gang activity, including narcotics trafficking and stolen or fraudulent goods peddling.[74] In many cases, street gang members who have converted while in prison serve as the link between the two groups.[75] Many state and local law enforcement entities possess a wealth of knowledge and experience on gangs, so they stand the best chance of dealing with this developing relationship between Islamic jihadists and gangs.

As discussed in Chapter 5, not every city faces a sufficient level of risk to justify the development of a counterterrorism capability. Of thirteen thousand law enforcement agencies in the United States, less than 25% of them possess more than twenty-five officers.[76] Roughly half of those agencies readily acknowledge that "the chance of a major terrorist incident occurring with their jurisdiction within the next five years as being very low."[77]

We must focus our finite resources on those jurisdictions where we know the risk of a terrorist attack exists. Only sixteen percent of local law enforcement agencies even possess counterterrorism units.[78] Of the thirty-seven urban areas listed in Chapter 5, very few have robust counterterrorism units. Hence, much work remains to be done to develop counterterrorism capabilities in higher-risk urban areas.

The organizational structure of state and local counterterrorism divisions should follow the recommendations contained in the *9/11 Commission Report* for the FBI. Specifically, state and local counterterrorism divisions should include "agents, analysts, linguists, and surveillance specialists who are recruited, and retained to ensure the development of an institutional culture imbued with a deep expertise in intelligence and national security."[79] Agents should receive training in both criminal justice and national security training and then "have the option to work such matters for their entire career."[80]

Counterterrorism divisions should focus on continuing education that emphasizes and rewards "advanced training courses and assignments to other intelligence agencies" at the federal level.[81] State and local law enforcement agencies "should fully implement a recruiting, hiring, and selection process for agents and analysts that enhances [their] ability to target and attract individuals with educational and professional backgrounds in intelligence, international relations, language, technology, and other relevant skills."[82]

State and local law enforcement agencies should report regularly to their government leaders on their activities, progress, and needs so that progress can be monitored and concerns with privacy and civil liberties can be minimized. States and localities "should make sure funding is available to accelerate the expansion of secure facilities... so as to increase their ability to use secure email systems and classified intelligence product exchanges."[83]

Finally, state and local law enforcement agencies should conform to the Law Enforcement Intelligence Unit's *Criminal Intelligence File Guidelines*.[84] Knowledge on counterterrorism legal parameters represents a vital foundation for successful programs.

For those state and local law enforcement entities interested in establishing a counterterrorism unit, David Carter's *Law Enforcement Intelligence: A Guide for State, Local, and Tribal Law Enforcement Agencies* is an excellent resource. Another key resource is *The National Criminal Intelligence Sharing Plan* developed by DOJ's Global Justice Information Sharing Initiative. The *Sharing Plan*, first published in October 2003 and revised in June 2005, contains twenty-eight recommendations that identify "system connections, personnel training, promulgation of model policies and standards, [and] outreach efforts."[85]

In terms of surveillance and other fieldwork activity, state and local counterterrorism units should adopt the guidelines contained in the *Handschu v. Special Services* settlement from 1985 as modified by Judge Charles S. Haight in 2003.[86] The 2003 modification adheres to the FBI's surveillance guidelines.[87] Because these guidelines apply to political activities where greater constitutional protections apply, it is safe to assume that using such guidelines for non-political activities is appropriate.

Because of past civil liberties violations, states and localities should create advisory councils that include members from groups who have historically defended the civil liberties of citizens.[88] Such advisory groups will ensure that policies and practices are designed to minimize the abuse of civil liberties by law enforcement.

With seven years of incremental movement behind us, it is time to leverage the power of the million-strong state and local law enforcement community. Those men and women represent the best chance America has to stop terrorists before they do more harm to our country and way of life.

CASE STUDY 6

Los Angeles' Counterterrorism Innovation

When it comes to counterterrorism and intelligence innovation, the federal government gets low marks as it continues to spin its wheels on turf wars and breaking down walls to increase the sharing of intelligence and information within the federal interagency. Any meaningful sharing of information with states and localities is still over the horizon.

The actions of the Greater Los Angeles urban area since September 11, 2001, demonstrates that the nation's toughest homeland security challenges will be solved by states and localities, not Washington. We should not be surprised. Rather than wait on Washington, the Greater Los Angeles urban area is charting its own course and, in doing so, serves as a national leader in bringing innovation to our homeland security counterterrorism efforts. The Greater Los Angeles area is home to over ten million residents and eighty-eight cities, as well as the busiest ports in America.[89]

Counterterrorism is not new to the Greater Los Angeles urban area. The Los Angeles Police Department (LAPD) has had a counterterrorism unit for decades, and prepared for possible terrorist activity in anticipation of the Summer Olympics in 1984. Following the Summer Olympics, Los Angeles created the Los Angeles Task Force on Terrorism, which brought together the FBI, the LAPD, and the Los Angeles Sheriff's Office (LASO).[90]

The first core innovation in Los Angeles occurred in October 1996 when Lieutenant John Sullivan of the LASO created the nation's first Terrorism Early Warning (TEW) group.[91] According to Los Angeles County Sheriff Lee Baca, "The TEW provide[d] a system to collect and process information across jurisdictional and disciplinary lines, and therefore, enable[d] a complete perspective beyond that of only traditional criminal intelligence."[92] The TEW group included traditional first preventers and first responders such as law enforcement and the fire service, as well as non-traditional disciplines such as public health and academia.[93] The TEW routinely interfaced with the Coast Guard, the Secret Service, and the Bureau of Alcohol, Tobacco and Firearms, as well as some foreign countries with diplomatic presence in Los Angeles.[94]

Functionally, the TEW "bridge[d] criminal and operational intelligence to support strategic and tactical users."[95] The TEW aimed to "identify emerging threats and provide early warning by integrating inputs and analysis from a multidisciplinary, interagency team."[96] Because each TEW participant group assigned a Terrorism Liaison Officer and private sector partners assigned Infrastructure Liaison Officers, a stable network of interagency government and private sector professionals existed who could focus on identifying threats and ensure that information reached those with a need to know.[97] The TEW was organized into six cells: Office-in-Charge, Analysis/Synthesis, Consequence Management, Investigative Liaison, Epidemiological Intelligence, and Forensic Intelligence Support.[98]

Finally, the TEW developed processes and operational procedures to facilitate the production and sharing of intelligence.[99] The TEW created target folders for "specific locations thought to be potential targets" and developed "playbooks detailing how to respond to specific threats."[100] This innovative approach resulted in the Greater Los Angeles urban area's TEW becoming the model for state and local government intelligence efforts after the September 11 attack. There are now roughly thirty TEW groups across the United States.

Another innovation involved the creation of the Homeland Security Advisory Council comprised of public and private members from Los Angeles County and Orange County.[101] The Council aimed to "provide direct interaction among senior executives from industry and the community with law enforcement and public safety services in support of Homeland Security, civil protection, and critical infrastructure protection."[102]

To strengthen ties to the local Muslim community, Sheriff Baca launched the Muslim American Homeland Security Congress in 2005 to "educate both Muslim and non-Muslim communities in an effort to discourage extremism within the Muslim community and hatred or discriminatory attitudes by the non-Muslim community against Muslims."[103] Although started by Sheriff Baca, the Muslim Congress is a national effort.

Lastly, through the ongoing efforts of Operation Safe Jails, LASO started several jail radicalization initiatives to detect and stop radicalization efforts in its prisons.[104] These efforts led to the discovery of the Folsom State Prison plot.

The pioneering work of the TEW led to the founding of the Joint Regional Intelligence Center (JRIC) in July 2006. The JRIC serves Southern California, which includes Los Angeles, Orange, Riverside, San Bernardino, Ventura, Santa Barbara, and San Luis Obispo counties.[105] The JRIC combines the LAPD's Major Crimes Division, the LASO's TEW, and the FBI's Field Intelligence Group.[106] The JRIC "collects information using an all-crimes approach, converts the information into operational and strategic intelligence, and disseminates the intelligence to prevent terrorist attacks and combat crime in the Central District of California."[107] The JRIC has thirty full-time staff from roughly fourteen participants, and produces daily, weekly, and monthly reports.[108]

More recently, the LAPD added another innovative tool to the Greater Los Angeles urban area's counterterrorism efforts. Chief Bratton leads the LAPD. Given his history of transforming how law enforcement approaches crime, this development likely will not be the last. Chief Bratton referred to this new program as "the 'heart and soul' of the LAPD's counterterrorism efforts."[109]

The LAPD program centers on the reporting of suspicious activities that could be proxies for terrorism.[110] The program routes suspicious activity reports (SARs) "to analysts at the LAPD's counterterrorism bureau who... assess them and assign codes so the new data could be studied [and] cross-referenced with other databases, to look for patterns."[111] The SARs focus on sixty-five activities, "such as photographing government buildings, espousing extremist views and displaying overt support for terrorist networks."[112] Critically, the SARs leverage the work being done every day by cops on the beat, finally integrating operational activities to information analysis.

Although some privacy advocates have raised concerns with the program, the LAPD inserted privacy protections to the SAR program, and received an opinion from the Director of National Intelligence that the program abided by privacy rules.[113] The LAPD is launching an education campaign—with support from the federal government—aimed at serving as the model for sixty-two large cities in the United States.

Together, these SAR programs will create a nationwide web. As we learned from the September 11 attack, the terrorists left clues across the United States, but because we lacked a web connecting suspicious activities, we failed to connect the dots in time to stop the attacks. The LAPD's newest tool, in conjunction with the work being done by the JRIC, gives it a fighting chance of stopping an attack in the Greater Los Angeles urban area.

The Greater Los Angeles urban area is blazing a trail of innovation that seems far more likely to get results than any program or initiative pushed out of Washington since the September 11 attack. Federalism works and wins because it unleashes the creative forces of those who are closest to the problem and possess the greatest interest in solving it.

10

The Role of the Community

Homeland security must be a priority in every city, every community and every neighborhood across America.

Secretary Tom Ridge[1]

Primum non nocere (First, do no harm).

Galen[2]

Do no harm—a simple concept. When it comes to securing the homeland after September 11, 2001, and Hurricane Katrina, it takes on profound importance. Whether it is the individual, family, community organizations, or the private sector, the primary role is to do no harm. What does this statement mean exactly? It means that the system cannot erode the ability of people to first take care of themselves so that our first responders can focus on those who have been harmed.

Nothing can be more detrimental to the response to a catastrophic event than for first responders to waste vital time and resources taking care of those who could have taken care of themselves. Every community has individuals who collectively form a sizable vulnerable population. Typically, the vulnerable population includes the mentally and physically disabled, the elderly, non-English speaking immigrants, and the poor. As we saw in Hurricane Katrina, we fail as a society when we fail those most in need.

Once each part of the community that is capable of doing so has taken care of themselves, then and only then can those parts of the community with the means engage with our first responders to lend a hand and become part of the broader community response. As the 9/11 Commission noted, "The "first" first responders on 9/11, as in most catastrophes, were private-sector civilians. Because 85 percent of our nation's critical infrastructure is controlled not by government but by the private sector, private-sector civilians are likely to be the first responders in any future catastrophes."[3]

It is the individual whose family is safe and secure who can volunteer at a disaster relief center. It is a not-for-profit community food bank whose supplies are protected that can resume its delivery of meals to those who cannot leave their homes. It is the big-box retailer whose employees are accounted for and stores are assessed for damage that can donate bottles of water and clothing to the victims of a disaster and reopen rapidly to serve its battered community.

We must, however, take a more realistic and pragmatic view on what actions community members should take based on the likelihood of various risks they may face. In the aftermath of the September 11 attack and Hurricane Katrina, so much of the national dialogue took a broad approach to preparedness by promoting the idea that every American should "make a list and buy a kit." This approach overstates the risk to most Americans, undermines the credibility of the government, and likely leads to a greater level of apathy than a more realistic approach would generate.

Many Americans struggle to meet their basic needs. This reality is especially true during tough economic times. For most businesses, money spent on homeland security directly impacts their profits. Given these competing needs for individuals and businesses, it becomes even more critical to assess risk realistically. It just makes no sense to ask a senior citizen who never ventures into a large urban area or who lives in an area that does not have many natural disasters to spend her resources on a disaster kit. The same dynamic applies to a business owner living under similar conditions.

Given the substantial interests in risk assessment capabilities by the federal government since the September 11 attack, the national laboratories, universities, and some private sector entities have developed sophisticated risk analysis tools to facilitate the performance of community risk assessments. For communities with over 100,000 people with higher population densities and more critical infrastructure, it makes sense for community members to expend some time and money preparing for a catastrophic event like a terrorist attack.

For smaller communities located outside of large urban areas, spending time and money preparing for a disaster simply does not make sense unless, as noted below, those communities face a known risk of a natural disaster or companies possess supply chain or other interdependencies linked to higher-risk areas. In these "front porch" communities, we should expect them to exercise vigilance, report suspicious individuals or activities, and take mitigation measures where appropriate, but otherwise live their lives as they always have.

Although not a perfect analogy due to geographic proximity to its enemies and the frequency of attacks, the Israeli people have adapted to their environment by being extremely vigilant. "The average Israeli is highly aware of suspicious packages, individuals, and actions that could pose a threat to public safety and does not hesitate to notify the police. As a result, ordinary citizens foil more than 80 percent of attempted terrorist attacks in Israel, including time bombs left by terrorists."[4] The American public would do well to adopt similar vigilance tendencies.

With terrorist threats, predictability is not high, so even sophisticated and costly risk analysis tools are vulnerable to the unknown. As noted in Chapter 5, one method to gauge the relative risk for larger communities within the United States is to use the urban areas that are deemed eligible by the UASI program each year as a rough guide on where the federal government deems the risk of terrorism to be the greatest.[5] To further analyze the relative risk within those thirty-seven higher-risk urban areas, a community can look at the amount of funds DHS has allocated historically and in the current year to each urban area to determine whether a particular urban area was at the upper or lower end on the risk list.[6]

When it comes to natural disasters, however, geography largely drives the relative risk to a community. Over the last fifty-four years, FEMA has compiled data on all of the larger natural disasters that have occurred in the United States. The information is publicly available, searchable by state or year, and contains details including impacted counties and news articles related to the disaster. Community members can use this actuarial data to develop a better understanding of the natural disasters likely to occur in their area and, therefore, make better decisions about what needs to be done for them to be prepared.

The remainder of this chapter will focus on those larger communities with higher risks of a terrorist attack or catastrophic natural disaster.

INDIVIDUALS AND FAMILIES SHOULD KEEP IT SIMPLE

The first step for many individuals is to get basic information on what actions they should take to prepare themselves and their families. There are multiple sources that provide information. The most well-known resource site is the Ready campaign (www.ready.gov) run by DHS. The Ready campaign aims to "educate and empower American citizens to prepare for and respond to potential terrorist attacks and other emergencies."[7] According to DHS, approximately 210 million people "have seen or read about" the Ready campaign.[8]

Based on multiple surveys and findings, the best method in which to communicate information to individuals and families is through a trusted community actor such as a popular news personality or community leader. The information communicated should be as specific as possible and tailored to the particular disaster.

Another important step is to utilize a tool such as the Readiness Quotient test developed by the Council for Excellence in Government to help individuals determine their readiness level.[9] The test asks ten questions aimed at gauging an individual's or family's preparedness for a disaster.[10] Based on the answers provided, the test scores the participant's readiness level and directs him to resources to close readiness level gaps.[11]

In many cases, the steps most individuals should take involve establishing a communication plan for family members and making sure basic supplies such as flashlights, batteries, a first aid kit, and a three-day supply of food and water are procured. For families with children, parents should create a plan on where they will meet if separated and appoint back-up relatives or friends who can pick the children up if needed. One other action that may be warranted is to gain or regain CPR certification.

After an individual has become individually prepared, then, for those who seek a greater degree of community involvement, joining a local Citizen Corps chapter or Community Emergency Response Team is a step in the right direction. The Citizen Corps program aims at helping "coordinate volunteer activities."[12] To date, the Citizen Corps program has focused too many resources on establishing as many chapters as possible across the United States, which has resulted in the few chapters in key jurisdictions not being truly operational.

For individuals seeking more official roles, the Community Emergency Response Team focuses on training citizens to serve on teams that supplement professional responders.[13] Specifically, the teams "provide immediate assistance to victims in their area, organize spontaneous volunteers who have not had the training, and collect disaster intelligence that will assist professional responders with prioritization and allocation of resources."[14] The program involves over seventeen hours of training on the following topics: disaster preparedness, disaster fire suppression, disaster medical operations, light search and rescue operations, and disaster psychology and team organization.[15] As with many effective organizations, it began as a local effort in 1985 by the Los Angeles City Fire Department.[16]

Other worthwhile programs where citizens can strengthen their communities include the Fire Corps, the Civilian Volunteer Medical Reserve Corps, the Volunteers in Police Service, and the USAonWatch program. To encourage volunteerism, state and local governments should modify Good Samaritan laws and other legal liability laws that inhibit action and will do little more than line the pockets of trial lawyers. As Peter Huber observed, "Germs no longer need to be smarter than our scientists, just faster than our lawyers."[17] We cannot allow the trial lawyers to undermine our homeland security efforts.

Another way citizens can get involved in community preparedness activities is to volunteer for or start a local organization that fills a gap. For example, in the days after Hurricane Katrina, seeing a disconnect between local faith-based groups and disaster recovery efforts in Mississippi, Leisha Pickering started HANDS: Helping Americans Needing Disaster Support. The group helps faith-based groups to assist the needy and first responders after a disaster.

With individuals taking actions to prepare themselves and their families and engaging in community-based efforts so that the "do no harm" principle is followed, a higher-risk community's resiliency will depend on whether its business community has taken steps to be prepared.

FIVE AFFORDABLE, PROACTIVE ACTIONS COMPANIES CAN TAKE TO BE PREPARED

Although many Fortune 500 companies can afford to hire Chief Risk Officers and top-shelf consultants to analyze their preparedness and develop plans to strengthen areas of weakness, most companies simply lack the resources to engage in such long-term strategic planning.[18] Nonetheless, it is important for all companies to do a basic level of preparedness analysis so that avoidable risks are eliminated and vulnerabilities minimized.[19] Importantly, these recommendations are directed at companies that do not possess critical infrastructure or key resources pursuant to the National Infrastructure Protection Plan. This more sensitive subset should continue to work with the federal government to determine the appropriate steps to safeguard those "national" assets.

For the remaining not-for-profit and for-profit companies, here are five proactive measures to stay ahead of today's threats. Most of these measures involve low-cost solutions that take advantage of the millions of dollars invested by the federal government to determine and minimize risk.

First, as noted above, companies should use a basic risk matrix to determine their risk levels. No company can afford to develop capabilities to deal with every possible threat. Even if a company could afford such a broad approach, it makes little sense to do so given that many of the threats will not happen. Such overinvesting in capabilities acquisitions will not decrease a company's risk or please investors.

By leveraging more work already done by the federal government to develop a list of representative scenarios, a basic risk matrix largely based on the National Planning Scenarios likely is sufficient to enable companies to identify their existing risk. For most companies, it does not make sense to segregate types of chemical or biological attacks (mustard gas, anthrax, etc.), as those are too hard to ascertain with any real confidence.[20] It does, however, make sense to add less severe threats like tornados, floods, and blizzards as those types of natural disasters routinely occur across the United States. For a particular company, the basic risk matrix will cover the key natural disasters, terrorist attacks, and naturally occurring threats to the degree necessary to help chart its relative risk.

As an example, a company based in Columbus, Ohio, with operations only in Ohio, Indiana, and Michigan, can use the UASI program for terrorism and the FEMA data for natural disasters to make an informed decision on the types of risks it may encounter. Because Columbus is on the UASI eligibility list, the company would know that it faced a higher level of terrorism risk than other cities in the United States. In light of Columbus receiving one of the smallest allocations from DHS out of the eligible urban areas in 2006, 2007, and 2008, however, the company could decide that the risk, although higher than a lot of cities, was still not high enough to demand specific action.

In addition, the FEMA data show that since 1953, there have been 117 declared natural disasters involving severe storms, flooding, blizzards, and tornadoes in Ohio (47), Indiana (39), and Michigan (31).[21] With an average of just over two disasters per year in those three states, it might make sense for the company to commit a small amount of resources to harden its operations from those specific threats.

Using a three-prong scale from low to high, the risk matrix might look like the one contained in Table 10.1. Based on this basic risk picture, the company should dedicate first available resources to ensure that its information technology systems are secure. Next, given the sheer impact a pandemic flu could have on the company, the company should commit resources to ensure that it can effectively continue to operate if a pandemic flu hits, including ensuring that the companies in its supply chain and other such interdependent entities (for example, power suppliers) have measures in place to deal with a pandemic flu outbreak.

Similarly, because an explosive device could result in multiple deaths and significant infrastructure destruction, a company should utilize security mechanisms such as security entry cards and surveillance cameras to harden its facilities. Then, the company should look at current insurance policies to see if damages from tornados, floods, and blizzards are covered. If those events are inadequately covered, then the company may look for supplemental coverage or take additional preventive steps to minimize the damage from one of those events. Lastly, due to the low likelihood of the remaining types of threats, the company should provide basic information to employees on those threats. FEMA's Web site contains background and "what to do" information on most types of natural disasters and terrorist attacks.

Next, companies should use exercises to baseline existing capabilities and test resiliency. For threats in the medium to high categories that could result in significant consequences, companies should allocate some resources to baseline and test the existing capabilities in place via a focused, limited exercise program. Fundamentally, the exercise program should aim to identify capability gaps so that the company can close those gaps *before* a crisis occurs. Over the course of one year, taking a few hours periodically to run a table top or simulated exercise will enable the company to enhance its overall resiliency.

TABLE 10.1 Basic Risk Matrix

Type of Threat	Low Risk	Medium Risk	High Risk
Cyber Attack			X
Pandemic Flu		X	
Hurricane	X		
Earthquake	X		
Tornado		X	
Severe Storm/Flood		X	
Blizzard		X	
Chemical Attack	X		
Biological Attack	X		
Radiological Attack	X		
Nuclear Attack	X		
Explosive Attack		X	

Because DHS has invested so much time and effort into developing the National Planning Scenarios, it should be easy to use its scenarios to develop appropriate-level exercises for private-sector companies to test capabilities. Many private-sector companies provide exercise services and have developed impressive simulations, so finding an entity willing to assist will be fairly easy.

Importantly, to gain the largest return on its investment, a company should leverage the exercise doctrine and policies (as appropriate) developed by DHS. DHS developed a four-volume guide that covers the following areas: overview and exercise program management, exercise planning and conduct, exercise evaluation and improvement planning, and a library of sample exercise materials.[22] These documents are free, so companies at a minimum should obtain the four-volume guide and determine how it can be used in a cost-effective manner to help strengthen key capabilities.[23]

Once a company determines its risks and broader baseline capability gaps, it can focus on ensuring critical business continuity issues. Regardless of the exact threat, every business has core, critical business capabilities that must continue for the company to remain viable. Although the exact critical continuity capabilities depend on the type of business, most companies need to ensure that all information technology and data systems have redundant, back-up systems in place. The redundant systems should be located at a separate site than the original systems, and ideally are in facilities that are secure and hardened from most threats.

As illustrated during Hurricane Katrina, those companies who were able to restore crisis communications and power capabilities quickly were able to help communicate with employees, corporate leaders, local authorities, and customers, as well as to maintain business operations.[24] Some of those companies were able to fill gaps left by the poor response of government entities and make a crucial difference in their communities.[25] At a minimum, companies should ensure that key corporate leaders are able to communicate during and immediately after a crisis so that vital decisions can be made to ensure continued viability of the company. If possible, companies should obtain backup power supplies so that minimal business operations can continue.

In the midst of an event, employees and their families will depend on the company to provide information to them. Even more importantly, for both continuity purposes and altruistic concerns, companies will want to have a system in place in which employees can report where they are and if they are okay. Such a system will allow the company to report missing employees to the appropriate authorities, as well as provide family members with either assurance when an employee has checked in or contact information for state or local agencies that are engaged in rescue operations. This action will ensure that first responders are not overwhelmed with telephone calls on individuals who are okay.

As an extra safety measure, companies with operations dependent on a working facility should establish contingent workspace contracts so that alternative work sites can be quickly set up and used to get the business back up and running as quickly as possible after an event has occurred. These contingent workspaces should include enough space for those operations identified as critical, a minimum number of telephone and data ports, and a place for displaced workers to gather to engage in recovery activities.

Another important resource is the National Fire Protection Association's Standard on Disaster/Emergency Management and Business Continuity Programs.[26] This standard has received the support of both the American National Standards Institute and the 9/11 Commission. Companies should use the standard to develop preparedness and continuity capabilities.

Finally, after taking care of preparedness issues, companies need to focus on several other issues. The first issue to address is the employment of illegal immigrants. With the substantial increase in employer raids by ICE, it simply is good business practice to voluntarily start using the E-Verify system for new employee screening. Because the E-Verify system is fast and inexpensive, adopting this practice will not pose an undue burden on companies.

The second issue to address is having an accurate picture of suppliers and customers. As evidenced by the DOJ case involving Chiquita Brands International (Chiquita) in which Chiquita paid a group with terrorist links to help provide security in Columbia, it is critical for companies to know who its suppliers and customers are so that corporate funds are not being provided to entities with ties to terrorists.[27] Due to its actions, Chiquita had to pay a $25 million fine.[28]

A simple solution to avoid this pitfall is to compare supplier and customer lists to the terrorist watch lists compiled by Dun & Bradstreet or other business information providers. Such entities routinely compile a master list from the various terrorist watch lists published by the United States and other key countries. Although this solution likely is unnecessary for companies with mostly U.S. suppliers and buyers, if a company's operations are global in nature or occur in countries with past terrorist activity, this solution will help the company manage its risk more effectively.

The key to such a solution is to ensure that the comparison happens on a routine basis such as once a quarter or once a month. This periodic approach will enable the company to deal quickly with a hit by clearing it or eliminating the entity as a supplier or customer. With a paper trail demonstrating the company's efforts to comply with federal law and the prompt, remedial action it took once a legitimate hit occurred, the company's goodwill compliance efforts can be used to eliminate or minimize any penalty or violation. Chiquita continued to provide funds to the terrorist group even after its outside legal counsel warned officers that the payments were illegal.[29] No company should put itself in a similar situation.

The third issue to address is to understand vulnerabilities across a company's supply chain. With the adoption of lean manufacturing and just-in-time inventory processes, most companies are at the mercy of the weakest link in their supply chains. Any delay upstream could result in lost profits or worse for the end-users. Spending a little time analyzing a supply chain is well worth it given the problems that could arise. The company should break down the supply chain to each of its component parts so it can identify critical links deserving of special attention to ensure that the entities controlling those links establish the appropriate continuity capabilities so that their failure does not lead to the end-user's failure.

When analyzing a supply chain, companies should take special care to identify those links that may be especially vulnerable to terrorist attacks or large-scale natural disasters. For example, roughly 8 percent of the global trade flows through the Suez Canal. Given the geopolitical instability in the region and proximity to state sponsors of terrorist groups, if a company's supply chain is largely dependent on shipments coming through the Suez Canal, then it might want to put in place alternative routing plans and alternative suppliers so that operational levels can be maintained in the event of a crisis. A low-cost, but effective tool that companies can use to monitor certain areas is to put in place Really Simple Syndication software that automatically checks and feeds pre-categorized information (for example, news articles on the Suez Canal) to users.

The last external issue to address is establishing a robust communication pipeline with local law enforcement. In any community, the ability of local law enforcement to detect and deter criminals is through receiving leads and other key pieces of information from the community, including the business community. Conversely, an effective law enforcement entity will share information with the business community so that they can serve as force multipliers in knowing what information might be useful.

Many experts and pundits have written extensively on the need for the private sector to do more to be prepared for a major event. Larger corporations have no problem absorbing the above-the-line costs of a risk management group; however, most companies just do not have excess resources available for such prophylactic measures. With just a little investment in time and money, most businesses can take all or most of the risk reduction steps noted above. With so much uncertainty in our ever-shrinking global economy, it is far better to be proactive and prepared then to be reactive and ill-equipped.

OTHER COMMUNITY ACTIONS

As discussed throughout this book, our first preventers and first responders are in need of educational and training courses geared toward knowledge and skills required to meet the challenges ahead. Because of the long histories of the fire service and emergency management, there appears to be a sufficient level of training programs for response capabilities. To supplement the existing training curriculum based on terrorism threats, the federal government created the National Domestic Preparedness Consortium as discussed in Chapter 6.

For law enforcement, however, because the need for domestic intelligence capabilities is largely a terrorism-driven requirement, the current offerings are quite limited. For example, America currently lacks the requisite level of trained analysts and linguists who can enhance our intelligence capabilities. Although the focus on closing this capability gap has been foreign intelligence operations, with the rise in fusion centers, JTTFs, and other state and local analysis capabilities, a domestic need also exists for these highly skilled individuals.

As the 9/11 Commission noted, "it takes five to seven years of training, language study, and experience to bring a recruit up to full performance."[30] Yet, "very few American colleges or universities offer... programs in Middle Eastern languages or Islamic studies. The total number of undergraduate degrees granted in Arabic in all U.S. colleges and universities in 2002 was six."[31] America cannot depend on just the federal training programs to meet its needs.

We need our colleges and universities to invest in developing degrees in homeland security and specialized skills such as intelligence and high-value foreign languages. As state and local law enforcement collect information, they will need linguists and translators fluent in Arabic, Bangla, Hindi, Urdu, Punjabi, Farsi, Turkish, Mandarin, and Russian. They will need individuals with high cultural awareness who can provide much-needed cultural intelligence.

Building these domestic, civilian capabilities will not occur overnight. As more institutions of higher learning rise to the occasion and develop the degrees and courses necessary to train tomorrow's domestic counterterrorism personnel, our capabilities gaps will close. Collectively, with a prepared citizenry, resilient private and not-for-profit companies, and our unparalleled higher education system all working to ensure that they have done their respective parts, our communities and country will be prepared for the future no matter what it holds.

CASE STUDY 7

Training Tomorrow's Prevention Forces Today at Michigan State University

The Michigan State University (MSU) Intelligence Program, led by Dr. David Carter, is one of the nation's top programs dedicated to building a robust domestic intelligence capability. The Intelligence Program is part of the School of Criminal Justice at MSU, which is the oldest degree-granting Criminal Justice program in America. Through its programs, MSU has assisted over 1,200 law enforcement agencies in forty-three states to understand and develop intelligence capabilities.

The Intelligence Program, started in 1988, offers multiple degrees, including an Online Master in Law Enforcement Intelligence Analysis and a Certificate in Law Enforcement Intelligence. The Master in Law Enforcement Intelligence Analysis is tailored for state and local law enforcement and private security officers. The course requires eight courses and two elective courses. The courses include: law enforcement intelligence operations; homeland security; proseminar in criminal justice; design and analysis in criminal justice research; counterterrorism and intelligence; analytic thinking and intelligence; quantitative methods in criminal justice research; policy analysis under conditions of change; crime causation, prevention and control; comparative criminal justice; globalization of crime; terrorism; and legal issues in criminal justice. In the two years since the Master's degree has been offered, MSU has enrolled approximately sixty students in the program.

The Certificate in Law Enforcement Intelligence involves four courses aimed at developing intelligence capabilities. The courses include law enforcement intelligence operations, public/private partnerships for emergency preparedness and homeland security, counterterrorism and intelligence, and terrorism. Each course involves roughly forty-five hours of class time. The certificate program is intended for state and local law enforcement personnel who do not have the ability to commit to the full Master's degree program. Roughly 100 individuals have earned certificates from MSU.

Because of its expertise, FEMA has contracted with MSU to provide a two-day training seminar around the country for state and local law enforcement focused on building intelligence capabilities. The Intelligence Toolbox Training takes a "hands-on" approach and provides attendees with actionable resources that they can use as soon as they return to their agencies. The course provides attendees with resource materials, guidance to avoid problems, details about intelligence products, and access to MSU's continuing education and technical assistance programs. To date, MSU has conducted forty-one seminars in twenty-five states where it trained 2,468 people representing forty-three states and 1,307 agencies. Additional seminars are booked well into 2009.

A follow-on course called Sustaining Intelligence Training seeks to solidify intelligence operations once established in a local law enforcement agency. As of August 2008, the Intelligence Program has conducted five seminars in five states where they trained 216 people representing seventeen states and 111 agencies. As with the Intelligence Toolbox Training, additional seminars are scheduled in 2009.

The Intelligence Program also provides its students with a rich set of resources including hundreds of links segmented by topic area, policy papers, publications like *Law Enforcement Intelligence: A Guide for State, Local and Tribal Law Enforcement*, and audio podcasts on intelligence issues.

Demonstrating its truly comprehensive approach to intelligence, MSU is developing two new intelligence programs aimed at non-traditional disciplines. First, the Intelligence Program has added an epidemiologist from the MSU School of Medicine to help develop intelligence courses and forecasting tools for public health and medicine, especially where public health needs involves law enforcement resources to handle an all-hazards threat. The second area is in environmental intelligence revolving around eco-terrorists. In that area, the Intelligence Program has added two faculty members from the Fisheries and Wildlife Department to work on adapting traditional intelligence tools to the eco-terrorism field.

Whether it is through traditional classroom coursework or seminars conducted online or offsite, MSU is actively doing all it can to produce domestic intelligence professionals who can help state and local law enforcement close their intelligence capability gaps.

Afterword

> It is not so much then for the purpose of undertaking to proclaim new theories and principles that this annual celebration is maintained, but rather to reaffirm and reestablish those old theories and principles which time and the unerring logic of events have demonstrated to be sound.
>
> President Calvin Coolidge[1]

This book discusses the principle of federalism, its importance in preserving our Constitution and our country, and its relevance in solving our complex challenges. Although many experts and pundits scoff at the notion that federalism remains a relevant concept, the alternative is continued centralization in Washington, which does not have a very impressive track record of transformation.

Today's antifederalists (ironically) mostly argue for an ever-expanding federal government because it is allegedly efficient—one big tax funds many big programs or one national policy is easier to deal with. As history has shown time and time again, big government is not efficient. It is bureaucratic, unaccountable, and opaque. With our security at stake, that just is not good enough.

The brilliance of our Founding Fathers is that they believed in the power of competition. As written in Proverbs 27:17, "Iron sharpens iron, so one man sharpens another." A monopolistic federal government has no competitor. By decentralizing functions back to the states, we can reduce the portion of government that lacks competition and, therefore, increase incentives for reducing costs and enhancing services.

At the same time, states are able to compete on a wide variety of goods and services. Rather than constituting a race to the bottom as predicted by antifederalists to scare voters, competition among the states forces our elected officials—like the private sector—to offer citizens the best good (security) or service (disaster response) at the lowest price (taxes). This competition becomes more meaningful if we can reduce the size of the federal government and the federal income tax that funds it because state income taxes would naturally increase as localities rediscovered their historical roles and responsibilities.

As state income taxes took a greater share and federal income taxes a lesser share of their paychecks, citizens would rightfully turn their attention back to states and localities. Because of geographic proximity and the ability to motivate similarly affected neighbors (read: James Madison's "factions"), imposing accountability on governors, mayors, and county commissioners is a lot easier than doing so in far off Washington. For proof of this accountability in action, just look at the number of school operating levies defeated in any given election year across the United States.

As governors, mayors, and county commissioners are forced to make tough choices on what is needed versus what is wanted, lacking the moral hazards that accompany federal funding and federal ownership, these elected officials will have to weigh the cost of a good or service against the benefit derived from it. The free lunch will be over.

For homeland security, this reality means that building capabilities will adhere more closely to

- what the actual risk of a jurisdiction is rather than to how much pork the federal government arbitrarily decides to send;
- a state's disaster management capabilities matching the state's actuarial risks rather than doing little and passing on the costs of routine natural disasters to taxpayers in other states;
- states with tough illegal immigration measures in employment, housing, identification, and criminality repelling illegal immigrants as states with weaker illegal immigration measures attract them; and
- jurisdictions with heightened terrorism risks expending the resources required to have the right number of cops on the beat, intelligence analysts, linguists, and counterterrorism capabilities to detect and defeat the terrorists who live in their cities and states.

The bottom line regardless of the issue will be that a state and its taxpayers will bear the costs of that state's decisions, and taxpayers will have a greater opportunity to have input into those decisions and to hold decision makers accountable for the good and bad decisions that they make. Results will come with accountability. With our very way of life at stake, we need results. With the federal government in charge, we just will not get the results we need as soon as we need them. We need federalism because those closest to the problems are better positioned to solve them. It has worked before. It will work again.

As the case studies vividly demonstrate, the use of federalism to solve our complex homeland security problems is not mere theory espoused by pointed-headed academics sitting in their ivory towers or flat-Earth society types who yearn for idyllic days gone by. Where there is leadership and the will to act, states and localities are taking the lead and getting results in preparedness, disaster management, illegal immigration, and counterterrorism. These brave change-agents are blazing a trail for others to follow.

More critically, we need federalism so that our Constitution will endure another 221 years. Today, a majority of Americans receive some form of transfer payment from the federal government. With the impending crises in Social Security, Medicare, and Medicaid, those dependent on the federal government will only increase while those with the means to pay for that dependency continue to decrease. As Scottish philosopher Alexander Tytler observed:

> A democracy is always temporary in nature; it simply cannot exist as a permanent form of government. A democracy will continue to exist up until the time that voters discover that they can vote themselves generous gifts from the public treasury. From that moment on, the majority always votes for the candidates who promise the most benefits from the public treasury, with the result that every democracy will finally collapse due to loose fiscal policy, which is always followed by a dictatorship ...
>
> The average age of the world's greatest civilizations from the beginning of history has been about 200 years. During those 200 years, these nations always progressed through the following sequence: from bondage to spiritual faith; from spiritual faith to great courage; from courage to liberty; from liberty to abundance; from abundance to complacency; from complacency to apathy; from apathy to dependence; from dependence back into bondage.[2]

Federalism is the only tool that can reverse our national dependency. Without it, we will slowly, but inevitably slip into bondage through the despotism of the majority.

The threat we face today from Islamic jihadists is a generational one, and requires the whole of a democratic society powered by federalism to defeat it. The Islamic jihadists and the despotism they seek to create through the use of terrorism are only worth fighting if what we are preserving is an inheritance for our children and grandchildren that remains an America where liberty and equality reign supreme.

Whether the challenge is the security of our homeland or the quality of our schools, federalism safeguards our rights and ensures that America remains a shining city on a hill.

Notes

PREFACE

1. Howard Zinn, *A People's History of the United States: 1492–Present* (New York: HarperCollins, 2003), 435.
2. Benjamin Franklin to Governor Thomas Penn, Philadelphia, November 11, 1755, *Reply to the Governor*.

CHAPTER 1

1. Sayyid Qutb, *Milestones* (Indianapolis: American Trust Publications, 1990), 112.
2. The Declaration of Independence, *Preamble*.
3. Ronald Reagan, *Speaking My Mind* (New York: Simon and Schuster, 1989), 118.
4. Caleb Carr, *The Lessons of Terror: A History of Warfare against Civilians: Why It Has Always Failed and Why It Will Fail Again* (New York: Random House, 2002), 223–224.
5. Carr, at 6.
6. For an historical picture of the players and activities that led to the September 11 attack, Lawrence Wright's *The Looming Tower: Al-Qaeda and the Road to 9/11* (New York: Knopf, 2006) is an excellent and well-written resource.
7. Richard P. Mitchell, *The Society of the Muslim Brothers* (London: Oxford University Press, 1969), 5–6.
8. Muslim Brotherhood, "Credo of the Muslim Brotherhood," *Muslim Brotherhood Movement Homepage* (2008); http://www.ummah.net/ikhwan (accessed on February 9, 2009).
9. Neil MacFarquhar, "Egyptian Group Patiently Pursues Dram of Islamic State," *New York Times*, January 20, 2002, 3.

10. Robin Hallett, *Africa Since 1875: A Modern History* (Ann Arbor: The University of Michigan Press, 1974), 138.

11. Robert S. Leiken and Steven Brooke, "The Moderate Muslim Brotherhood," *Foreign Affairs* 86 (March/April 2007): 108.

12. Ibid.

13. Lawrence Wright, *The Looming Tower: Al-Qaeda and the Road to 9/11* (New York: Knopf, 2006), 10, 14, 16, 22.

14. Ibid., 23.

15. Ibid.

16. Ibid., 24.

17. Ibid., 29.

18. Qutb, 69.

19. Wright, 30.

20. Ibid., 30–31.

21. Ibid., 31.

22. Leiken and Brooke, 110.

23. Giles Kepel, *The War for Muslim Minds: Islam and the West* (Cambridge, MA: Harvard University Press, 2004), 174–175.

24. Ibid.

25. Marc Sageman, *Understanding Terror Networks* (Philadelphia: University of Pennsylvania Press, 2004), 63.

26. Wright, 37.

27. Ibid., 39.

28. Ibid., 54–57.

29. Ibid., 53.

30. Ibid., 58–59.

31. Nimrod Raphaeli, "'Ayman Muhammad Rabi' Al-Zawahiri: The Making of an Arch Terrorist," *Terrorism and Political Violence* 14 (Winter 2002): 20–22.

32. Wright, 127.

33. Ibid., 125.

34. Ibid., 130.

35. Ibid.

36. Ibid.

37. Ibid., 185.

38. Ibid., 179–198. As additional proof of America's inability to secure its borders, the story of Ali Abdelsoud Mohammed is both illustrative of that inability and damning. As Wright notes in his book, Mohammed accompanied Zawahiri on his fundraising trip in the United States. Mohammed had been placed in the State Department watch list by the Central Intelligence Agency. Not only did Mohammed gain entry into the United States, he enrolled in the Army, went to special warfare school, left to "kill Russians" in Afghanistan, returned to the United States, worked for a defense contractor, disappeared infrequently to train bin Ladin and others, warned the FBI about al Qaeda, became a key intelligence operative for al Qaeda, and played a major role in the bombing of the American embassies in Nairobi and Dar es Salaam. Mohammed finally was arrested in 1998 and pled guilty to five counts of conspiracy to kill Americans and other related changes. Lance Williams and Eric McCormick, "Al Qaeda Terrorist Worked with FBI," *San Francisco Chronicle*, November 4, 2001, A-1.

39. Wright, 179.
40. Ibid., 186.
41. Ibid., 249.
42. Ibid., 250.
43. Ibid., 75.
44. Ibid., 75–76.
45. Ibid., 76.
46. Ibid., 79–80.
47. Ibid., 96.
48. Ibid., 97.
49. Ibid., 111.
50. Ibid., 141–142.
51. Ibid., 153–154.
52. Ibid., 157–158.
53. Ibid.
54. Ibid., 159.
55. Ibid., 161.
56. Ibid., 164–165.
57. Ibid., 174–175.
58. Ibid.
59. Ibid., 189.
60. Ibid., 195.
61. Ibid., 221–222.
62. Ibid., 223–225.
63. Osama bin Laden, *Declaration of War against the Americans Occupying the Land of the Two Holy Places*, August 1996; http://www.pbs.org/newshour/terrorism/international/fatwa_1996.html (accessed on February 9, 2009).
64. Ibid.
65. Ibid.
66. World Islamic Front, *Jihad against Jews and Crusaders*, February 23, 1998; http://www.pbs.org/newshour/terrorism/international/fatwa_1998.html (accessed on February 9, 2009).
67. Ibid.
68. Ibid.
69. George Friedman, *America's Secret War: Inside the Hidden Worldwide Struggle between America and Its Enemies* (New York: Broadway Books, 2004), 34.
70. bin Laden, *Declaration of War*.
71. Wright, 174.
72. Ibid.
73. Bin Laden, *Declaration of War*.
74. Wright, 177.
75. Ibid.
76. National Commission on Terrorist Attacks upon the United States. *Final Report of the National Commission on Terrorist Attacks upon the United States* [hereafter cited as *9/11 Commission Report*]. New York: W.W. Norton & Company, 2004, 72.
77. Ibid.
78. Wright, 57.

79. Ibid., 138.
80. *The 9/11 Commission Report*, 60.
81. Bin Laden, *Declaration of War*.
82. *The 9/11 Commission Report*, 73.
83. Ibid.
84. Ibid.
85. Ibid., 60.
86. Ibid.
87. Wright, 237.
88. Ibid.
89. *The 9/11 Commission Report*, 109.
90. Wright, 270–271.
91. Id, 272.
92. Ibid., 282–283.
93. Ibid., 297.
94. Ibid.
95. Ibid., 319–320.
96. *The 9/11 Commission Report*, 196.
97. Friedman, 57.
98. *The 9/11 Commission Report,* 215.
99. Ibid., 215–253.
100. Ibid.
101. For a comprehensive description of the September 11 attack, see *The 9/11 Commission Report*.
102. *The 9/11 Commission Report,* 46
103. Ibid., 326.
104. Ibid., 336–337.
105. Ibid., 350.
106. Ibid.
107. Donald Rumsfeld, "A New Kind of War," *New York Times*, September 27, 2001, A-2.

CHAPTER 2

1. Dwight D. Eisenhower, *Farewell Address to the Nation*, January 17, 1961.
2. U.S. Constitution, amendment X, December 15, 1791.
3. The Declaration of Independence, *Preamble*, July 4, 1776.
4. John F. Kennedy, *Inaugural Address*, January 20, 1961.
5. Paul Johnson, *A History of the American People* (New York: HarperCollins, 1997), 77.
6. Robert Beverley, *The History and Present State of Virginia: A Selection* (Indianapolis & New York: The Bobbs-Merrill Company, Inc., 1971), 21–22.
7. Ibid.
8. Ibid.
9. Ibid.
10. Johnson, 77–78.

11. *Journals of the Continental Congress, 1774–1789 (2nd)*, July 18, 1775, 187–190.

12. Alan D. Watson, "The Committees of Safety and the Coming of the American Revolution in North Carolina, 1774–1776," *The North Carolina Historical Review* (April 1996): 132.

13. Johnson, 160.

14. Ibid.

15. Elwyn A. Mauck, "History of Civil Defense in the United States," *The Bulletin of the Atomic Scientists* 6 (September 1950): 270.

16. Thomas J. Kerr, *Civilian Defense in the U.S.* (Boulder, CO: Westview Press, 1983), 10.

17. Ibid., 12.

18. Mauck, 270.

19. Kerr, 12.

20. Ibid.

21. Mauck, 265.

22. Wladislava S. Frost, "Cities and Towns Mobilize for War," *American Sociological Review* 9 (February 1944): 87–88.

23. Ibid., 88.

24. Mauck, 266.

25. Ibid.

26. Ibid.

27. Mauck, 266.

28. James M. Landis, "The Need for Civilian Protection," *Vital Speeches of the Day* 8 (March 1, 1942): 319–320.

29. Landis, 319.

30. Ibid.

31. Ibid.

32. Frost, 87.

33. Landis, 319.

34. Mauck, 268.

35. Ibid.

36. Frost, 86–87.

37. Ibid., 86.

38. Mauck, 267.

39. Frost, 89.

40. Mauck, 266.

41. Ibid., 268.

42. Ibid.

43. U.S. War Department, *United States Strategic Bombing Survey Summary Report (Pacific War)* (Washington, DC: GPO, July 1, 1946), 20.

44. Mauck, 269.

45. Ibid.

46. Ibid.

47. Ibid.

48. Ibid.

49. Ibid.

50. Ibid.

51. Ibid.
52. Wayne B. Blanchard, *American Civil Defense 1945–1984: The Evolution of Programs and Policies* (Washington, DC: GPO, 1986), 2.
53. Mauck, 269.
54. Ibid., 270.
55. Blanchard, 2.
56. Ibid.
57. Walter G. Green III, ed., "Civil Defense: The Truman Administration," *Electronic Encyclopaedia of Civil Defense and Emergency Management* (August 12, 2003), Entry 0113.
58. Ibid.
59. Ibid.
60. Clyde A. Hutchison, Jr., "Civil Defense News," *Bulletin of the Atomic Scientists* 6 (1950): 382.
61. John F. Kennedy, Executive Order no. 10952, *Federal Register* 26 (July 20, 1961): 6577.
62. Richard M. Nixon, Executive Order no. 11725, *Federal Register* 38 (June 29, 1973): 17175.
63. Jimmy Carter, Executive Order no. 12127, *Federal Register* 44 (April 3, 1979): 19367.
64. Federal Emergency Management Agency, *FEMA History* (September 20, 2007), 1; http://www.fema.gov/about/history.shtm.
65. James B. Simpson, *Simpson's Contemporary Quotations* (Boston: Houghton Mifflin Company, 1988), Number 183.
66. It is true that there were several instances when the Germans or Japanese were able to penetrate the continental United States, but those were fairly minor incidents that pale in comparison to a nuclear detonation.
67. James Jay Carafano, "The Pentagon Crisis of 2015," *Commentary* (Washington, DC: The Heritage Foundation, May 15, 2007).
68. Ibid.
69. Senate Committee on Governmental Affairs, *The Local Role in Homeland Security*, 107th Cong., 1st sess., 2001.
70. The National Commission on Terrorist Attacks upon the United States, *Final Report of the National Commission on Terrorist Attacks upon the United States* (New York: W.W. Norton & Company, 2004), 284.

CHAPTER 3

1. Lyndon B. Johnson, *State of the Union*, speech, January 8, 1964.
2. Ronald Reagan, *Remarks to the American Dental Association*, speech, October 29, 1972.
3. National Commission on Terrorism, *Countering the Changing Threat of International Terrorism* (Washington, DC: GPO, June 7, 2000), ii.
4. Ibid.

5. National Commission on Terrorist Attacks upon the United States. *Final Report of the National Commission on Terrorist Attacks upon the United States* [hereafter cited as *9/11 Commission Report*]. New York: W.W. Norton & Company, 2004, xvi

6. Roberta Wohlstetter, *Pearl Harbor: Warning and Decision* (Palo Alto, CA: Stanford University Press, 1962), vii.

7. *The 9/11 Commission Report*, 327.

8. Ibid.

9. *Uniting and Strengthening America by Providing Appropriate Tools Required to Intercept and Obstruct Terrorism Act of 2001*, Public Law 107–56, *U.S. Statutes at Large* 115 (2001): 272.

10. Ibid.

11. Ibid.

12. The White House, *National Strategy for Homeland Security* (Washington, DC: GPO, July 2002).

13. Ibid., 2.

14. Ibid., vii–xiii.

15. *Homeland Security Act of 2002*, Public Law 107–296, *U.S. Statutes at Large* 116 (2002): 2135.

16. Ibid.

17. Congressional Research Service, "Department of Homeland Security Reorganization: The 2SR Initiative," *CRS Report for Congress Order Code RL33042* (August 19, 2005), CRS-2.

18. *Department of Homeland Security Appropriation Act of 2004*, Public Law 108–90, *U.S. Statutes at Large* 117 (2003): 1137.

19. *Homeland Security Act of 2002*, §§ 821, 888, and 451.

20. Ibid., Title IV.

21. Ibid., Title V.

22. Ibid., Title II.

23. Ibid., Titles III, VII.

24. Tom Ridge, *Letter to Senator Susan Collins*, letter on the reorganization of the U.S. Department of Homeland Security, January 26, 2004.

25. Ibid.

26. Ibid.

27. Michael Chertoff, *U.S. Department of Homeland Security Second Stage Review Remarks*, speech, July 13, 2005.

28. Ibid.

29. Ibid.

30. Michael Chertoff, *Letter to the Representative Christopher Cox*, letter on the reorganization of the U.S. Department of Homeland Security, July 13, 2005.

31. *Post-Katrina Emergency Management Reform Act of 2006*, Public Law 109–295, *U.S. Statutes at Large* 120 (2006): 1394.

32. The White House, *National Strategy for Homeland Security* (Washington, DC: GPO, October 2007).

33. Inspector General, *Major Management Challenges Facing the Department of Homeland Security*, audit on the management of the U.S. Department of Homeland Security, January 4, 2008, 1 (Washington, DC: OIG).

34. Ibid., 16.

35. Ibid.
36. Ibid., 10–11.
37. Ibid., 19.
38. *The 9/11 Commission Report*, 361.
39. U.S. Constitution, art. I, sec. 8.
40. U.S. Constitution, Amendment XIV.
41. *The 9/11 Commission Report*, 383.
42. Ibid.
43. *Major Management Challenges*, 32.
44. *The 9/11 Commission Report*, 390–391.
45. U.S. Customs and Border Protection, *Customs-Trade Partnership Against Terrorism (C-TPAT) Fact Sheet*, June 2007 (Washington, DC: CBP). CBP launched the Customs-Trade Partnership against Terrorism program just two months after the September 11 attack. CBP promotes it as a "partnership [that] develops and adopts security measures that add security but do not have a chilling effect on trade." To date, CBP has certified over 7,000 entities for the program thereby "extending the United States' zone of security to the point of origin."
46. U.S. Customs and Border Protection, *Container Security Initiative Fact Sheet*, March 2007 (Washington, DC: CBP). CBP launched the Container Security Initiative program only four months after the September 11 attack. CBP promotes that program as "working bilateral partnerships with foreign authorities to identify high-risk cargo containers at ports throughout the world before they are loaded on vessels destined for the United States." CBP aimed to have fifty-eight CSI-designated ports by 2008, which would cover over 90 percent of all U.S-bound cargo traffic.
47. U.S. Customs and Border Protection, *Inspection Technology Fact Sheet*, May 2006 (Washington, DC: CBP).
48. *Major Management Challenges*, 32.
49. Brian Grow et al., "The New E-spionage Threat," *Businessweek*, April 21, 2008, 32.
50. Ibid.
51. Gordon Corera, "Al-Qaeda's 007: The Extraordinary Story of the Solitary Computer Geek in a Shepherds Bush Bedsit Who Became the World's Most Wanted Cyber-Jihadist," *The London Times*, January 16, 2008, 4
52. Ibid.
53. Ibid.
54. Ibid.
55. *Major Management Challenges*, 24.
56. U.S. Department of Homeland Security, *Interim National Infrastructure Protection Plan* (February 2005), 1.
57. Ibid.
58. U.S. Department of Homeland Security, *National Infrastructure Protection Plan* (Washington, DC: DHS, June 2006), i.
59. U.S. Department of Homeland Security, *DHS Completes Key Framework for Critical Infrastructure Protection*, press release, May 21, 2007.
60. *National Infrastructure Protection Plan*, 3.
61. *Major Management Challenges*, 18.
62. Ibid., 23.

63. Katherine McIntire Peters, "Congressional Oversight of Homeland Security Comes under Fire Again," *Government Executive*, July 30, 2008; http://www.govexec.com/dailyfed/0708/07300kpl.htm (accessed on February 9, 2009).

64. Michael Chertoff, *U.S. Department of Homeland Security 2007 Achievements and 2008 Priorities*, speech, December 12, 2007.

65. *Major Management Challenges*, 15.

66. Ibid., 3.

67. Ibid., 2.

68. Federal Bureau of Investigation, *Protecting America against Terrorist Attack: A Close Look at the FBI's Joint Terrorism Task Forces* (Washington, DC: DoJ, December 1, 2004), 1.

CHAPTER 4

1. Ronald J. Pestritto, ed., *Woodrow Wilson: The Essential Political Writings* (Lanham, MD: Lexington Books, 2005), 121.

2. Daniel Webster, *Speech at Niblo's Saloon*, New York City, March 15, 1837.

3. Briefing, "The American Right: Under the Weather," *The Economist*, August 9, 2007, 20–2.

4. Eugene W. Hickok, *Why States? The Challenge of Federalism* (Washington, DC: The Heritage Foundation, 2007), 70.

5. Republican Members of the U.S. House of Representatives, *Republican Contract with America*, Washington, D.C., 1994.

6. Chris Edwards, "Pork: A Microcosm of the Overspending Problem," *Tax & Budget Bulletin* 24 (Washington, DC: CATO Institute, August 2005); Jeffrey H. Birnbaum, "The Road to Riches Is Called K Street," *Washington Post*, June 22, 2005, A01.

7. Hickok, 17.

8. U.S. Constitution, Articles ix, x.

9. Clinton Rossiter, ed., *The Federalist Papers* (New York: Signet Classics, 1999), 289.

10. Ibid., 320.

11. Ibid., 79.

12. Ibid., 376.

13. Hickok, 52.

14. Pestritto, 227.

15. Hickok, 66.

16. Gina M. Scott, "Study Says Real ID Act Will Cost $11 Billion, Be Logistics Nightmare," *Government Technology*, September 21, 2006; http://www.govetech.com/gt/articles/101128 (accessed February 9, 2009).

17. U.S. House of Representatives, *Final Vote Results for Roll Call 161 on H.R. 1268*, May 5, 2005; U.S. Senate, *Roll Call Votes 109th Congress, 1st Session on the Conference Report H.R. 1268*, May 10, 2005.

18. Associated Press, "Ohio's Governor Blames National Economy," *Forbes*, February 7, 2008; http://www.forbes.com/feeds/Afx/2008/02/07/afx4630120.html (accessed on February 9, 2009).

19. Pete Du Pont, "Good Buy, Columbus: Ohioans May Revolt against Higher Taxes and Spending," *Wall Street Journal*, October 27, 2003; http://www.opinionjournal.com/columnists/dupont/?id+110004221 (accessed on February 9, 2009).

20. Editorial, "Texas v. Ohio," *Wall Street Journal*, March 3, 2008, A16.

21. Ohio History Central, "Biography of Ted Strickland," *Ohio Historical Society*, March 14, 2008.

22. Jeb Bush, "Think Locally on Relief," *Washington Post*, September 30, 2005, A19.

23. Robert Nolin, Linda Kleindienst, and Brittany Wallman, "Gov. Bush Accepts Blame for Slow Relief Response Days after Wilma," *Florida Sun-Sentinel*, October 27, 2005; http://www.sun-sentinel.com/news/local/southflorida/sfl-wilma,0.1180061.story (accessed on February 9, 2009).

24. U.S. Conference of Mayors, *Mayors 2004 Agenda: "Keeping America Strong,"* press release, February 9, 2004.

25. U.S. Conference of Mayors, *2005 National Action Plan on Safety and Security in America's Cities*, working paper, October 25, 2005.

26. James Jay Carafano and Richard Weitz, "Learning from Disaster: The Role of Federalism and the Importance of Grassroots Response," *Backgrounder* (Washington, DC: The Heritage Foundation, March 21, 2006): 1.

CHAPTER 5

1. Donald Rumsfeld, *U.S. Defense Department Briefing*, transcript, February 12, 2002.

2. Aesop, "The Ant and the Grasshopper," *The Fables of Aesop* (New York: Book of the Month Club, 1995), 6.

3. *The New Oxford American Dictionary*, 2nd ed. (New York: Oxford University Press, May 2005), s.v. "Risk."

4. For this book, the type of risk discussed focuses on risk associated with insurable events such as death, injury, or destruction caused by a natural disaster or terrorist attack. It does not involve risk in the financial markets and the various credit crises caused by failures to accurately evaluate the risks associated with non-insurance related financial instruments.

5. Nassim Nicholas Taleb, *The Black Swan: The Impact of the Highly Improbable* (New York: Random House, 2007), 211.

6. *Terrorism Risk Insurance Act of 2002*, Public Law 107–197, *U.S. Statutes at Large* 116 (2002): 274.

7. *Terrorism Risk Insurance Program Reauthorization Act of 2007*, Public Law 110–160, *U.S. Statutes at Large* 121 (2007): 1839.

8. Federal Emergency Management Agency, "Disaster Search," Disaster Information, http://www.fema.gov/news/disasters.fema (accessed on March 31, 2008).

9. Ibid.
10. Ibid.
11. Ibid.
12. Ibid.
13. Ibid.

14. Todd Masse et al., "The Department of Homeland Security's Risk Assessment Methodology: Evolution, Issues, and Options for Congress," *CRS Report for Congress* (Washington, DC: GPO, February 2, 2007), CRS-5-CRS-6, CRS-11.

15. National Commission on Terrorist Attacks upon the United States. Final Report of the National Commission on Terrorist Attacks upon the United States. New York: W.W. Norton & Company, 2004, 396.

16. Michael Chertoff, Second State Review Remarks, speech, July 13, 2005.

17. Paul Rosenzweig and Alane Kochems, "Risk Assessment and Risk Management: Necessary Tools for Homeland Security," Backgrounder (Washington, DC: The Heritage Foundation, October 25, 2005): 3.

18. Masse et al., CRS-6.

19. Ibid., CRS-11.

20. Michael Chertoff, Press Conference on the Fiscal Year 2006 Urban Areas Security Initiative Grants, speech, January 3, 2005.

21. Ibid.

22. Masse et al., CRS-7.

23. Ibid.

24. Ibid.

25. John Mueller, "A False Sense of Insecurity: How Does the Risk of Terrorism Measure up against Everyday Dangers," Regulation (Washington, DC: CATO Institute, Fall 2004): 42.

26. John Lewis Gaddis, The Cold War: A New History (New York: The Penguin Press, 2005), 46–47.

27. Mueller, 43.

28. Although explosives should be a focus due to the frequency and ease of use, our enemies have expressed a desire to acquire weapons of mass destruction. Because the development of the TCL used fifteen scenarios across the chemical, biological, radiological, nuclear, and explosive spectrum, the capabilities that comprise the TCL should allow states and localities to handle the full range of potential threats—expected and unexpected.

29. U.S. Department of Homeland Security, Fiscal Year 2005 Homeland Security Grant Program: Program Guidelines and Application Kit (Washington, DC: GPO, December 2004), 6.

30. Ibid., 4.

31. U.S. House Committee on Appropriations Subcommittee on Homeland Security, Homeland Security: Applying Risk Management Principles to Guide Federal Investments, 110th Cong., 1st sess., 2007, 3.

32. Chertoff, Urban Areas Security Initiative Grants.

33. Tracy Henke, Press Conference by Under Secretary George Foresman and Assistant Secretary Tracy Henke on the FY 06 Homeland Security Grant Program, speech, May 31, 2006.

34. James Jay Carafano and Matt A. Mayer, "Spending Smarter: Prioritizing Homeland Security Grants by Using National Standards and Risk Criteria," Backgrounder (Washington, DC: The Heritage Foundation, May 10, 2007): 3–4.

35. U.S. House Committee on Appropriations, Applying Risk Management, 15.

36. Chertoff, Urban Areas Security Initiative Grants.

37. Eric Lipton, "Security Cuts for New York and Washington," New York Times, June 1, 2006, A1.

38. Al Baker and Diane Cardwell, "City Has Itself to Blame for Terror Cuts, U.S. Says," New York Times, June 2, 2006, A1.

39. U.S. Department of Homeland Security, DHS Announces $1.7 Billion in Homeland Security Grants: Grants Will Build States' and Urban Areas' Preparedness—Attachment B, press release, May 31, 2006.

40. Ibid.

41. Ibid. Because those eleven jurisdictions did not make the full eligibility list, clearly their respective risk rankings fell below those jurisdictions that did make the full eligibility list.

42. U.S. Department of Homeland Security, FY 2007 Homeland Security Grant Program (Washington, DC: GPO, July 18, 2007), 9.

43. Although many have erroneously laid the blame for allocation errors on the risk aspect of DHS's risk and need allocation process, the fury of the Congress and recipients did not occur when the eligible UASI jurisdictions were announced in January 2006, which was determined by the relative risk scores of jurisdictions; rather, the fury occurred when the allocations occurred in May 2006 based on the secretive and subjective needs analysis of the investment justifications, which resulted in both New York City and the National Capital Region receiving substantially fewer funds then in years past.

44. U.S. Department of Homeland Security, Fiscal Year 2004 Urban Areas Security Initiative Grant Program: Program Guidelines and Application Kit (Washington, DC: GPO, 2003), 5; U.S. Department of Homeland Security, Fiscal Year 2005 Homeland Security Grant Program: Program Guidelines and Application Kit (Washington, DC: GPO, December 2004), 6.

45. U.S. Department of Homeland Security, DHS Announces $1.7 Billion; U.S. Department of Homeland Security, FY 2007 Homeland Security Grant Program, 9.

46. Michael Chertoff, Press Conference with Secretary Chertoff to Announce $1.7 Billion in Homeland Security Grants, speech, July 18, 2007.

47. Ibid.

48. The case involves convicted terrorists Nuradin Abdi and Christopher Paul who had plotted to blow up a mall in the Columbus area and assisted al Qaeda for over a decade. Jodi Andes, "Somali Man Pleads Guilty to Plot," Columbus Dispatch, August 1, 2007, O1A; Jodi Andes, "Local Terrorist's Steps Detailed," Columbus Dispatch, June 4, 2008, O1A.

CHAPTER 6

1. Franklin D. Roosevelt, *Second Inaugural Address*, speech, January 20, 1937.

2. Amity Shlaes, *The Forgotten Man: A New History of the Great Depression* (New York: HarperCollins Publishers, 2007), 243.

3. George W. Bush, *Homeland Security Presidential Directive 8, "National Preparedness,"* December 17, 2003.

4. Ibid., § 2(h).

5. *The New Oxford American Dictionary*, 2nd ed. (New York: Oxford University Press, May 2005), v. "Resiliency."

6. Robert J. Samuelson, *The Good Life and Its Discontents: The American Dream in the Age of Entitlement 1945–1995* (New York: Times Books, 1995), 148.

7. Shlaes, 202.
8. Ibid., 11.
9. U.S. Conference of Mayors, *National Action Plan on Safety and Security in America's Cities* (October 25, 2005).
10. The United Kingdom uses this approach to improve its resiliency to a terrorist attack. As stated on its Web site, the "Government has a national risk assessment capability which identified risks to the United Kingdom as a whole over a five-year period, and assesses their likelihood and impact [which] forms the basis for decisions about emergency preparedness and about capability planning." Interestingly, the Resilience Office also used capabilities-based planning tools to arrive at a set of eighteen capability workstreams (as compared the DHS' thirty-seven critical capabilities)—three structural, ten functional, and five essential services.
11. Bush, *Homeland Security Presidential Director 8*, § 5.
12. Ibid., § 6.
13. U.S. Government Accountability Office, *Homeland Security: DHS' Efforts to Enhance First Responders' All-Hazards Capabilities Continue to Evolve* (Washington, DC: GPO, July 2005), 18.
14. U.S. Department of Homeland Security, *Universal Task List: Version 2.1* (Washington, DC: GPO, May 23, 2005), 2.
15. Ibid.
16. U.S. Department of Homeland Security, *Comprehensive List of Staffing Requirements for National Preparedness Goal, Universal Task List (UTL), and Target Capabilities List (TCL)*, February 2005, 1.
17. Ibid., 1.
18. Ibid., 5.
19. Ibid.
20. Ibid., 2, 6–7. There were three Integrated Concept Teams: Balanced Investments; Training, Exercises, and Lessons Learned; and Assessment and Reporting. Each team consisted of federal, state, and local government representatives. State and local entities that participated on the teams included: the Fraternal Order of Police, the National Association of City & County Health Officials, the International Association of Emergency Managers, the National Volunteer Fire Council, the New York State Emergency Management Office, the American Public Works Association, the International Association of Chiefs of Police, the International Association of Fire Chiefs, the Council of State Governments, the National Sheriffs' Association, and the Association of State and Territorial Health Officials.
21. U.S. Government Accountability Office, *All-Hazards Report*, 16–17.
22. For the terrorist scenarios, DHS developed the Universal Adversary to serve as the enemy. The Universal Adversary replicates terrorist networks and simulates intelligence gathering and analysis. Because the National Planning Scenarios are response-oriented, DHS also created the prevention prequels and detailed attack trees to test the prevention capabilities of local, state, and federal government exercise participants.
23. U.S. Department of Homeland Security, *National Planning Scenarios* (Washington, DC: GPO, April 2005), ii.
24. Ibid., ii-v.
25. Ibid., vii.
26. U.S. Department of Homeland Security, *Comprehensive List*, 2.

27. Ibid.
28. Ibid.
29. Ibid., 8–15.
30. Ibid., 2.
31. U.S. Department of Homeland Security, *Universal Task List*, 2.
32. Ibid.
33. U.S. Government Accountability Office, *All-Hazards Capabilities*, 18.
34. U.S. Department of Homeland Security, *National Preparedness Guidelines*, report, September 2007, 4–5.
35. Federal Emergency Management Agency, *National Preparedness System: Current Prototype & Proposed Implementation Approach*, report, undated, 12.
36. U.S. Department of Homeland Security, *Comprehensive List*, 3.
37. Ibid.
38. Ibid.
39. Ibid.
40. Ibid., 4.
41. Ibid., 1.
42. Ibid.
43. Ibid.
44. Ibid.
45. Ibid.
46. Ibid., 2.
47. For example, New York City clearly needs a Search and Rescue capability resourced for a large urban city, while Des Moines may only need a Search and Rescue capability with a quarter of the resources possessed by New York City. Conversely, as a large urban city, New York City likely does not need a heavily-resourced Food and Agriculture Safety and Defense capability, whereas Des Moines likely should have a heavily-resourced Food and Agriculture Safety and Defense capability given the large presence of animals and agriculture that enter our food supply from Iowa. The key is to create a robust, flexible system that can accommodate the particular needs of each jurisdiction.
48. For example, the Interim vision statement stated:

> To engage Federal, State, local, and tribal entities, their private sector and nongovernmental partners, and the general public to achieve and sustain risk-based target levels of capability to prevent, protect against, respond to, and recover from major events in order to minimize the impact on lives, property, and the economy.
>
> —U.S. Department of Homeland Security, Interim National Preparedness Goal, report, March 2005, 3.

The Guidelines vision statement stated:

> A NATION PREPARED with coordinated capabilities to prevent, protect against, respond to, and recover from all hazards in a way that balances risk with resources and need.
>
> —U.S. Department of Homeland Security, Guidelines, 1.

Other than shortening the various entities listed in the Interim vision by using the word "Nation" in the Guidelines vision and restating "risk-based" as "balances risk with resources and need," the Guidelines vision is largely identical.

49. The TCL has three types of critics. The first type, and the one with the fewest critics, is the group of individuals who sincerely see flaws in the TCL. These critics tend to participate in the process to improve the TCL. The second type is the group of individuals who resist anything they did not create. The final type is the group of individuals who see the TCL for exactly what it is; namely, a strategic document that will drive accountability and transparency. The TCL is not the panacea, but it is as close to a consensus and objective blueprint on what capabilities are needed to secure the homeland as has been developed yet. As with any endeavor, it is far easier to serve as a problem-citer than it is to be a problem-solver. For those who criticize the TCL, when asked what they would replace it with (and if there is a better way then critics should articulate it), the silence is deafening.

50. U.S. Government Accountability Office, *All-Hazards Capabilities*, 14.

51. Bush, *Homeland Security Presidential Directive 8*, §§17, 18.

52. Federal Emergency Management Agency, *Training Overview*, report, March 10, 2008, 1.

53. The consortium includes the Center for Domestic Preparedness in Anniston, Alabama; the Academy of Counter-Terrorist Education in Baton Rouge, Louisiana; the National Emergency Response and Rescue Training Center in College Station, Texas; the Energetic Materials Research and Testing Center in Socorro, New Mexico; and the National Center for Exercise Excellence in Las Vegas, Nevada.

54. U.S. Department of Homeland Security, *Homeland Security Exercise and Evaluation Program (HSEEP)* (Washington, DC: GPO, February 2007), v.

55. U.S. House Subcommittee on Emergency Communications, Preparedness, and Response, *National Exercise Program*, 110th Cong., 1st sess., 2007, 4.

56. Bush, *Homeland Security Presidential Directive 8*, § 19.

57. George W. Bush, *Homeland Security Presidential 8 Annex 1, "National Planning,"* December 3, 2007.

58. Ibid., § 31.

59. Each Federal Preparedness Coordinator has the following functions: integration of preparedness missions; contingency planning modernization; preparedness review and monitoring; preparedness planning; exercise coordination and review; information sharing; strengthen local relationships; situational awareness; public communications; and special event planning. U.S. Department of Homeland Security, *Preparedness Integration with the Regions*, report, August 9, 2007, 9.

60. Michael Chertoff, *Press Availability on 2008 Homeland Security Grant Guidance*, speech, February 1, 2008.

61. U.S. Government Accountability Office, *All-Hazards Capabilities*, 39.

62. The most recent example of this squandering involves the FY 2008 UASI allocations where DHS failed to use either risk or capability needs to allocate funds to the higher-risk jurisdiction. Instead, DHS simply cut all but four urban areas by 3 percent from the allocations they had received in FY 2007.

63. U.S. Government Accountability Office, *DHS Risk-Based Grant Methodology Is Reasonable, But Current Version's Measure of Vulnerability Is Limited*, audit on risk-based grant methodology (Washington, DC: GPO, June 2008) 25,

64. Bush, *Homeland Security Presidential Directive 8*, § 9.

65. U.S. Government Accountability Office, *DHS Risk-Based Grant*, 47.

66. Joey Nowak, "Hazmat Vehicle Just Sitting in Garage," *Columbus Dispatch*, July 13, 2008, B3.

67. Rexford B. Sherman, *Seaport Governance in the United States and Canada*, report by the American Association of Port Authorities, undated, 3.

68. U.S. Government Accountability Office, *All-Hazards Capabilities*, 21.

69. U.S. Department of Homeland Security, *Analysis of Federal Requirements Final Report*, report on the requirements forced on states and localities (Washington, DC: DHS, October 2007), MATRIX-1 to MATRIX-48.

70. Ibid., EX-6.

71. Ibid., SOIR-8.

72. U.S. Government Accountability Office, *Management of First Responder Grant Programs and Efforts to Improve Accountability Continue to Evolve*, audit on federal homeland security grants (Washington, DC: GAO, April 12, 2005), 14.

73. U.S. Department of Homeland Security, *Analysis of Federal Requirements*, EX-4.

74. Ibid., MATRIX-23 to MATRIX-29.

75. National Governors Association, *2007 State Homeland Security Directors Survey*, report on views of state homeland security advisors, December 18, 2007, 1.

76. U.S. Department of Homeland Security, *Analysis of Federal Requirements*, SOIR-7.

77. Ibid.

78. U.S. Government Accountability Office, "Emergency Preparedness and Response: Some Issues and Challenges Associated with Major Emergency Incidents," audit on disaster response capabilities (Washington, DC: GAO, February 2006), 13.

79. Inspector General, *Major Management Challenges*, 15.

80. For example, an audit in Colorado revealed a systemic failure to assure "adequate oversight of program activities" and "ineffective" internal controls, subgrantee compliance, and program readiness. Inspector General, *Audit of the State of Colorado Homeland Security Grant Program*, audit on Colorado's financial management capabilities (Washington, DC: OIG, December 2007), 1.

81. Inspector General, *Major Management Challenges*, 15.

82. Otto Nelson, *Non-Military Defense in the Shadow of Nuclear Attack*, speech to the Industrial College of the Armed Forces, May 15, 1956.

83. Cynthia Dold, *King County Healthcare Coalition*, report, undated, 2.

84. Ibid.

85. Ibid.

86. Seattle/King County Public Health, *Community Communication Network Vulnerable Populations Action Team (VPAT)*, report, undated, 1.

87. Ibid.

88. Ibid.

89. Ibid., 2.

90. U.S. Department of Homeland Security, *Good Story: Public Health—Seattle & King County's Vulnerable Populations Action Team*, report on Seattle/King County's preparedness activities, 2007, 1.

91. Ibid., 2.

92. Ibid.

93. Ibid.

94. Seattle/King County and United Way of King County, *Katrina's Lessons: Reach Our Vulnerable Residents Now*, report on the lessons of Hurricane Katrina (Seattle: Seattle/King County, December 15, 2006), 1.

95. Seattle/King County Public Health and Vulnerable Populations System Coordination Steering Committee, *Community Based Organizations: Standards and Indicators for Emergency Preparedness and Response*, report on standards and indicators for disaster response (Seattle: Seattle/King County, May 2008), 1.

96. Ibid., 2–3.

97. Ibid., 3.

98. Ibid.

99. Seattle/King County Public Health, *VPAT*, 6.

100. Ibid., 7, 9.

101. King County Healthcare Coalition, *Involuntary Isolation or Quarantine Legal Team Protocol*, report on procedures for mass care (Seattle: Seattle/King County Healthcare Coalition, April 12, 2006), 1.

102. Seattle/King County Public Health, *VPAT*, 13.

103. King County Healthcare Coalition, *Business Resiliency Workshop for Healthcare Providers* .Seattle: KCHC, 2008.

104. Seattle/King County Public Health, *Windstorm 2006: After Action Report*, report on mitigation efforts, February 2, 2007, 2.

105. Ibid., 7–13.

106. Seattle and King County Public Health, *Business Not as Usual: Preparing for Pandemic Flu*. Seattle: S/KCPH, 2008. The recommendations are the following: adopt social distancing practices; expect a reduced workforce; plan for months not weeks; prioritize critical functions; verify suppliers have pandemic flu plans; understand interdependencies; assume no mutual aid; develop internal and external messages; decide what you will do, reduce, and suspend; cross-train employees; prepare for human resources issues; demonstrate leadership; anticipate supply chain issues; stockpile supplies; educate employees on how to prepare at home; prioritize critical functions; determine how to keep critical functions running; create partnerships; test and revise your plan; communicate your plan to employees; emphasize stop germ behaviors; and identify resources to help with planning.

CHAPTER 7

1. Samuelson, 218, 232.

2. Adam Nossiter, "Nagin Re-elected as New Orleans Mayor," *New York Times*, May 21, 2006.

3. U.S. House Select Bipartisan Committee to Investigate the Preparation for and Response to Hurricane Katrina, *A Failure of Initiative: Final Report of the Select Bipartisan Committee to Investigate the Preparation for and Response to Hurricane Katrina*, report, February 15, 2006; The White House, *The Federal Response to Hurricane Katrina: Lessons Learned*, report, February 23, 2006; U.S. Senate Committee on Homeland Security and Governmental Affairs, *Hurricane Katrina: A Nation Still Unprepared*, report, May 2006.

4. Michael Chertoff, *National Emergency Management Association Mid-Year Conference,* remarks, February 13, 2006.

5. Ibid.

6. *Post-Katrina Emergency Management Reform Act*, Public Law 109–295, *U.S. Statute at Large* 120 (2006): 1355. The legislation put back into FEMA those elements

taken out in October 2006 and merged ODP into FEMA. The rest of the Preparedness Directorate remained outside of FEMA.

7. Ibid.

8. Bush, "Think Locally on Relief," A19.

9. Bill Nichols and Richard Benedetto, "Govs to Bush: Relief Our job," *USA Today*, October 2, 2005, 1A.

10. Michael Grunwald and Susan B. Glasser, "Brown's Turf Wars Sapped FEMA's Strength," *Washington Post*, December 23, 2005. A1.One of the famous electronic mail messages occurred between Brown and his Chief of Staff Patrick Rhode in which Rhode said: "Let them play their reindeer games as long as they are not turning around and tasking us with their stupid questions." This attitude pervaded FEMA resulting in FEMA "ignoring DHS requests for information."

11. Ibid.

12. U.S. House Committee on Oversight and Government Reform, *FEMA Preparedness in 2007 and Beyond*, 110th Cong., 1st sess., 2007, 1–2; U.S. House Committee on Transportation and Infrastructure Subcommittee on Economic Development, Public Buildings, and Emergency Management, *Recovering After Katrina: Ensuring That FEMA Is Up to the Task*, 109th Cong., 1st sess., 2005, 2.

13. House Committee, *FEMA Preparedness*, 1–2.

14. Ibid, 1; House Committee, *Recovering After Katrina*, 2.

15. House Committee, *Recovering After Katrina*, 2.

16. Michael, *Second Stage Review Remarks*.

17. Carl Limbacher et al., "1999 Hurricane Swamped Clinton' FEMA," *NewsMax*, September 7, 2005. http://archive.newsmax.com/archives/ic/2005/9/7/134914.shtml (accessed February 10, 2009)

18. Ibid.

19. Ibid.

20. Jon Elliston, *A Disaster Waiting to Happen*, Independent Weekly (September 22, 2004); http://www.indpweek.com/gyrobase/Content?oid+oid%3A22664 (accessed on February 10, 2009).

21. National Emergency Management Agency, "Emergency Management," *NEMA-WEB*, 2008, 3.

22. House Committee, *FEMA Preparedness*, 2.

23. National Emergency Management Agency, 1.

24. Ibid.

25. Samuelson, 149.

26. Grover Cleveland, 49th Cong., 2d Sess., *Congressional Record* vol. xviii, Pt. II (1887):1875.

27. Lawrence W. Reed, "Grover Cared: Taking Disaster Relief Lessons from a Compassionate Conservative," *National Review Online* (March 2, 2006).

28. National Emergency Management Agency, 1.

29. Ibid.

30. Ibid.

31. John McQuaid and Mark Schleifstein, "Washing Away: Part 4: Tempting Fate," *New Orleans Times-Picayune*, June 26, 2002; http://www.nola.com/hurricane/content.ssf?/washingaway/part4.html (accessed on February 10, 2009).

32. Ibid.

33. Federal Emergency Management Agency, *FEMA History*, report, 2008.
34. Ibid.
35. Ibid.
36. James J. Carafano and Matt A. Mayer, "FEMA and Federalism: Washington Is Moving in the Wrong Direction," *Backgrounder* (Washington, DC: The Heritage Foundation, May 8, 2007), 2.
37. Ibid.
38. National Emergency Management Agency, 3.
39. Ibid., 3–4.
40. Carafano and Mayer, 2.
41. Ibid.
42. Ibid.
43. *Robert T. Stafford Disaster Relief and Emergency Assistance Act*, Public Law 93–288, 100th Cong., 2d sess. (November 23, 1988), codified at *U.S. Code* 42 (1988), § 5121.
44. *Robert T. Stafford Disaster Relief and Emergency Assistance Act*, § 5170b.
45. Carafano and Mayer, 2.
46. Ibid.
47. Ibid.
48. Ibid.
49. Ibid.
50. Ibid.
51. Ibid.
52. Ibid.
53. Ibid.
54. Federal Emergency Management Agency, "Disaster Search," Disaster Information, http://www.fema.gov/news/disasters.fema. (accessed on June 11, 2008).
55. Ibid.
56. Carafano and Mayer, 2.
57. Ibid.
58. Ibid.
59. Congressional Research Service, *FEMA and Disaster Relief* (Washington, DC: GPO, 1998).
60. Carafano and Mayer, 2.
61. NewsMax Wires, "Bush Aims to Be Unlike Dad in Storm Response," *NewsMax*, August 16, 2004; http://www.archive.newsmax.com/archives/articles/2004/8/15/174950.shtml (accessecd February 10, 2009).
62. Carafano and Mayer, 3.
63. Federal Emergency Management Agency, "Disaster Search," (accessed on June 11, 2008).
64. Carafano and Mayer, 3.
65. Ibid.
66. Ibid.
67. Ibid.
68. Ibid.
69. Grunwald and Glasser, A01.
70. Ibid.
71. Ibid.

72. Ibid.

73. Ibid.

74. Carafano and Mayer, 3.

75. Christopher Cooper and Robert Block, *Disaster: Hurricane Katrina and the Failure of Homeland Security* (New York: Times Book, 2006), 64.

76. Congress's recent changes to the requirements for the FEMA Administrator are a solid step in the right direction, but getting FEMA back to its historical origins is even more critical. Congress also should strengthen FEMA's financial oversight by providing for an in-house Inspector General with adequate staffing and greater access to FEMA decision making. Such internal monitoring will ensure that attempts to politicize FEMA are stopped before taxpayer resources are used frivolously.

77. George W. Bush, *Homeland Security Presidential Directive 5: "Management of Domestic Issues,"* February 28, 2003.

78. Ibid.

79. U.S. Department of Homeland Security, *National Response Plan*, December 2004, v–viii. The federal government did not make the same procedural error with the National Response Framework, which replaced the National Response Plan in January 2008.

80. Bush, *Homeland Security Presidential Directive 5*, para. 4.

81. Ibid.

82. House Committee, *FEMA Preparedness*, 3.

83. Robert T. Stafford Disaster Relief and Emergency Assistance Act, §517ob.

84. House Committee, FEMA, *Preparadness*, 1.

85. R. David Paulison, conversation with author, September 26, 2007.

86. U.S. Senate Committee on Homeland Security and Government Affairs, *FEMA's Level of Preparedness*, 110th Cong., 2d sess., 2008, 1–2.

87. Ibid., 4. The nine critical areas are overall planning, coordination and support, interoperable communication, logistics, evacuations, housing, disaster workforce, mission assignments, and acquisition management.

88. Ibid.

89. The refinement of FEMA's existing regional structure is different than some of the discussions inside the Beltway that push for a more robust regional structure involving all governments. First, states and localities are already understaffed, so there is no realistic chance that those governments will deploy permanent staff to a regional government entity. Next, without states and localities, the entity simply becomes another federal regional office, which just creates another layer of bureaucracy to micromanage, add costs, and build empires. Lastly, the vast majority of disasters are not interstate or regional disasters, so, in most cases, each state and its local governments should be able to handle the disaster. If, on occasion, additional support is needed, then the state can seek assistance by leveraging an Emergency Management Assistance Compact.

90. Christopher Cooper, "Forget Austerity, State Spending Ratchets Up," *Wall Street Journal*, February 24–25, 2007, A1.

91. National Commission on Terrorist Attacks upon the United States. *Final Report of the National Commission on Terrorist Attacks upon the United States* [hereafter cited as *9/11 Commission Report*]. New York: W.W. Norton & Company, 2004, 97.

92. Cooper, A1.

93. The reasoning behind the attempt to unify preparedness programs outside of FEMA centered on insulating preparedness activities from the operational tempo of an

inherently response-centric organization. After the September 11 attack, it made little sense to allow preparedness activities to wither on the vine or be mothballed because all resources were needed to respond to one of the 130 disaster declarations each year.

94. While simplistic, this population per disaster ratio is derived by dividing a state's total population by the number of disaster declarations. By normalizing large and small states and disaster declarations, comparisons can be made that show that a state like California may have a lot of disaster declarations, but, because of its large population, it has a fairly high population to disaster ratio. Arguably, this means that California residents are paying more in federal taxes for federal disaster assistance than they receive due to disaster declarations. Similarly, a large state like Michigan that has few disaster declarations, but lots of people also will pay more in federal taxes for the disaster assistance that it receives. In contrast, a state like North Dakota with a moderate level of disaster declarations, but few people will underpay in federal taxes for the disaster assistance it receives.

95. Federal Emergency Management Agency, "Disaster Search," (accessed on June 11, 2008).

96. Ohio Emergency Management Agency, *Application Packet for the State Disaster Relief Program* (Columbus: OEMA, September 2007), 1.

97. Ohio Emergency Management Agency, *Public Assistance Handbook* (Columbus: OEMA, September 2007).

98. Ohio Emergency Management Agency, *State of Ohio Individual Assistance Program* (Columbus: OEMA, November 2, 2006), 1.

99. Ohio Emergency Management Agency, *EMA Preliminary Damage Assessment Field Guide* (Columbus: OEMA, October 2006).

100. Ibid.

101. Ibid.

102. Ohio Emergency Management Agency, *Assistance Toolbox* (Columbus: OEMA, August 2005), 1.

103. Ibid.

104. Ohio Emergency Management Agency, *Cost Documentation Workshop*, July 2007; Ohio Emergency Management Agency, *Damage Assessment Workshop*, May 2007.

105. Ohio Emergency Management Agency, *Recovery from Disaster: Role of Local Government* (Columbus: OEMA, March 2008).

106. Ohio Emergency Management Agency, *Ohio Response System*, undated, 1–2 (Columbus: OEMA).

107. Ibid., 1–3.

108. Ohio Emergency Management Agency, *Plan Development and Review Guidance for Local Emergency Operations Plans*, May 2008; Ohio Emergency Management Agency, *Continuity of Operations Plan (All Hazards) Overview and Guidance for Local Government* (Columbus: OEMA, September 2006).

CHAPTER 8

1. Mexican American Legal Defense and Educational Fund, "Civil Rights Coalition Challenges Arizona Employer Sanctions Law," *ACLU Immigrants' Right Project*,

September 4, 2007; http://www.maldef.org/news/press.cfu?zd=431 (accessed February 10, 2009).

2. Joseph Story, *Commentaries on the Constitution of the United States with a Preliminary Review of the Constitutional History of the Colonies and States before the Adoption of the Constitution* (Boston: Hilliard, Gray and Company, 1833), 191.

3. Lawrence Downes, "What Part of 'Illegal' Don't You Understand?," *New York Times*, October 28, 2007, WK11.

4. U.S. House of Representatives Committee on the Judiciary Subcommittee on Immigration, Citizenship, Refugees, Border Security, and International Law, *Summary of U.S. Immigration History*, 110th Cong., 1st sess., 2007, 3.

5. Ibid., 5.

6. Ibid.

7. *Chinese Exclusion Act of 1882*, Public Law 71, 50th Cong., 2d sess. (May 6, 1882).

8. House Committee, *Immigration History*, 6.

9. Ibid.

10. Margaret Sanger, "A Plan for Peace," *Birth Control Review* (April 1932): 107–108.

11. *Buck v. Bell*, 274 U.S. 200, 207 (1927).

12. House Committee, *Immigration History*, 6.

13. Ibid., 8.

14. Ibid.

15. Ibid., 6–7.

16. Sanger, 107–108.

17. House Committee, *Immigration History*, 7.

18. Ibid., 9.

19. Ibid., 10.

20. United States and Mexico, "For the Temporary Migration of Mexican Agricultural Workers to the United States as Revised on April 26, 1943, by an Exchange of Notes between the American Embassy at Mexico City and the Mexican Ministry for Foreign Affairs," *The Official Bracero Agreement* (August 4, 1942).

21. House Committee, *Immigration History*, 11.

22. Ibid.

23. Ibid., 12.

24. *Immigration and Nationality Amendments of 1965*, Public Law 89–236, 89th Cong., 1st sess., *U.S. Statutes at Large* 20 (1965): 1151.

25. Ibid.

26. House Committee, *Immigration History*, 12.

27. *Immigration Reform and Control Act of 1986*, Public Law 99–603, 99th Cong., 2d sess., *U.S. Statutes at Large* 8 (1986): 1101, codified at *United States Code* 8, § 1401 et seq.

28. House Committee, *Immigration History*, 14.

29. Betsy Cooper and Kevin O'Neill, "Lessons from the Immigration Reform and Control Act of 1986," *MPI Policy Brief* (August 2005): 3.

30. Congressional Budget Office, *Report on Senate Amendment 1150 to S. 1348: the Comprehensive Immigration Reform Act of 2007*. Washington, DC: GPO, June 4, 2007, 26.

31. U.S. Constitution, art. I, § 8; art. IV, § 3; amend. XIV.

32. Eileen Sullivan, "21,000 Slipped Past Borders Illegally," *USA Today*, November 5, 2007, http://www.usatoday.com/news/Washington/2007-11-05-1051006212.xhtm (accessed February 10, 2009).

33. Julie Preston, "Employers Fight Tough Measures on Immigration," *The New York Times*, July 6, 2008, A1.

34. The reality on the wage suppression aspect of illegal immigration is that wages would rise without the cheaper labor provided by illegal immigrants, but those wage increases would not be enough to attract the requisite number of Americans to fill all of the jobs needed in those lower paying jobs.

35. Anne Broache, "Annual H-1B Visa Cap Met—Already," *cnetnews.com*, April 3, 2007.

36. David A. Vise, "Gates Cites Hiring Woes, Criticizes Visa Restrictions," *Washington Post*, April 28, 2005, E05.

37. James J. Carafano and Matt A. Mayer, "Better, Faster, Cheaper Border Security Requires Better Immigration Services," *Backgrounder* (Washington, DC: The Heritage Foundation, February 28, 2007), 1–5.

38. The European Union is taking steps to make it easier for highly skilled workers to go to Europe, so we must not fall behind in competing for these workers.

39. For example, in FY 2002, ICE only had twenty-five arrests and 485 administrative arrests during worksite enforcement actions. Michael Chertoff, *Homeland Security Secretary Michael Chertoff on the State of Immigration*, speech, November 6, 2007.

40. Miriam Jordan, "Crackdown on Illegal Immigrants Spurs Backlash among Locals," *Wall Street Journal*, April 17, 2008, A4.

41. U.S. Department of Homeland Security, *State of the Border—Border Security and Immigration Efforts Successful in Fiscal Year 2007*, report, November 6, 2007.

42. Emily Bazar, "Workplace Raids Ensnare Kids in Net, Too," *USA Today*, November 1, 2007, 13A.

43. U.S. Immigration and Customs Enforcement, *Fact Sheet: The ICE T. Don Hutto Family Residential Facility: Maintaining Family Unity, Enforcing Immigration Laws*, report, April 2007.

44. U.S. Constitution, amend. I, cl. 3.

45. The White House, *Fact Sheet: Improving Border Security and Immigration within Existing Law*, report, August 10, 2007.

46. Ibid.

47. Peter Micek, "Access Washington: Lawsuit Targets Homeland Security 'No Match' Rule," *New America Media* (September 19, 2007), 1.

48. U.S. Department of Homeland Security, *U.S. Government Seeks to End Litigation Undermining Expedited Removal of Salvadorans*, report (Washington, DC: DHS< November 17, 2005).

49. U.S. Department of Homeland Security, *State of the Border*.

50. Ibid.

51. Marianne Kolbasuk McGee, "Could Europe's New 'Blue Card' Cause Global Tech Talent to Shun U.S.?" *InformationWeek*, October 26, 2007; http://www.eetimes.eu/uk.202601886 (accessed on February 12, 2009). Alix Kroeger, "EU pins Skills Hopes on 'Blue Card,'" *BBC News*, October 23, 2007; http://news.bbc.co.uk/2/hi/Europe/7057730.stm (accessed on February 10, 2009).

52. Katrin Bennhold, "France Uses Money, Not Manacles, for Deportation," *International Herald Tribune*, December 20, 2006; http://www.iht.com/articles/2006/12/20/news/migr.de.php (accessed on February 10, 2009).

53. Darryl Fears, "Judge Blocks City's Ordinances against Illegal Immigration," *Washington Post*, July 27, 2007, A02.

54. In 2006, state legislatures filed 570 bills on illegal immigration issues involving employment, law enforcement, public benefits, education, and identification issues. Raymond Rico, "Immigration Was Key in 2006 State Legislation and Ballot Measures," *Immigrants' Rights Update*, March 29, 2007. Of those bills, 90 bills were passed, 84 were signed into law, and six were vetoed. Additionally, many states had referenda on their ballots; many of which passed overwhelmingly, 1–5.

55. Congressional Research Service, *Report for Congress: Enforcing Immigration Law: The Role of State and Local Law Enforcement*. Washington, DC: GPO, August 30, 2007, CRS-2.

56. Ibid.

57. Ibid., CRS-4.

58. U.S. Constitution, art. VI, cl. 2.

59. Congressional Research Service, *Enforcing Immigration Law*, CRS-5.

60. Ibid.

61. *California Division of Labor Standards Enforcement v. Dillingham Construction, N.A., Inc.*, 519 U.S. 316, 325 (1997).

62. *Immigration Reform and Control Act of 1986*, § 1324a(h)(2).

63. *De Canas v. Bica*, 424 U.S. 351, 357 (1976).

64. *Cipollone v. Liggett Group, Inc.*, 505 U.S. 504, 516 (1992).

65. *Manigault v. Springs*, 199 U.S. 473, 480 (1905).

66. *Sturges v. Crowninshield*, 17 U.S. 122, 193 (1819).

67. *Lynch v. Cannatella*, 810 F.2d 1363, 1371 (5th Cir. 1987).

68. Congressional Research Service, *Enforcing Immigration Law*, CRS-4.

69. Federal News Service, *Press Conference with United States Attorney General John Ashcroft and Immigration and Naturalization Service Commissioner James Zigler*, Re: Tracking of Foreign Visitors, June 5, 2002.

70. *Enforcing Immigration Law*, CRS-7.

71. Kris W. Kobach, "The Quintessential Force Multiplier: The Inherent Authority of Local Police to Make Immigration Arrests," *Albany Law Review* (Vol. 69, 2005): 183.

72. Ibid., 183–186.

73. Ibid., 188.

74. U.S. Department of Homeland Security, *Partners: Section 287(g), Immigration and Nationality Act; Delegation of Immigration Authority*, report (Washington, DC: DHS, April 1, 2008).

75. *De Canas*, 356.

76. Ibid., 356–357.

77. *Plyler v. Doe*, 457 U.S. 202, 228 n.23 (1982).

78. *Gray v. City of Valley Park, Missouri*, Case No. 4:07CV00881 ERW, Memorandum and Order by Judge E. Richard Webber (E.D. Mo. 2008), 9.

79. Ibid., 16–17.

80. Ibid., 15.

81. *Chicanos Por La Causa, Inc. v. Napolitano*, No. 07–17272, 13081 (9th Cir. 2008).

82. *Ibid.*, 13077.

83. *Ibid.*, 13074.

84. *South Carolina State Highway Department v. Barnwell Brothers, Inc.*, 303 U.S. 177, 190–191 (1938).

85. Immigration Reform Law Institute, *Planning for State Immigration Enforcement Legislation*, 2006, 1.
86. Ibid., 1–7.
87. Robert Rector, "White House Report Hides the Real Costs of Amnesty and Low Skill Immigration," *Web Memo No. 1523* (Washington, DC: The Heritage Foundation, June 26, 2007), 1.
88. Robert Rector, "Amnesty Will Cost U.S. Taxpayers at Least $2.6 Trillion," *Web Memo No. 1490* (Washington, DC: The Heritage Foundation, June 6, 2007), 1–2.
89. Ibid., 2.
90. Rector, *Web Memo No. 1523*, 1.
91. James Jay Carafano, *Border Security and State Safety and Security: Addressing Common Agendas*, speech, 2008.
92. For example, when former New York Governor Elliott Spitzer unilaterally decided to issue drivers licenses to illegal immigrants without the support of the legislature, the people of New York sent him a clear message that they did not support his reckless move. Nicholas Confessore, "Senate Votes to Stop Spitzer Plan to Give Illegal Immigrants Driver's Licenses," *New York Times*, October 23, 2007, B1. With the proviso "Not for federal purposes" stamped on the license, there was serious doubts as to whether many illegal immigrants would "come out of the shadow" as the document would be like wearing a Scarlet letter. Danny Hakim, "Bloomberg Opposes Spitzer's Latest Plan for Drivers," *New York Times*, November 2, 2007, B5. In polls taken after the action, 72 percent of New Yorkers adamantly opposed the decision. WNBC-TV, "Poll: New Yorkers Oppose Plan to Allow Illegal Aliens Driver's Licenses," *MSNBC.com*, October 15, 2007. Spitzer failed to heed the lessons from states like North Carolina, which had enormous problems with fraud and a mass influx of illegal immigrant when it decided to give them a driver's license. Yilu Shao, "The Law: Illegal Aliens Travel to Other States for Driver's Licenses," *New York Times*, March 2, 2003, B5.
93. Az. Rev. Code, § 13–2319 (West 2005).
94. Terry Goddard, *Border Trafficking Team to Combat Human Smuggling and Drugs*, speech, March 23, 2006.
95. Paul Gilbin, "Arpaio Claims 1,000th Arrest under Smuggling Law," *East Valley Tribune*, June 18, 2008; http://www.eastvalleytribune.com/story/118882 (accessed February 10, 2009).
96. Mike Sunnucks, "Tough Employer Sanctions Measure Pushed for Ballot," *The Phoenix Business Journal*, April 20, 2007, 1.
97. *Arizona Contractors Association, Inc. et al. v. Napolitano, et al.*, Case no. CV07-02496-PHX-NVW, Findings of Fact, Conclusions of Law and Order by Judge Neil V. Wake (D.Ct. Az. 2008), 2–3.
98. Ibid., 26–29.
99. *Arizona Contractors Association, Inc. et al. v. Napolitano, et al.*, Case no. CV07-02496-PHX-NVW, Notice of Appeal (D.Ct. Az. 2008).
100. *Arizona Contractors Association, Inc. et al. v. Napolitano, et al.*, Case no. 07–17272, Unofficial Transcript of Oral Argument (9th Cir. 2008).
101. *Chicanos Por La Causa, Inc.*, 13081.
102. AFP, "Toughest Sheriff in US Vows No Let Up in Immigration Fight," *brietbar.com*, June 16, 2008; http:nfp.google.com/article/ALegM5g7LYJ9PceMCAle00t_A-Wj_now7A (accessed on February 10, 2009).
103. Ibid., 2.

CHAPTER 9

1. Friedman, 61.
2. Malcolm Gladwell, "Open Secrets: Enron, Intelligence, and the Perils of Too Much Information," *The New Yorker*, January 8, 2007, 53.
3. For example, Mohammed Bouyeri, the jihadist who killed Theo Van Gogh in The Netherlands in November 2004, did not become radicalized by visiting a mosque; rather, Bouyeri turned to the Internet and jihadi Web sites to feed his thirst for radical teachings. Ian Buruma, *Murder in Amsterdam: The Death of Theo van Gogh and the Limits of Tolerance* (New York: Penguin Press, 2006), 211–212.
4. John Poindexter, "Overview of the Information Awareness Office," *DARPA-Tech 2002 Conference*, speech, August 2, 2002; Mark Clayton, "U.S. Plans Massive Data Sweep," *The Christian Science Monitor*, February 9, 2006, 1.
5. Jerry Seper, "Counterterror Staff Falls to 62 percent as FBI Seeks Volunteers," *Washington Times National Weekly Edition*, May 26, 2008, 1, 23.
6. John P. Sullivan, "Analytical Approaches for Sensing Novel and Emerging Threats," *49th Annual ISA Convention*, speech, March 29, 2008.
7. International Association of Chiefs of Police, "Criminal Intelligence Sharing: A National Plan for Intelligence-Led Policing at the Local, State and Federal Level," *IACP Intelligence Summit*, report, August 2002, 1.
8. Gladwell, 2.
9. Ibid.
10. Ibid., 7. As Gladwell points out, a group of Cornell business school students did ask the right questions about Enron using the information already public and concluded in 1998 that Enron likely was cooking its books. Those students recommended owners of Enron stock sell their stock, which was then trading at half the price it would reach before the collapse in 2001.
11. Gerald R. Murphy and Martha R. Plotkin, "Volume 1: Local-Federal Partnerships," *Protecting Your Community from Terrorism: Strategies for Local Law Enforcement* (Washington, DC: Police Executive Research Forum, March 2003), 12.
12. Herman Goldstein, "What Is POP," *Center for Problem-Oriented Policing*, report, 2001.
13. William de Lint, "Intelligence in Policing and Security: Reflections on Scholarship," *Policing & Society* 16 (March 2006): 1–6.
14. David L. Carter, "A Brief History of Law Enforcement Intelligence: Past Practice and Recommendations for Change," *Law Enforcement Intelligence: A Guide for State, Local, and Tribal Law Enforcement Agencies* (Washington, DC: Office of Community Oriented Policing Services, 2004), 22.
15. Ibid., 23.
16. Ibid., 24.
17. Ibid., 24–25.
18. Ibid., 25.
19. Ibid., 26.
20. Ibid., 31.
21. Ibid., 32.
22. National Commission on Terrorist Attacks upon the United States. *Final Report of the National Commission on Terrorist Attacks upon the United States* [hereafter cited as *9/11 Commission Report*]. New York: W.W. Norton & Company, 2004, 82.

23. Ibid., 73.
24. Ibid., 74.
25. Ibid., 265.
26. Ibid., 390.
27. Inspector General, *The Department of Justice's Terrorism Task Forces*, report (Washington, DC: OIG, June 2005, 15).
28. Federal Bureau of Investigation, *Protecting America against Terrorist Attack: A Closer Look at the FBI's Joint Terrorism Task Forces*, report (Washington, DC: DoJ, December 1, 2004).
29. The 9/11 Commission Report, 81–82.
30. Ibid.
31. Murphy and Plotkin, 31.
32. *The 9/11 Commission Report*, 81–82.
33. Ibid.
34. The White House, *National Strategy for Information Sharing*, report (Washington, DC: The White House, October 2007), 8.
35. Federal Bureau of Investigation, *Joint Terrorism Task Forces*, 15.
36. Ibid., 20.
37. Carter, *Law Enforcement Intelligence*, 16.
38. U.S. Senate Committee on Homeland Security and Governmental Affairs, *Present View of the Terrorist Threat*, 109th Cong., 2d sess., 2006, 3.
39. Ibid., 20.
40. Ibid.
41. Murphy and Plotkin, 33.
42. U.S. Department of Homeland Security, *Fiscal Year 2005 Homeland Security Grant Program: Program Guidelines and Application Kit* (Washington, DC: GPO, 2004), 27.
43. U.S. Department of Homeland Security, *FY 2007 Homeland Security Grant Program: Supplemental Resource—Fusion Capability Planning Tool* (Washington, D.C.: GPO, January 2007), 1.
44. The White House, *National Strategy for Information Sharing*, 20.
45. Siobhan Gorman, "Intelligence Sharing Still Lacking," *Wall Street Journal*, February 26, 2008, A12.
46. Government Security News, "Uncle Sam Should Provide Ongoing Support to State and Local Fusion Centers, Says GAO," *Hot News*, May 2008, 14.
47. The FBI launched the Law Enforcement Online system, which has over 40,000 users, in 1995 and the Regional Information Sharing System, which links more than 7,000 law enforcement entities, in 1974. Stephan A. Loyka, Faggiani, Donald A., and Karchmer, Clifford, "Volume 4: The Production and Sharing of Intelligence," *Protecting Your Community from Terrorism: The Strategies for Local Law Enforcement Series* (Washington, DC: Police Executive Research Forum, February 2005), 37–38.
48. *The 9/11 Commission Report*, 412.
49. Ibid.
50. The White House, *National Strategy for Information Sharing*, 13.
51. Some critics of this consolidation will argue that JTTFs and fusion centers are not competitive entities, but rather complementary efforts. Even experts in the field note that the JTTF is an example of a fusion center, so either critics are wrong or law

enforcement experts at all levels of government are confused. Loyka, Faggiani, and Karchmer, 38.

52. U.S. House Committee on Homeland Security, Subcommittee on Intelligence, Information Sharing, and Terrorism Risk Assessment, *The Way Forward with Fusion Centers: Challenges and Strategies for Change*, 110th Cong., 1st sess., 2007, 3.

53. Ibid.

54. Federal Bureau of Investigation, *Joint Terrorism Task Forces*, 131–132.

55. U.S. Government Accountability Office, *Homeland Security: Federal Efforts Are Helping to Alleviate Some Challenges Encountered by State and Local Information Fusion Centers (GAO-08-35)*, report (Washington, DC: GPO, October 2007), 7.

56. U.S. Department of Homeland Security, *Analysis of Federal Requirements*, EX-9 (Washington, DC: DHS).

57. Murphy and Plotkin, 12.

58. William A. Forsyth, *State and Local Intelligence Fusion Centers: An Evaluative Approach in Modeling a State Fusion Center* (Monterey, CA: Naval Post Graduate School, September 2005), 6.

59. Senate Committee, *Present View of the Terrorist Threat*, 19.

60. Jim Harper, "Fusion Centers: Leave 'Em to the States," *techknowledge* (Washington, DC: CATO Institute, March 13, 2007).

61. U.S. Department of Justice, *The National Criminal Intelligence Sharing Plan* (Washington, DC: DoJ report, June 2005), 2.

62. Ibid.

63. Senate Committee, *Present View of the Terrorist Threat*, 19.

64. U.S. Department of Justice, *Criminal Intelligence Sharing*, 2.

65. Ibid.

66. Forsyth, *State and Local Information Fusion Centers*, 5.

67. U.S. Department of Justice, "Prison Inmates at Midyear 2007," *Bureau of Justice Statistics Bulletin* NCJ 221944 (June 2008): 1; U.S. Department of Justice, "Jail Inmates at Midyear 2007," *Bureau of Justice Bulletin* NCJ 221945 (June 2008): 1.

68. Ibid.

69. U.S. Department of Justice, *Bureau of Justice Statistics Bulletin* NCJ 221944, 3; U.S. Department of Justice, *Bureau of Justice Bulletin* NCJ 221945, 4.

70. U.S. House Subcommittee on Intelligence, Information Sharing, and Terrorism Risk Assessment, *Homegrown Terrorism*, 110th Cong., 1st sess., 2007, 4.

71. Mitchell D. Seiber and Arvin Bhatt, *Radicalization in the West: The Homegrown Threat* (New York: NYPD, report, 2007), 6.

72. Ibid., 8.

73. Ibid., 20.

74. U.S. Senate Committee on Homeland Security and Governmental Affairs, *Counterfeit Goods: Easy Cash for Criminals and Terrorists*, 109th Cong., 1st sess., (2005).

75. U.S. Senate Committee on Homeland Security and Government Affairs, *Prison Radicalization: Are Terrorist Cells Forming in U.S. Cell Blocks?*, 109th Cong., 2d sess., (2006).

76. U.S. Department of Justice, *Criminal Intelligence Sharing*, 10.

77. Lois M. Davis et al., *When Terrorism Hits Home: How Prepared Are State and Local Law Enforcement* (Los Angeles: RAND Corporation, 2004), xvii.

78. Ibid., 44.

79. *The 9/11 Commission Report*, 426–427.
80. Ibid.
81. Ibid.
82. Ibid.
83. Ibid.
84. Carter, *Law Enforcement Intelligence*, 94.
85. U.S. Department of Justice, *Criminal Intelligence Sharing*, 4.
86. *Handschu v. Special Services Division*, 2003 U.S. Dist. LEXIS 2134 (S.D.N.Y. 2003).
87. Ibid.
88. U.S. Department of Justice, *Criminal Intelligence Sharing*, 5.
89. Sunchlar M. Rust, *Collaborative Network Evolution: The Los Angeles Terrorism Early Warning Group* (Monterey, CA: Naval Post Graduate School, March 2006), 21.
90. Ibid., 24.
91. U.S. House of Representatives Committee on the Judiciary, *How Does Illegal Immigration Impact American Taxpayers and Will the Reid-Kennedy Amnesty Worsen the Blow*, 109th Cong., 2d sess., 2006.
92. Ibid.
93. Ibid.
94. Rust, 37.
95. John Sullivan, "Terrorism Early Warning and Co-Production of Counterterrorism Intelligence," *Canadian Association for Security and Intelligence Studies CASIS 20th Anniversary Conference*, speech, October 21, 2005, 1.
96. Ibid.
97. Ibid., 4.
98. Ibid., 3.
99. Ibid., 1.
100. Rust, 25.
101. Ibid., 35.
102. Ibid.
103. Ibid., 37–38.
104. Mead, 6–7.
105. Rust, 38.
106. Forsyth, *State and Local Information Fusion Centers*, 58.
107. Ibid.
108. Ibid., 8–59.
109. Siobhan Gorman, "LAPD Terror-Tip Plan May Serve as Model," *Wall Street Journal*, April 15, 2008, A3.
110. Ibid.
111. Ibid.
112. Ibid.
113. Ibid.

CHAPTER 10

1. Tom Ridge, *Public/Private Sector Program on Emergency Preparedness*, remarks, September 28, 2004, 1.

2. Galen was a famous Greek physician who lived from 129 A.D. to 200 A.D.

3. National Commission on Terrorist Attacks upon the United States. *Final Report of the National Commission on Terrorist Attacks upon the United States* [hereafter cited as *9/11 Commission Report*]. New York: W.W. Norton & Company, 2004, 317.

4. Jonathan B. Tucker, "Strategies for Countering Terrorism: Lessons from the Israeli Experience," *Journal of Homeland Security* (March 2003): 3.

5. U.S. Department of Homeland Security, *FY 2007 Homeland Security Grant Program: Program Guidance and Application Kit,* report (Washington, DC: DHS, January 2007), 47–51.

6. As discussed in Chapter 5, although not a perfect method to determine risk, the reality is that urban areas receiving larger amounts of funding are likely to be getting those awards because the risk for those urban areas as calculated by DHS is much higher than the urban areas receiving smaller amounts of funding.

7. U.S. Department of Homeland Security, *Fact Sheet: Ready Campaign*, report (Washington, DC: DHS, October 1, 2004), 1.

8. Ibid.

9. The Council for Excellence in Government, *Are We Ready? Introducing the Public Readiness Index: A Survey-Based Tool to Measure the Preparedness of Individuals, Families and Communities*, report (Washington, DC: CEG, December 14, 2006), 20.

10. Ibid.

11. Ibid.

12. U.S. Department of Homeland Security, *About Citizen Corps*, report (Washington, DC: DHS, 2008), 1.

13. U.S. Department of Homeland Security, *About CERT*, report (Washington, DC: DHS, 2008), 1.

14. Ibid.

15. Ibid., 2.

16. Ibid., 1.

17. Peter Huber, "The Coming Plague," *The Wall Street Journal*, April 10, 2007, A19.

18. Geoffrey Colvin, "An Executive Risk Handbook: Five Ways Managers Can Use Scenario Planning to Prepare for Disasters," *Fortune*, October 3, 2005, 69.

19. A useful resource for small and medium sized businesses is DHS's Ready Business Web site (www.ready.gov/business/).

20. In certain cases, such as grocery stores, it would make sense to specify biological events such as foodborne pathogens.

21. Federal Emergency Management Agency, "Disaster Search," http://www.fema.gov/news/disasters.fema (accessed on March 31, 2008).

22. Ibid.

23. Although not currently available to private sector entities, another tool would be DHS's Lessons Learned Information Sharing web site, www.llis.gov.

24. Ellen Florian Kratz, "For FedEx, It Was Time to Deliver: Years of Coping with Calamity Have Taught the Huge Supplier to Improvise," *Fortune*, October 3, 2005, 83.

25. Devin Leonard, *The Only Lifeline Was the Wal-Mart: The World's Biggest Company Flexed Its Massive Distribution Muscle to Deliver Vital Supplies to Victims of Katrina*, Fortune (October 3, 2005), 74–80.

26. National Fire Protection Association, *NFPA 1600: Standard on Disaster/Emergency Management and Business Continuity Programs* (2007 Edition).

27. U.S. Department Justice, *Chiquita Brands International Pleads Guilty to Making Payments to a Designated Terrorist Organization and Agrees to Pay $25 Million Fine*, press release (Washington, DC: DoJ, March 19, 2007).
28. Ibid.
29. Ibid.
30. *The 9/11 Commission Report*, 90.
31. Ibid., 92.

AFTERWORD

1. Calvin Coolidge, *On the Occasion of the One Hundred and Fiftieth Anniversary of the Declaration of Independence*, speech, July 5, 1926.
2. This quote is widely attributed to Tytler. Loren Collins, *The Truth about Tytler*, http://lorencollins.net/tytler.html (accessed September 10, 2008).

Bibliography

Aesop, "The Ant and the Grasshopper." *The Fables of Aesop*. New York: Book of the Month Club, 1995, http://AFP.google.com/article/ALeqMSg7LY59PczMLAle0DP_A-Wj_now7A (accessed on February 10, 2009).
AFP. "Toughest Sheriff in US vows No Let Up in Immigration Fight." *brietbard.com*. June 16, 2008.
"The American Right: Under the Weather." *The Economist*. August 9, 2007.
Andes, Jodi. "Somali Man Pleads Guilty to Plot." *Columbus Dispatch*. August 1, 2007, 01A.
———. "Local Terrorist's Steps Detailed." *Columbus Dispatch*. June 4, 2008, 01A.
Arizona Contractors Association, Inc. et al. v. Napolitano, et al. Case no. CV07-02496-PHX-NVW, Findings of Fact, Conclusions of Law and Order. D.Ct. Az. 2008.
———. Notice of Appeal. D.Ct. Az. 2008.
———. Case no. 07-17272. Unofficial Transcript of Oral Argument. 9th Cir. 2008.
Arizona Revised Code. § 13-2319. West 2005.
Associated Press. "Ohio's Governor Blames National Economy." *Forbes*. February 7, 2008; http://www.forbes.com/feeds/AFx/2008/02/07/Afx4630170.html (accessed on February 10, 2009).
Baker, Al and Diane Cardwell. "City Has Itself to Blame for Terror Cuts, U.S. Says." *New York Times*. June 2, 2006, A1.
Bazar, Emily. "Workplace Raids Ensnare Kids in Net, Too." *USA Today*. November 1, 2007, 13A.
Bennhold, Katrin. "France Uses Money, Not Manacles, for Deportation." *International Herald Tribune*. December 20, 2006; http://www.iht.com/articles/2006/12/20/news/migrate.php (accessed on February 10, 2009).
Beverley, Robert. *The History and Present State of Virginia: A Selection*. Indianapolis & New York: The Bobbs-Merrill Company, Inc., 1971.

Bin Laden, Osama. *Declaration of War against the Americans Occupying the Land of the Two Holy Places.* August 1996; http://www.pbs.org/newshour/terrorism/international/fatwa_1996.html (accessed on February 10, 2009).

Birnbaum, Jeffrey H. "The Road to Riches Is Called K Street." *Washington Post.* June 22, 2005, A01.

Blanchard, Wayne B. *American Civil Defense 1945–1984: The Evolution of Programs and Policies.* Washington, DC: GPO, 1986.

Broache, Anne. "Annual H-1B Visa Cap Met—Already." *cnetnews.com.* April 3, 2007.

Buck v. Bell. 274 U.S. 200, 207. 1927.

Buruma, Ian. *Murder in Amsterdam: The Death of Theo van Gogh and the Limits of Tolerance.* New York: Penguin Press, 2006.

"Bush Aims to Be Unlike Dad in Storm Response." *NewsMax.* August 16, 2004; http://archive.newsmax.com/archives/articles/2004/8/15/174950.shtml (accessed on February 10, 2009).

Bush, George W. *Homeland Security Presidential Directive 8, "National Preparedness."* December 17, 2003.

———. *Homeland Security Presidential 8 Annex 1, "National Planning."* December 3, 2007.

———. *Homeland Security Presidential Directive 5: "Management of Domestic Issues."* February 28, 2003.

Bush, Jeb. "Think Locally on Relief." *Washington Post.* September 30, 2005, A19.

California Division of Labor Standards Enforcement v. Dillingham Construction, N.A., Inc. 519 U.S. 316. 1997.

Carafano, James Jay. "The Pentagon Crisis of 2015." *Commentary.* Washington, DC: The Heritage Foundation, May 15, 2007.

———. *Border Security and State Safety and Security: Addressing Common Agendas.* 2008.

Carafano, James Jay and Matt A. Mayer. "Better, Faster, Cheaper Border Security Requires Better Immigration Services." *Backgrounder.* Washington, DC: The Heritage Foundation, February 28, 20071–5.

———. "FEMA and Federalism: Washington Is Moving in the Wrong Direction." *Backgrounder.* Washington, DC: The Heritage Foundation, May 8, 2007, 2.

———. "Spending Smarter: Prioritizing Homeland Security Grants by Using National Standards and Risk Criteria." *Backgrounder.* Washington, DC: The Heritage Foundation, May 10, 2007, 3–4.

Carafano, James Jay and Richard Weitz. "Learning from Disaster: The Role of Federalism and the Importance of Grassroots Response." *Backgrounder.* Washington, DC: The Heritage Foundation, March 21, 2006, 1.

Carr, Caleb. *The Lessons of Terror: A History of Warfare against Civilians: Why It Has Always Failed and Why It Will Fail Again.* New York: Random House, 2002.

Carter, "A Brief History of Law Enforcement Intelligence: Past Practice and Recommendations for Change." *Law Enforcement Intelligence: A Guide for State, Local, and Tribal Law Enforcement Agencies.* Washington, DC: Office of Community Oriented Policing Services, 2004.

Carter, James. Executive Order 12127. *Federal Register* 44. April 3, 1979.

Chertoff, Michael. *Letter to the Representative Christopher Cox.* July 13, 2005.

———. *Homeland Security Secretary Michael Chertoff on the State of Immigration*. November 6, 2007.
———. *National Emergency Management Association Mid-Year Conference*. February 13, 2006.
———. *Remarks at a Press Availability on 2008 Homeland Security Grant Guidance*. February 1, 2008.
———. *Remarks by Homeland Security Michael Chertoff at a Press Conference on the Fiscal Year 2006 Urban Areas Security Initiative Grants*. January 3, 2006.
———. *Transcript of Press Conference with Secretary Chertoff to Announce $1.7 Billion in Homeland Security Grants*. July 18, 2007.
———. *U.S. Department of Homeland Security 2007 Achievements and 2008 Priorities*. December 12, 2007.
———. *U.S. Department of Homeland Security Second Stage Review Remarks*. July 13, 2005.
Chicanos Por La Causa, Inc. v. Napolitano. No. 07-17272. Ninth Circuit. 2008.
Chinese Exclusion Act of 1882. Public Law 71, 50th Cong., 2d sess. May 6, 1882.
Cipollone v. Liggett Group, Inc. 505 U.S. 504. 1992.
Clayton, Mark. "US Plans Massive Data Sweep." *The Christian Science Monitor*. February 9, 2006, 1.
Cleveland, Grover. 49th Cong., 2d Sess., *Congressional Record,* vol. xviii, Pt. II. 1887.
Collins, Loren. *The Truth about Tytler*. http://lorencollins.net/tytler.html (accessed December 10, 2008).
Colvin, Geoffrey. "An Executive Risk Handbook: Five Ways Managers Can Use Scenario Planning to Prepare for Disasters." *Fortune*. October 3, 2005, 69.
Congressional Budget Office. *Report on Senate Amendment 1150 to S. 1348: the Comprehensive Immigration Reform Act of 2007*. Washington, DC: GPO, June 4, 2007.
Confessore, Nicholas. "Senate Votes to Stop Spitzer Plan to Give Illegal Immigrants Driver's Licenses." *New York Times*. October 23, 2007, B1.
Congressional Research Service. "FEMA and Disaster Relief." Washington, DC: GPO, 1998.
———. *Department of Homeland Security Reorganization: The 2SR Initiative*. CRS Report for Congress Order Code RL33042 CRS-2. August 19, 2005.
———. *Report for Congress: Enforcing Immigration Law: The Role of State and Local Law Enforcement*. Washington, DC: GPO, August 30, 2007.
The Constitution of the United States. Philadelphia, 1787.
Coolidge, Calvin. *On the Occasion of the One Hundred and Fiftieth Anniversary of the Declaration of Independence*. July 5, 1926.
Cooper, Betsy and Kevin O'Neill. "Lessons from the Immigration Reform and Control Act of 1986." *MPI Policy Brief*. August 2005.
Cooper, Christopher. "Forget Austerity, State Spending Ratchets Up." *Wall Street Journal*. February 24–25, 2007, A1.
Cooper, Christopher and Robert Block. *Disaster: Hurricane Katrina and the Failure of Homeland Security*. New York: Times Book, 2006.
Corera, Gordon. "Al-Qaeda's 007: The Extraordinary Story of the Solitary Computer Geek in a Shepherds Bush Bedsit Who Became the World's Most Wanted Cyber-Jihadist." *The London Times*. January 16, 2008, 4.

Council for Excellence in Government. *Are We Ready? Introducing the Public Readiness Index: A Survey-Based Tool to Measure the Preparedness of Individuals, Families and Communities*. December 14, 2006.

Davis, Lois M., et al. *When Terrorism Hits Home: How Prepared Are State and Local Law Enforcement*. Los Angeles: RAND Corporation, 2004.

De Canas v. Bica. 424 U.S. 351. 1976.

Declaration of Independence. Philadelphia, July 4, 1776.

De Lint, William. "Intelligence in Policing and Security: Reflections on Scholarship." *Policing & Society* 16. March 2006, 1–6.

Department of Homeland Security Appropriation Act of 2004. Public Law 108–90, *U.S. Statutes at Large* 117. 2003.

Dold, Cynthia. *King County Healthcare Coalition*. undated.

Downes, Lawrence. "What Part of 'Illegal' Don't You Understand?," *New York Times*. October 28, 2007, WK-11.

Du Pont, Pete. "Good Buy, Columbus: Ohioans May Revolt against Higher Taxes and Spending." *Wall Street Journal*. October 27, 2003; http://www.opinionjournal.com/columnists/pdupont/?id=110004221 (accessed on February 10, 2009).

Edwards, Chris. "Pork: A Microcosm of the Overspending Problem." *Tax & Budget Bulletin* 24. Washington: CATO Institute, August 2005, 1–2.

Eisenhower, Dwight D. *Farewell Address to the Nation*. January 17, 1961.

Elliston, Jon. "A Disaster Waiting to Happen." *Independent Weekly*. September 22, 2004; http://www.indyweek.com/gyrobase/content?oid+oid%3A23664 (accessed on February 10, 2009).

Fears, Darryl. "Judge Blocks City's Ordinances against Illegal Immigration." *Washington Post*. July 27, 2007, A02.

Federal Bureau of Investigation. *Protecting America against Terrorist Attack: A Close Look at the FBI's Joint Terrorism Task Forces*. December 1, 2004.

Federal Emergency Management Agency. *FEMA History*. Washington, DC; http://www.fema.gov/about/history.shtm (accessed on September 20, 2007).

———. "Disaster Search." Disaster Information. http://www.fema.gov/news/disasters.fema. Accessed on March 31, 2008.

———. "Disaster Search." Disaster Information. http://www.fema.gov/news/disasters.fema. Accessed on June 11, 2008.

———. *FEMA History*. 2008, Washington, DC: DHS.

———. *National Preparedness System: Current Prototype & Proposed Implementation Approach*. Undated, Washington, DC: DHS.

———. *Training Overview*. March 10, 2008, Washington, DC: DHS.

Federal News Service. *Press Conference with United States Attorney General John Ashcroft and Immigration and Naturalization Service Commissioner James Zigler*. June 5, 2002.

Forsyth, William A. *State and Local Intelligence Fusion Centers: An Evaluative Approach in Modeling a State Fusion Center*. Monterey, CA: Naval Post Graduate School, September 2005.

Franklin, Benjamin. *Letter to Governor Thomas Penn*. Philadelphia, November 11, 1755.

Friedman, George. *America's Secret War: Inside the Hidden Worldwide Struggle between America and Its Enemies*. New York: Broadway Books, 2004.

Frost, Wladislava S. "Cities and Towns Mobilize for War." *American Sociological Review* 9. February 1944, 87–88.
Gaddis, John Lewis. *The Cold War: A New History*. New York: The Penguin Press, 2005.
Gilbin, Paul. "Arpaio Claims 1,000th Arrest under Smuggling Law." *East Valley Tribune*. June 18, 2008; http://www.eastvalleytribune.com/story/118882 (accessed on February 10, 2009).
Gladwell, Malcolm. "Open Secrets: Enron, Intelligence, and the Perils of Too Much Information." *The New Yorker*. January 8, 2007, 53.
Goddard, Terry. *Border Trafficking Team to Combat Human Smuggling and Drugs*. March 23, 2006.
Goldstein, Herman. "What Is POP." *Center for Problem-Oriented Policing*. Madison: CPOP, 2001.
Gorman, Siobhan. "Intelligence Sharing Still Lacking." *Wall Street Journal*. February 26, 2008, A12.
———. "LAPD Terror-Tip Plan May Serve as Model." *Wall Street Journal*. April 15, 2008, A3.
Government Security News. "Uncle Sam Should Provide Ongoing Support to State and Local Fusion Centers, Says GAO." *Hot News*. May 2008, 14.
Gray v. City of Valley Park, Missouri. Case No. 4:07CV00881 ERW. E.D. Mo. 2008.
Green III, Walter G., ed. "Civil Defense: The Truman Administration." *Electronic Encyclopaedia of Civil Defense and Emergency Management*. August 12, 2003, 32.
Grow, Brian, et al. "The New E-spionage Threat." *Businessweek*. April 21, 2008, A1.
Grunwald, Michael and Susan B. Glasser. "Brown's Turf Wars Sapped FEMA's Strength." *Washington Post*. December 23, 2005, A1.
Hakim, Danny. "Bloomberg Opposes Spitzer's Latest Plan for Drivers." *New York Times*. November 2, 2007, B5.
Hallett, Robin. *Africa Since 1875: A Modern History*. Ann Arbor: The University of Michigan Press, 1974.
Handschu v. Special Services Division. 2003 U.S. Dist. LEXIS 2134. S.D.N.Y. 2003.
Harper, Jim. "Fusion Centers: Leave 'Em to the States." *Techknowledge*. Washington, DC: CATO Institute, March 13, 2007.
Henke, Tracy. *Press Conference by Under Secretary George Foresman and Assistant Secretary Tracy Henke on the FY 06 Homeland Security Grant Program*. May 31, 2006.
Hickok, Eugene W. *Why States? The Challenge of Federalism*. Washington, DC: The Heritage Foundation, 2007.
Homeland Security Act of 2002. Public Law 107–296, *U.S. Statutes at Large* 116, 2002.
Huber, Peter. "The Coming Plague." *Wall Street Journal*. April 10, 2007, A19.
Hutchinson, Jr., Clyde A. "Civil Defense News." *Bulletin of the Atomic Scientists* 6. 1950, 382.
Immigration and Nationality Act of 1965. Public Law 89–236, 89th Cong., 1st sess. October 3, 1965.
Immigration Reform and Control Act of 1986. Public Law 99–603, 99th Cong., 2d sess. 1986.
Immigration Reform Law Institute. *Planning for State Immigration Enforcement Legislation*. 2006.

Inspector General. *The Department of Justice's Terrorism Task Forces (Report I-2005-007)*. June 2005, Washington, DC, OIG.

———. *Audit of the State of Colorado Homeland Security Grant Program*. December 2007, Washington, DC, OIG.

———. *Major Management Challenges Facing the Department of Homeland Security*. January 4, 2008, Washington, DC, OIG.

International Association of Chiefs of Police. "Criminal Intelligence Sharing: A National Plan for Intelligence-Led Policing at the Local, State, and Federal Level." *IACP Intelligence Summit*. August 2002.

Johnson, Paul. *A History of the American People*. New York: HarperCollins, 1997.

Jordan, Miriam. "Crackdown on Illegal Immigrants Spurs Backlash among Locals." *Wall Street Journal*. April 17, 2008, A4.

Journals of the Continental Congress, 1774–1789 (2nd). July 18, 1775.

Kennedy, John F. *Inaugural Address*. January 20, 1961.

———. Executive Order 10952. *Federal Register* 26. July 20, 1961.

Kepel, Giles. *The War for Muslim Minds: Islam and the West*. Cambridge, MA: Harvard University Press, 2004.

Kerr, Thomas J. *Civilian Defense in the U.S.* Boulder, CO: Westview Press, 1983.

Kobach, Kris W. "The Quintessential Force Multiplier: The Inherent Authority of Local Police to Make Immigration Arrests." *Albany Law Review* 69. 2005, 183.

King County Healthcare Coalition. *Involuntary Isolation or Quarantine Legal Team Protocol*. Seattle: KCHC, April 12, 2006.

———. *Business Resiliency Workshop for Healthcare Providers*. Seattle: KCHC, 2008.

Kratz, Ellen Florian. "For FedEx, It Was Time to Deliver: Years of Coping with Calamity Have Taught the Huge Supplier to Improvise." *Fortune*. October 3, 2005. 83.

Kroeger, Alix. "EU Pins Skills Hopes on 'Blue Card.'" *BBC News*. October 23, 2007; http://news.bbc.co.uk/2/hi/Europe/7057730.stm (accessed on February 10, 2009).

Landis, James M. "The Need for Civilian Protection." *Vital Speeches of the Day* 8. March 1, 1942.

Leiken, Robert S., and Steven Brooke. "The Moderate Muslim Brotherhood." *Foreign Affairs* 86. March/April 2007, 108.

Leonard, Devin. "The Only Lifeline Was the Wal-Mart: The World's Biggest Company Flexed Its Massive Distribution Muscle to Deliver Vital Supplies to Victims of Katrina." *Fortune*. October 3, 2005, 74–80.

Limbacher, Carl et al. "1999 Hurricane Swamped Clinton' FEMA." *NewsMax*. September 7, 2005; http://archive.newsmax.com/archives/ic/2005/9/7/134914.shtml (accessed on February 10, 2009).

Lipton, Eric. "Security Cuts for New York and Washington." *New York Times*. June 1, 2006, A1.

Loyka, Stephan A., Donald A. Faggiani, and Clifford Karchmer. "Volume 4: The Production and Sharing of Intelligence." *Protecting Your Community from Terrorism: The Strategies for Local Law Enforcement Series*. Washington, DC: Police Executive Research Forum, February 2005.

Lynch v. Cannatella. 810 F.2d 1363. 5th Cir. 1987.

MacFarquhar, Neil. "Egyptian Group Patiently Pursues Dram of Islamic State." *New York Times*. January 20, 2002, 3.

Manigault v. Springs. 199 U.S. 473. 1905.
Masse, Todd, et al. "The Department of Homeland Security's Risk Assessment Methodology: Evolution, Issues, and Options for Congress." *CRS Report for Congress.* Washington, DC: GPO, February 2, 2007.
Mauck, Elwyn A. "History of Civil Defense in the United States." *The Bulletin of the Atomic Scientists* 6. September 1950, 265–70.
McGee, Marianne Kolbasuk. "Could Europe's New 'Blue Card' Cause Global Tech Talent to Shun U.S.?." *InformationWeek.* October 26, 2007; http://www.eetimes.eu/uk/202601886 (accessed on February 10, 2009).
McQuaid, John and Mark Schleifstein. "Washing Away: Part 4: Tempting Fate." *New Orleans Times-Picayune.* June 26, 2002; http://www.nola.com/hurricane/content.scf?/washingaway/part4.html (accessed on February 10, 2009).
Mexican American Legal Defense and Educational Fund. "Civil Rights Coalition Challenges Arizona Employer Sanctions Law." *ACLU Immigrants' Right Project.* September 4, 2007; http://www.maldef.org/news/press.cfu?20=431 (accessed on February 10, 2009).
Micek, Peter. *Access Washington: Lawsuit Targets Homeland Security 'No Match' Rule.* September 19, 2007; New America Media, 1.
Mitchell, Richard P. *The Society of the Muslim Brothers.* London: Oxford University Press, 1969.
Mueller, John. "A False Sense of Insecurity: How Does the Risk of Terrorism Measure up against Everyday Dangers." *Regulation.* Washington, DC: CATO Institute, Fall 2004, 42.
Murphy, Gerald R. and Martha R. Plotkin. "Volume 1: Local-Federal Partnerships." *Protecting Your Community from Terrorism: Strategies for Local Law Enforcement.* Washington, DC: Police Executive Research Forum, March 2003.
Muslim Brotherhood. "Credo of the Muslim Brotherhood." *Muslim Brotherhood Movement Homepage.* 2008; http://www.ummah.net/ikhwa (accessed on February 10, 2009).
National Emergency Management Agency. "Emergency Management." *NEMAWEB.* 2008, 3.
National Commission on Terrorism. *Countering the Changing Threat of International Terrorism.* Washington, DC: GPO, June 7, 2000.
The National Commission on Terrorist Attacks upon the United States. *Final Report of the National Commission on Terrorist Attacks upon the United States.* New York: W.W. Norton & Company, 2004.
National Fire Protection Association. *NFPA 1600: Standard on Disaster/Emergency Management and Business Continuity Programs.* 2007 Edition, Washington, DC: NFPA.
Nelson, Otto. *Non-Military Defense in the Shadow of Nuclear Attack.* May 15, 1956.
New Oxford American Dictionary, 2nd ed. New York: Oxford University Press, s.v. "Risk," May 2005.
———. s.v. "Resiliency."
Nichols, Bill and Richard Benedetto. "Govs to Bush: Relief Our Job." *USA Today.* October 2, 2005, 1A.
Nixon, Richard M. Executive Order 11725. *Federal Register* 38. June 29, 1973.

Nolin, Robert, Linda Kleindienst, and Brittany Wallman. "Gov. Bush Accepts Blame for Slow Relief Response Days after Wilma." *Florida Sun-Sentinel*. October 27, 2005; http:/www.sun-sentinal.com/news/local/southflorida/sflwilma,0,1170061.story (accessed on February 10, 2009).

Nossiter, Adam. "Nagin Re-elected as New Orleans Mayor." *New York Times*. May 21, 2006, A1.

Nowak, Joey. "Hazmat Vehicle Just Sitting in Garage." *Columbus Dispatch*. July 13, 2008, B3.

Ohio Emergency Management Agency. *Assistance Toolbox*. Columbus: OEMA, August 2005.

———. *Application Packet for the State Disaster Relief Program*. Columbus: OEMA, September 2007.

———. *Continuity of Operations Plan (All Hazards) Overview and Guidance for Local Government*. Columbus: OEMA, September 2006.

———. *Cost Documentation Workshop*. Columbus: OEMA, July 2007

———. *Damage Assessment Workshop*. Columbus: OEMA, May 2007.

———. *EMA Preliminary Damage Assessment Field Guide*. Columbus: OEMA, October 2006.

———. *Ohio Response System*. Columbus: OEMA, undated.

———. *Plan Development and Review Guidance for Local Emergency Operations Plans*. Columbus: OEMA, May 2008.

———. *Public Assistance Handbook*. Columbus: OEMA, September 2007.

———. *Recovery from Disaster: Role of Local Government*. Columbus: OEMA, March 2008.

———. *State of Ohio Individual Assistance Program*. Columbus: OEMA, November 2, 2006.

Ohio History Central. "Biography of Ted Strickland." *Ohio Historical Society*. March 14, 2008, 1.

Pestritto, Ronald J. *Woodrow Wilson: The Essential Political Writings*. Lanham, MD: Lexington Books, 2005.

Peters, Katherine McIntire. "Congressional Oversight of Homeland Security Comes under Fire Again." *Government Executive*. July 30, 2008; http://www.govexec.com/dailyfed0708/073008kpl.htm (accessed on February 9, 2009).

Preston, Julie. "Employers Fight Tough Measures on Immigration." *New York Times*. July 6, 2008, A1.

Poindexter, John. "Overview of the Information Awareness Office." *DARPATech 2002 Conference*. August 2, 2002.

Post-Katrina Emergency Management Reform Act of 2006. Public Law 109–295, *U.S. Statutes at Large* 120. 2006.

Plyler v. Doe. 457 U.S. 202. 1982.

Qutb, Sayyid. *Milestones*. Indianapolis: American Trust Publications, 1990.

Raphaeli, Nimrod. "Ayman Muhammad Rabi' Al-Zawahiri: The Making of an Arch Terrorist." *Terrorism and Political Violence* 14. Winter 2002, 20–22.

Reagan, Ronald. *Speaking My Mind*. New York: Simon and Schuster, 1989.

———. *Remarks to the American Dental Association*. October 29, 1972.

Rector, Robert. "Amnesty Will Cost U.S. Taxpayers at Least $2.6 Trillion." *Web Memo No. 1490*. Washington, DC: The Heritage Foundation, June 6, 2007, 1–2.

———. "White House Report Hides the Real Costs of Amnesty and Low Skill Immigration." *Web Memo No. 1523.* Washington DC: The Heritage Foundation, June 26, 2007, 1.
Reed, Lawrence W. "Grover Cared: Taking Disaster Relief Lessons from a Compassionate Conservative." *National Review Online.* March 2, 2006.
Republican Members of the U.S. House of Representatives. *Republican Contract with America.* Washington, DC, 1994.
Rico, Raymond. "Immigration Was Key in 2006 State Legislation and Ballot Measures." *Immigrants' Rights Update.* March 29, 2007, 1–5.
Ridge, Tom. *Letter to Senator Susan Collins.* January 26, 2004.
———. *Public/Private Sector Program on Emergency Preparedness.* September 28, 2004.
Robert T. Stafford Disaster Relief and Emergency Assistance Act. Public Law 93–288, 100th Cong., 2d sess. November 23, 1988.
Roosevelt, Franklin D. *Second Inaugural Address.* January 20, 1937.
Rosenzweig, Paul and Alane Kochems. "Risk Assessment and Risk Management: Necessary Tools for Homeland Security." *Backgrounder.* Washington, DC: The Heritage Foundation, October 25, 2005.
Rossiter, Clinton, ed. *The Federalist Papers.* New York: Signet Classics, 1999.
Rumsfeld, Donald. "A New Kind of War." *New York Times.* September 27, 2001.
———. *U.S. Defense Department Briefing.* February 12, 2002, A21.
Rust, Sunchlar M. *Collaborative Network Evolution: The Los Angeles Terrorism Early Warning Group.* Monterey, CA: Naval Post Graduate School, March 2006.
Sageman, Marc. *Understanding Terror Networks.* Philadelphia: University of Pennsylvania Press, 2004.
Samuelson, Robert J. *The Good Life and Its Discontents: The American Dream in the Age of Entitlement 1945–1995.* New York: Times Books, 1995.
Sanger, Margaret. "A Plan for Peace." *Birth Control Review.* April 1932, 107–8.
Scott, Gina M. "Study Says Real ID Act Will Cost $11 Billion, Be Logistics Nightmare." *Government Technology.* September 21, 2006; http://www.govtech.com/gt/articles/101128 (accessed on February 10, 2009).
Seattle/King County Public Health. *Community Communication Network Vulnerable Populations Action Team (VPAT).* Seattle: S/KCPH, undated.
———. *Windstorm 2006: After Action Report.* Seattle: S/KCPH, February 2, 2007.
———. *Business Not as Usual: Preparing for Pandemic Flu.* Seattle: S/KCPH, 2008.
Seattle/King County Public Health and the Vulnerable Populations System Coordination Steering Committee. *Community Based Organizations: Standards and Indicators for Emergency Preparedness and Response.* Seattle: S/KCPH, May 2008.
Seattle, King County, and the United Way of King County. *Katrina's Lessons: Reach Our Vulnerable Residents Now.* Seattle: S/KCPH, December 15, 2006.
Seiber, Mitchell D. and Arvin Bhatt. *Radicalization in the West: The Homegrown Threat.* 2007, New York City: NYPD.
Seper, Jerry. "Counterterror Staff Falls to 62 Percent as FBI Seeks Volunteers." *Washington Times National Weekly Edition.* May 26, 2008, 1–3.
Sherman, Rexford B. *Seaport Governance in the United States and Canada.* Undated, Washington, DC: AAPA, 3.

National Governors Association. *2007 State Homeland Security Directors Survey.* December 18, 2007.

Shao, Yilu. "The Law: Illegal Aliens Travel to Other States for Driver's Licenses." *New York Times.* March 2, 2003, 14WC-5.

Shlaes, Amity. *The Forgotten Man: A New History of the Great Depression.* New York: HarperCollins Publishers, 2007.

Simpson, James B. *Simpson's Contemporary Quotations.* Boston: Houghton Mifflin Company, 1988.

South Carolina State Highway Department v. Barnwell Brothers, Inc.. 303 U.S. 177. 1938.

Story, Joseph. *Commentaries on the Constitution of the United States with a Preliminary Review of the Constitutional History of the Colonies and States before the Adoption of the Constitution.* Boston: Hilliard, Gray and Company, 1833.

Sturges v. Crowninshield. 17 U.S. 122. 1819.

Sullivan, Eileen. "21,000 Slipped Past Borders Illegally." *USA Today.* November 5, 2007; http://www.usatoday.com/news/Washington/2007-11-05-1051006212_x.htm (accessed on February 10, 2009).

Sullivan, John P. "Terrorism Early Warning and Co-Production of Counterterrorism Intelligence." *Canadian Association for Security and Intelligence Studies CASIS 20th Anniversary Conference.* October 21, 2005.

———. "Analytical Approaches for Sensing Novel and Emerging Threats." *49th Annual ISA Convention.* March 29, 2008.

Sunnucks, Mike. "Tough Employer Sanctions Measure Pushed for Ballot." *The Phoenix Business Journal.* April 20, 2007, 1.

Taleb, Nassim Nicholas. *The Black Swan: The Impact of the Highly Improbable.* New York: Random House, 2007.

Terrorism Risk Insurance Act of 2002. Public Law 107–197, *U.S. Statutes at Large* 116. 2002.

Terrorism Risk Insurance Program Reauthorization Act of 2007. Public Law 110–160, *U.S. Statutes at Large* 121. 2007.

"Texas v. Ohio." *Wall Street Journal.* Editorial. March 3, 2008, A16.

Tucker, Jonathan B. "Strategies for Countering Terrorism: Lessons from the Israeli Experience." *Journal of Homeland Security.* March 2003, 3.

United States and Mexico. "For the Temporary Migration of Mexican Agricultural Workers to the United States as Revised on April 26, 1943, by an Exchange of Notes between the American Embassy at Mexico City and the Mexican Ministry for Foreign Affairs." *The Official Bracero Agreement.* August 4, 1942.

Uniting and Strengthening America by Providing Appropriate Tools Required to Intercept and Obstruct Terrorism Act of 2001. Public Law 107–56, *U.S. Statutes at Large* 115, 2001.

U.S. Conference of Mayors. *Mayors 2004 Agenda: "Keeping America Strong.* February 9, 2004.

———. *2005 National Action Plan on Safety and Security in America's Cities.* October 25, 2005.

U.S. Customs and Border Protection. *Inspection Technology Fact Sheet.* Washington, DC, May 2006.

———. *Container Security Initiative Fact Sheet.* Washington, DC, March 2007.

———. *Customs-Trade Partnership Against Terrorism (C-TPAT) Fact Sheet*. Washington, DC, June 2007.

U.S. Department of Homeland Security. *Fiscal Year 2004 Urban Areas Security Initiative Grant Program: Program Guidelines and Application Kit*. Washington, DC: GPO, 2003.

———. *About CERT*. Washington, DC: DHS. 2008.

———. *About Citizen Corps*. Washington, DC: DHS. 2008.

———. *Analysis of Federal Requirements Final Report*. Washington, DC: DHS. October 2007.

———. *Comprehensive List of Staffing Requirements for National Preparedness Goal, Universal Task List (UTL), and Target Capabilities List (TCL)*. Washington, DC: DHS, February 2005.

———. *DHS Announces $1.7 Billion in Homeland Security Grants: Grants Will Build States' and Urban Areas' Preparedness—Attachment B*. Washington, DC: DHS, May 31, 2006.

———. *DHS Completes Key Framework for Critical Infrastructure Protection*. Washington, DC: DHS, May 21, 2007.

———. *Fact Sheet: Ready Campaign*. Washington, DC: DHS, October 1, 2004.

———. *Fiscal Year 2005 Homeland Security Grant Program: Program Guidelines and Application Kit*. Washington, DC: GPO, December 2004.

———. *FY 2007 Homeland Security Grant Program*. Washington, DC: GPO, July 18, 2007.

———. *FY 2007 Homeland Security Grant Program: Program Guidance and Application Kit*. Washington, DC: DHS, January 2007.

———. *FY 2007 Homeland Security Grant Program: Supplemental Resource – Fusion Capability Planning Tool*. Washington, DC: GPO, January 2007.

———. *Good Story: Public Health—Seattle & King County's Vulnerable Populations Action Team*. Washington, DC: DHS, 2007.

———. *Homeland Security Exercise and Evaluation Program (HSEEP)*. Washington, DC: GPO, February 2007.

———. *Interim National Infrastructure Protection Plan*. Washington, DC: DHS, February 2005.

———. *Interim National Preparedness Goal*. Washington, DC: DHS, March 31, 2005.

———. *National Infrastructure Protection Plan*. Washington, DC: DHS, June 2006.

———. *National Planning Scenarios*. Washington, DC: DHS, April 2005.

———. *National Preparedness Guidelines*. Washington, DC: DHS, September 2007, 4–5.

———. *National Response Plan*. Washington, DC: DHS, December 2004.

———. *Partners: Section 287(g), Immigration and Nationality Act; Delegation of Immigration Authority*. April 1, 2008.

———. *Preparedness Integration with the Regions*. Washington, DC: DHS, August 9, 2007.

———. *State of the Border—Border Security and Immigration Efforts Successful in Fiscal Year 2007*. Washington, DC: DHS, November 6, 2007.

———. *U.S. Government Seeks to End Litigation Undermining Expedited Removal of Salvadorans*. Washington, DC: DHS, November 17, 2005.

———. *Universal Task List: Version 2.1*. Washington: GPO, May 23, 2005.

U.S. Department of Justice. *The National Criminal Intelligence Sharing Plan.* June 2005.

———. *Chiquita Brands International Pleads Guilty to Making Payments to a Designated Terrorist Organization and Agrees to Pay $25 Million Fine.* March 19, 2007.

———. "Jail Inmates at Midyear 2007." *Bureau of Justice Bulletin* NCJ 221945. June 2008, 1.

———. "Prison Inmates at Midyear 2007." *Bureau of Justice Statistics Bulletin* NCJ 221944. June 2008, 1.

U.S. Government Accountability Office. *Management of First Responder Grant Programs and Efforts to Improve Accountability Continue to Evolve.* Washington, DC: GPO, April 12, 2005.

———. *Homeland Security: DHS' Efforts to Enhance First Responders' All-Hazards Capabilities Continue to Evolve.* Washington, DC: GPO, July 2005.

———. *Homeland Security: Federal Efforts Are Helping to Alleviate Some Challenges Encountered by State and Local Information Fusion Centers.* Washington, DC: GPO, October 2007.

———. *DHS Risk-Based Grant Methodology Is Reasonable, but Current Version's Measure of Vulnerability Is Limited.* Washington, DC: GPO, June 2008.

U.S. House Committee on Appropriations Subcommittee on Homeland Security. *Homeland Security: Applying Risk Management Principles to Guide Federal Investments.* February 7, 2007.

———. "Emergency Preparedness and Response: Some Issues and Challenges Associated with Major Emergency Incidents." Washington, DC: GAO, February 2006.

U.S. House of Representatives. *Final Vote Results for Roll Call 161 on H.R. 1268.* 2005.

———. Committee on Homeland Security, Subcommittee on Intelligence, Information Sharing, and Terrorism Risk Assessment. *The Way Forward with Fusion Centers: Challenges and Strategies for Change.* 110th Cong., 1st sess., 2007.

———. Committee on the Judiciary. *How Does Illegal Immigration Impact American Taxpayers and Will the Reid-Kennedy Amnesty Worsen the Blow.* 109th Cong., 2d sess., 2006.

———. Committee on the Judiciary Subcommittee on Immigration, Citizenship, Refugees, Border Security, and International Law. *Summary of U.S. Immigration History.* 110th Cong., 1st sess., 2007.

———. Committee on Oversight and Government Reform. *FEMA Preparedness in 2007 and Beyond.* 110th Cong., 1st sess., 2007.

———. Committee on Transportation and Infrastructure Subcommittee on Economic Development, Public Buildings, and Emergency Management. *Recovering after Katrina: Ensuring That FEMA Is Up to the Task.* 109th Cong., 1st sess., 2005.

———. Select Bipartisan Committee to Investigate the Preparation for and Response to Hurricane Katrina. *A Failure of Initiative: Final Report of the Select Bipartisan Committee to Investigate the Preparation for and Response to Hurricane Katrina.* 2006.

———. Subcommittee on Intelligence, Information Sharing, and Terrorism Risk Assessment. *Homegrown Terrorism.* 110th Cong., 1st sess., 2007.

U.S. Immigration and Customs Enforcement. *Fact Sheet: The ICE T. Don Hutto Family Residential Facility: Maintaining Family Unity, Enforcing Immigration Laws.* Washington, DC: DHS, April 2007.

U.S. Senate. Roll Call Votes 109th Congress, 1st Session. *On the Conference Report H.R. 1268.* 2005.

———. Committee on Governmental Affairs. *The Local Role in Homeland Security.* 107th Cong., 1st sess., 2001.

———. Committee on Homeland Security and Governmental Affairs. *Counterfeit Goods: Easy Cash for Criminals and Terrorists.* 109th Cong., 1st sess., 2005.

———. Committee on Homeland Security and Government Affairs. *Prison Radicalization: Are Terrorist Cells Forming in U.S. Cell Blocks?.* 109th Cong., 2d sess., 2006.

———. Committee on Homeland Security and Governmental Affairs. *Hurricane Katrina: A Nation Still Unprepared*, Washington, DC: GPO, 2006.

———. Committee on Homeland Security and Government Affairs. *FEMA's Level of Preparedness.* 110th Cong., 2d sess., 2008.

———. Committee on Homeland Security and Governmental Affairs. *Present View of the Terrorist Threat.* 109th Cong., 2d sess., 2006.

U.S. War Department. *United States Strategic Bombing Survey Summary Report (Pacific War).* Washington, DC: GPO, July 1, 1946.

Vise, David A. "Gates Cites Hiring Woes, Criticizes Visa Restrictions." *Washington Post.* April 28, 2005, E05.

Watson, Alan D. "The Committees of Safety and the Coming of the American Revolution in North Carolina, 1774–1776." *The North Carolina Historical Review.* April 1996, 132.

Webster, Daniel. *Speech at Niblo's Saloon.* New York City, March 15, 1837.

The White House. *National Strategy for Homeland Security.* Washington, DC: GPO, July 2002.

———. *Fact Sheet: Improving Border Security and Immigration within Existing Law.* Washington, DC: The White House, August 10, 2007.

———. *The Federal Response to Hurricane Katrina: Lessons Learned.* Washington, DC: The White House, February 23, 2006.

———. *National Strategy for Homeland Security.* Washington, DC: GPO, October 2007.

———. *National Strategy for Information Sharing.* Washington, DC: The White House, October 2007.

Williams, Lance, and Eric McCormick. "Al Qaeda Terrorist Worked with FBI." *San Francisco Chronicle.* November 4, 2001, A-1.

WNBC-TV. "Poll: New Yorkers Oppose Plan to Allow Illegal Aliens Driver's Licenses." *MSNBC.com.* October 15, 2007.

Wohlstetter, Roberta. *Pearl Harbor: Warning and Decision.* Palo Alto, CA: Stanford University Press, 1962.

World Islamic Front. *Jihad against Jews and Crusaders.* February 23, 1998; http://www.pbs.org/newshour/terrorism/international/fatwa_1998.html (accessed February 9, 2009).

Wright, Lawrence. *The Looming Tower: Al-Qaeda and the Road to 9/11.* New York: Knopf, 2006.

Zinn, Howard. *A People's History of the United States: 1492–Present.* New York: HarperCollins, 2003.

Index

10+2 Rule, 33
24-hour Rule, 33
2005 National Action Plan on Safety and Security in America's Cities, 48
42 U.S.C. section 1983, 130
96-hour Advance Notice of Arrival Rule, 33

Abdi, Nuradin, 168n48
Academy of Counter-Terrorist Education, 171n53
Advanced Targeting System, 33
Aeneid, 14
Al Qaeda, xiv, 7, 11, 158n38; bombing of Khost training camps, 12; bombing in Yeman, 8; estimating al Qaeda's capabilities, 11; exploitation of weakened security, 130; first attack on WTC, 7, 10, 22–23, 82; first known bombing, 10; focus of al Qaeda, 9, 81; historical record, 64; Khobar Towers attack, 11; Saudi Arabia National Guard center attack, 11; search for bin Laden, 12; September 11, 2001, attack, 12; ties to Columbus, Ohio, 168n48; training camps, 7; U.S. embassy bombings, 11; U.S.S. Cole bombing, 11; use of the Internet, 126
Allbaugh, Joe, 27; appointment to FEMA, 132; career experience, 98; fight to keep FEMA out of DHS, 27; political use of FEMA, 98
American Civil Liberties Union, 115
American National Standards Institute, 148
American Public Works Administration, 169n20
Analysis, Dissemination, Visualization, Insight, and Semantic Enhancement system, 126
Animal and Plant Health Inspection Service, 28
Anti-Federalists, 153
Arizona Human Smuggling Act, 123
Arizona Proposition 200, 123
Arizona Proposition 203, 122
Arpaio, Joseph, 123, 124
Ashcroft, John, 119
Ashwood, Albert, 93; blaming DHS for FEMA failures, 93; federalization mindset of, 100
Assistant Secretary for Civil Defense Liaison, 20
Association of State and Territorial Health Officials, 169n20
Atta, Mohammed, 119
Augustus, 128
Azzam, Abdullah, 7

Baca, Lee, 138
Bacon, Nathaniel, 14–15
Bacon's Rebellion, 15
al-Banna, Hassan, 5, 6; death of, 5; founding of Muslim Brotherhood, 5; nature of Islam, 5;
Battle of Antietam, xiv
Battle of Concord, 15
Battle of Lexington, 15
Battle of Thermopylae, 3
Beltway, x, xiv, 47, 96, 122, 126, 176n89
Beverley, Roger, 14
Biannual Strategy Implementation Report, 85
Bill of Rights, 16, 45
Bin Laden, Osama, xiv, 7, 11, 13; in Afghanistan, 7; America as weak, 8, 10, 11, 12; confiscation of assets by Sudanese government, 8; first fatwa against America, 8–9; loss of citizenship and inheritance, 8; in Pakistan, 8; offer to defend Saudi Arabia, 8; radicalization of, 7; return to Afghanistan, 8; return to Saudi Arabia, 8; second fatwa against America, 9; in Sudan, 8; upbringing in Saudi Arabia, 7
bomb shelters, 20–21
Border and Transportation Security Directorate, 28; elimination of, 29
border security, xiv, 27, 32, 51, 52, 112, 117
Bouyeri, Mohammed, 182n3
Bracero Program, 111; union opposition to, 112
Brandeis, Justice Louis, xiv; opposition to centralization, 71
Bratton, William, 129, 139
British, 15; apprehension of cyber terrorist, 35; passage of the Metropolitan Police Act, 128; use of capabilities-based planning, 169n10
Broken Windows, 129
Brown, Michael, 27, 174n10; appointment to FEMA, 98; blaming DHS for FEMA failures, 92–93; career experience, 98; failure to use National Response Plan, 92; fight against Second Stage Review changes, 29; fight to keep grants from moving to ODP, 29; lack of emergency management experience, 27; loss of job after Hurricane Katrina, 92; political use of FEMA, 98; refusal to communicate with DHS, 92; validation from Congress, 29; White House encouragement to circumvent DHS, 92
Bull Report, 19
Bulletin of the Atomic Scientists, 21
Bureau of Customs and Border Protection (CBP), 28, 32, 34; creation of Container Security Initiative, 33; creation of Customs-Trade Partnership Against Terrorism program, 33; partnership with Texas, 52–53; Secure Border Initiative, 32; Secure Freight Initiative, 33; securing commerce, 33; securing the borders, 32
Bureau of Immigration and Customs Enforcement (ICE), 25, 28, 29, 31; increase in activities, 114–115; interior enforcement activities, 34; number of agents, 39; opening of the Don T. Hutto Detention Center, 115; staffing levels, 117; use of 287(g) agreements, 117, 119
Bureau of Public Roads, 96
Bush Doctrine, 12
Bush, George H.W., 98
Bush, George W., 12; appointment of Joe Allbaugh to FEMA, 98; appointment of Michael Brown to FEMA, 98; appointment of Tom Ridge to head the Homeland Security Council, 27; creating the Department of Homeland Security, 27; increase in disaster declarations, 97; issuance of HSPD-8, 72; issuance of HSPD-8 Annex 1, 79; lessons learned from failed response to Hurricane Andrew, 97–98; record on civil defense, 14
Bush, Jeb, 47; defense of state sovereignty, 48, 91–92

capabilities-based planning, 49, 74, 78, 169n10
cargo security, xiv, 32, 33, 164n46

INDEX

Carr, Caleb, 4
Carter, David, 137; 150
Carter, Jimmy, 21; creation of FEMA, 21, 96
Categorical Assistance Progress Report, 85
Center for Domestic Preparedness, 171n53
Central Intelligence Agency, 158n38
Chemical, Biological, Radiological, and Nuclear Countermeasures Program, 28
Chiquita Brands International, 148
Citizen Corps, 14, 144
Citizens Defense Corps, 18
Citizenship and Immigration Services (CIS), 28, 29, 31, 32; backlog of work, 34; transformation of, 114
Civil Air Patrol, 18
Civil Defense Agency, 19
Civil Defense Board (*see also* Bull Report), 19
Civilian Volunteer Medical Reserve Corps, 144
Civilian War Services Branch, 18
Chertoff, Michael, 29; creation of "super" UASI jurisdictions, 62; fixing FEMA, 91, 101; inability to review NPG, 77; lack of information from FEMA, 92; on burdensome congressional oversight, 36; movement to risk-based funding formulas, 62; reform of immigration activities, 114–115; relationship with Michael Brown, 92; Second Stage Review, 29, 93–94; speech at NEMA, 91; use of TCL to allocate grants, 67
Chinese Exclusion Act of 1882, 111
Clark, Tom, xiii
Cleveland, Grover, 95
Clinton, Bill, 12; acceptance of welfare reform, 58; appointment of James Lee Witt, 98; bin Laden on, 11; criticism from Jesse Jackson, 94; deployment of military, 22; failure to enforce immigration laws, 114; government shutdown of 1995, 44; his peace dividend defense cuts, 22; increase in disaster declarations, 96–97; lessons learned from failed response to Hurricane Andrew, 98; record for single year issuance of disaster declarations, 98
Coast Guard, 28, 32, 34, 138; securing commerce, 33; securing the waterways, 32; Integrated Deepwater program, 32
Cold War, 3, 10, 13, 20, 22, 28, 23, 64, 72, 87, 99
Colonial Period, 13, 14–15
Commission of the Accreditation of Law Enforcement Agencies, 130
Committees of Correspondence and Safety, 15
Community Emergency Response Team, 14, 144
Community Policing, 129, 134, 135
Congress, 16, 20, 21, 23; additional FEMA reforms, 91–92, 101, 103; attempted passage of comprehensive immigration reform, 112; burdensome oversight of DHS, 36; cessation of the *Bracero* program, 112; creation of the *Bracero* program, 111; exemptions from immigration laws for Mexican migrants, 112; funding of CIS, 34; fury over grant allocations, 169n43; minimizing the dilution of UASI funds, 80–81; need to permit use of No Match letters by DHS, 115; passage of literacy test and head tax for admission into America, 111; passage of national origin quotas, 111; passage of the Chinese Exclusion Act of 1882, 111; passage of the Homeland Security Act of 2002, 27; passage of the Immigration and Nationality Act of 1952, 112; passage of the Immigration Reform and Control Act of 1986, 112; passage of the PATRIOT Act, 27; passage of the Robert T. Stafford Disaster Relief and Emergency Assistance Act, 96; passage of the Terrorism Risk Insurance Act, 56–57; passage of the Texas Seed Act, 95; power to pass private legislation, 115; reform of SHSP and UASI, 81–83; reorganization of DHS, 29; unfunded mandates, 37; validation of Michael Brown, 29

Congressional Budget Office, 112
Container Security Initiative (CSI), 33, 164n46
Continental Army, 15
Contract with America, 44
Coolidge, Calvin, 153
Cooperative Agreements, 86–87, 103
Cooperative Training Outreach Program, 78
Corrective Action Program, 78
Council for Excellence in Government, 143
Council of National Defense, 16–17
Council of State Governments, 169n20
counterterrorism, xii, 25, 50, 51, 53, 54, 125, 134, 136, 137, 138–139, 154; building capabilities of, 126–127, 130; FBI as lead federal agency, 132–133; focus on data mining, 126; historical failure of intelligence community, 125; need for intelligence analysts, 150; need for linguists, 150
Countering the Changing Threat of International Terrorism, 25
Criminal Intelligence File Guidelines, 136
Customs Service, 28
Customs-Trade Partnership Against Terrorism (C-TPAT), 33, 164n45
cyber jihadists, 35
cyber security, 34–35, 127

Dar es Salaam, Tanzania, 11
Darwinism, 43, 111
De Canas v. Bica, 119–120, 171
Declaration of Independence, 3
Declaration of War against Americans Occupying the Land of the Two Holy Places, 8
Defense Civil Preparedness Agency, 21
Defense Councils, 17, 19
Delamare, Nicolas, 128
Democracy Corps, 43
Director of National Intelligence, 139
disaster management, xi, xiv, 107, 154; building capabilities, 50, 55; centralization and federalization of, 38, 49; focus on money, 100

District of Columbia (see Beltway), 16
Division of State and Local Cooperation, 17
Domestic Emergency Support Team, 28
domestic intelligence, xiv (see counterterrorism)
Domestic Nuclear Detection Office, 32–33
Don T. Hutto Detention Center, 115
Dossier System, 130
Dragani, Nancy, 105
Dun & Bradstreet, 148

E-Verify, 34, 124; as a good business practice, 148; mandatory element of LAWA, 123; reauthorization of, 116; use by the private sector, 116; use of constitutional, 120, 123
Egyptian Islamic Jihad, 6, 7; losing the Muslim Street, 7
Eisenhower, Dwight D., 13, 98
Electoral College, 64, 98
Elsenboss, Carina, 88
Emergency Preparedness and Response Directorate, 28, elimination of, 29
Energetic Materials Research and Testing Center, 171n53
Energy Security and Assurance Program, 28
Enron, 125, 128, 182n10
Environmental Measures Laboratory, 28
Executive Order 8757, 17
eugenics, 111
European Union, 179n38

al-Faisal, Turki, 8
Farouq mosque, 10
fatwa, 8, 9, 10
FBInet, 133
Federal Bureau of Investigation (FBI), 10, 158n38; as lead federal agency on state and local intelligence, 39, 132, 133; conducting background checks, 116; conflict with DHS, 39–40, 132–133; establishment of JTTFs, 131–132; information sharing systems, 133; investigation of active cases, 126; landmark plot, 10; modification of surveillance

guidelines, 137; staffing level, 126; use of Field Intelligence Groups, 133, 139
Federal Civil Defense Act of 1950, 20
Federal Civil Defense Administration, 20
Federal Computer Incident Response Center, 28
Federal Disaster Assistance Administration, 21
Federal Emergency Management Agency (FEMA), 21, 26; as direct report to the Secretary, 29; blaming DHS for failures, 29, 92–93; budget issues, 93, 98; creation of, 27, 96; continued management challenges, 38, 101; expansion of powers, 48; failure to collaborate in developing NIMS, 85; federalization of disasters, 38, 49–50, 66, 94, 103; fight against Second Stage Review changes, 29; fight to keep grants from moving to ODP, 28–29; fight to keep it out of DHS, 27; history of poor performance, 29, 86; increase in disaster declarations, 96–98; limiting FEMA's ability to issue declarations, 99, 101–103; merger into DHS, 23, 98; response to Hurricane Andrew, 29, 94, 97, 98, 99; response to Hurricane Floyd, 29, 94; response to Hurricane Katrina, 21, 27, 29, 38, 75, 91–93, 100–101, 103; takeover of ODP, 39; troubled relationship with DHS, 27, 174n10; use of actuarial data, 56, 101–102, 104, 143, 154; use of cooperative agreements, 86; use of data by the private sector, 145
Federal Government, x, xi, xii; approach to risk, 58–63; as coordinator, consolidator, and policy arbiter, xv; expansion of, 17, 46, 96; flawed model for certain issues, xv, 25, 126; historical role during disasters, 95–99; inflation of risk, 63; lack of response to multiple al Qaeda attacks, 11; Potomac Fever, 43, 132
Federal Insurance Administration, 21
Federal Law Enforcement Training Center, 28
Federal Preparedness Agency, 21

Federal Preparedness Agency of the General Services Administration, 21
Federal Preparedness Coordinators, 79, 171n59
Federal Protective Service, 28
federalism, ix, 16, 31, 45; adherence to, 73; crossroad of, 50; defense of, 91; failure to follow, xv, 134; founders concept of, xi; number of state and local personnel, 116–117; relevance today, 153–155; victory of, 120; weakening of during the Progressive Era, 46–47
Federalist 10, 45
Federalist 17, xii
Federalist 51, 45
Fi Zilial al-Qur'an, 6
Field Intelligence Groups, 133, 139
Fire Corps, 144
First Battle of Mogadishu, 10
First Gulf War, 8
Folsom State Prison, 135, 157
Founding Fathers, x, xv, 14, 16, 45, 47, 118, 153
Fourteenth Amendment, 32
Franklin, Benjamin, xiii
Fraternal Order of Police, 169n20
Freeman, Michael, 74
Friedman, George, 11, 125
Fujita Scale, 103
Fusion Center, 40; conflict with JTTFs, 40; creation of, 132–133; difficulty staffing, 134; merge into JTTS, 40; weakness of, 133

Gaddis, John Lewis, 64
Galen, 141
Gates, Bill, 114
Gingrich, Newt, 43
Giuliani, Rudy, 23
Gladwell, Malcolm, 125, 182n10; conclusions on Enron, 128; on the difference between a puzzle and a mystery, 127–128
Global Justice Information Sharing Initiative, 137
Gold Mohur Hotel, 10

Great Depression, 17
Great Society, 46

H-1B, 114
HANDS: Helping Americans Needing Disaster Support, 144
Handschu v. Special Services, 137
Hanjour, Hani, 119
Hayak, Friedrich, 134
al-Hazmi, Nawaf, 119
Henke, Tracy, 67; changing allocation component from the TCL to effectiveness, 67; noting no change in risk to New York City, 68
Holland and Lincoln Tunnel attack, 10
Holmes, Oliver Wendell, 111
Homeland Security Act of 2002, 27, 28
Homeland Security Advisory Council, 138
Homeland Security Advisory Council Emergency Response Senior Advisory Committee, 77
Homeland Security Advisory Council State and Local Senior Advisory Committee, 77
Homeland Security Council, 27, 29; bureaucratic intransigence of, 77; lack of experience, 77
Homeland Security Data Network, 133
Homeland Security Exercise and Evaluation Program, 78, 147
Homeland Security Information Network, 40, 133
Homeland Security Presidential Directive-5 (HSPD-5), 99; creation of the National Response Plan, 99; role of the federal government, 99–100
Homeland Security Presidential Directive-8 (HSPD-8), 72; development of lessons learned system, 79; development of national exercise program, 78; development of national training program, 78; development of the National Preparedness Goal, 73–78; new definition of preparedness, 72; Senior Steering Committee, 74, 77
Homeland Security Presidential Directive-8 Annex 79
Hopley Report, 19–20
House of Representatives, 44; design of, 45; vote on Real ID Act, 47
HSPD-8 Senior Steering Committee, 74, 77
Huber, Peter, 144
Hurricane Andrew, 29, 94, 99; lessons learned, 97, 98
Hurricane Dean, 101
Hurricane Floyd, 29, 94; failure of FEMA, 94
Hurricane Katrina, 11, 20, 21, 27, 29, 37, 38, 47, 48, 57, 93, 94, 97, 99, 101, 103, 141, 142; confirmation of TCL capabilities list, 75; insurance industry response, 78; omissions in White House report, 92; reshuffling of federal agencies after, 91–92; resiliency of the private sector, 147
Hurricane Wilma, 48

Illegal Immigration Reform and Immigrant Responsibility Act of 1996, 50; use of section 287(g), 50, 117, 119
Illusion of Peace, 22–23
Immigration, 34, 48, 50; explosion of illegal immigration, 112; federal role, 114–116; history of immigration, 110–112; state and local role, 116–122; three-legged stool of, 113–114
Immigration and Nationality Act of 1952 (INA), 112, 121; illegal presence as a civil violation, 117; use of section 287(g), 50, 117, 119
Immigration and Naturalization Service, 28
Immigration Reform and Control Act of 1986 (IRCA), 112, 120, 123
In the Shades of the Qur'an, 6
Information Analysis, 28, 29
Information Analysis and Infrastructure Protection Directorate, 28, 40
Information Sharing Environment, 131, 133
Infrastructure Protection, 28, 29
Inspector General (IG), 30, 87; cyber security challenges, 35; FEMA failures,

38; financial management challenges, 30; financial oversight and accountability challenges, 30–31; grant recipient challenges, 37, 87
Intelligence Community (IC), 126
Intelligence-led Policing, 129–130
Interim National Infrastructure Protection Plan, 35
Interim National Preparedness Goal (*see also* National Preparedness Goal), 68, 77
interior illegal immigration enforcement, xiv, 37, 50, 112, 113, 114, 116, 117, 122
Internal Revenue Service, 121
International Association of Chiefs of Police, 127, 135, 169n20
International Association of Emergency Managers, 169n20
International Association of Fire Chiefs, 169n20
Investment Justification, 67–69, 86, 87
al-Iraqi, Abu Hajer 8
Islamic jihadism, x, 3, 4, 6, 7, 14, 23, 54, 128, 135, 136, 155

Jackson, Jesse, 94
Jadwat, Omar, 109
Jam'iyyat Ul-Islam Is-Sheeh, 135
Jamestown Settlement, 14
Jarrah, Ziad, 119
jihad, 5, 6, 7, 9, 35
Johnson, Lyndon B., 25; decrease in disaster declarations, 97
Joint Regional Intelligence Center, 139
Joint Terrorism Task Force (JTTF), 39, 40, 54; establishment of, 131–132; need for more resources, 150; reform of, 133–134; takeover of fusion centers, 134; use in first WTC bombing, 131

Keenan, George, 64
Kelling, George L., 129
Kempthorne, Dirk, 74
Khobar Towers, 11
Khrushchev, Nikita, 22, 48

La Guardia, Fiorello, 17–18
Laboratories of democracy, xiv, 40
Landis, James M., 18–19
Laocoön, 14
Law Enforcement Intelligence: A Guide for State, Local, and Tribal Law Enforcement Agencies, 137
Law Enforcement Intelligence Unit, 136
Law Enforcement Online, 133, 183n47
Legal Arizona Workers Act (LAWA), 123; legislative fight with Governor Janet Napolitano, 123; mandatory use of E-Verify system, 123; upheld by federal appellate court, 123; upheld by federal district court, 123
Lessons Learned Information Sharing website, 79, 88
Letter to the Annual Meeting of Quakers, 15
Long War, 5, 14
Los Angeles Fire Department, 144
Los Angeles Police Department, 138; development of Suspicious Activity Reports, 139; preparation for Summer Olympics, 138
Los Angeles Sheriff's Office, 138; creation of Terrorist Early Warning group, 138
Louis XIV, 128

Ma'alim fi-l-Tariq, 6
Madison, James, 45, 46, 154
Management Directorate, 28
maritime security, xiv
Martin, Dean, 124
McCraw, Steve, 51
Metropolitan Police Act, 128–129
Michigan State University, 150–151
Milestones, 6
Millennium attacks, 11
Mexican-American War, 16, 46
Miller, Karen, 74
Mohammed, Ali Abdelsoud, 158n38
Mohammed, Khalid Sheikh, 10–11
Mujahideen, 6, 7, 8
Muslim American Homeland Security Congress, 138
Muslim Brotherhood, 5, 6, 9

Nagin, Ray, 91
Napolitano, Janet, 123; loss of legislative battle on LAWA, 123; veto of additional illegal immigration mezasures, 124
Nasser, Gamal Abdel, 6
National Association of City & County Health Officials, 169n20
National Bio-weapons Defense Analysis Center, 28
National Center for Exercise Excellence, 171n53
National Commission on Terrorism, 25
National Commission on Terrorist Attacks Upon the United States (9/11 Commission), 12; comment of first responders, 141; comments on securing transportation system, 33; conflict between DHS and DOJ/FBI, 133; counterterrorism capabilities needs, 150; failure by the federal government to change policies to prevent the 9/11 attack, 12; federal focus, 31, 32; first use of JTTF, 131; lack of career path in intelligence, 130; on congressional reform, 36; on federal government's approach to risk and grants, 62; on New York City's location of emergency operations center in World Trade Center, 23; on Nunn-Lugar-Domenici reforms, 102; recommendations on FBI reform, 136
National Communications System, 28
National Criminal Intelligence Sharing Plan, 137
National Data Exchange, 133
National Domestic Preparedness Consortium, 96, 150
National Domestic Preparedness Office, 28
National Emergency Management Agency, 91, 94; creation of, 96
National Emergency Response and Rescue Training Center, 171n53
National Exercise Program, 78–79
National Fire Prevention and Control Administration, 21
National Fire Protection Association, 148

National Incident Management System, 85
National Infrastructure Protection Center, 28
National Infrastructure Protection Plan, 35, 145
National Planning Scenarios, 74, 79; creation of prevention prequels and attack trees, 169n22; use in developing task list and TCL, 74–75; use by the private sector, 145, 147; use in National Exercise Program, 78
National Preparedness Goal (NPG), 68, 74; change to guidelines, 77; change to interim status, 77; collaborative national effort to develop, 77; delay in finalizing, 77; development of, 76–79; little difference between interim and guidelines versions, 77, 170n48; release for national review, 77; review by Homeland Security Advisory Council Emergency Response Senior Advisory Committee, 77; review by Homeland Security Advisory Council State and Local Senior Advisory Committee, 77; review by HSPD-8 Senior Steering Committee, 77; review by State, Local, and Tribal Working Group, 77; use of Integrated Concept Teams, 169n20
National Preparedness Guidelines (*see also* National Preparedness Goal), 77, 170n48
National Preparedness System, 49, 78; components of, 78
National Response Plan, 74, 92, 99
National Security Resources Board, 20
National Sheriffs' Association, 169n20
National Strategy for Homeland Security, 27, 29
National Strategy for Information Sharing, 132–133
National Volunteer Fire Council, 169n20
National Weather Service Community Preparedness Program, 21
Nationwide Plan Review, 79, 102
New Deal, 46; expansion of disaster response, 96; similarity to today's federal government, 72

New Federalism, 43
New York Police Department (NYPD), 129; commissioner statement on importance of JTTF, 132; criticism of DHS, 132; membership in JTTF, 131–132
New York State Emergency Management Office, 169n20
Ninth Amendment, 45, 118
Nixon, Richard, 43
Nokrashi, Mahmud Fahmi, 5
Nuclear Incident Response Team, 28

Office for Domestic Preparedness (ODP), 21, 28; adherence to federalism principles, 73; collaborative effort in developing the TCL and NPG, 73–78; creation of one-stop shop and first name change, 28–29; FEMA's attempt to takeover, 27; FEMA's takeover of, 29; lead in implementing HSPD-8, 73; relationship with FBI and DOJ, 39–40; unification of preparedness, 29; use of grants, 40, 86; use of state and local subject matter experts to develop the TCL, 74; use of workshops to development task list and TCL, 74–77
Office of Civil and Defense Mobilization, 21
Office of Civil Defense Planning, 19–20
Office of Civilian Defense, 17–18, 19
Office of Emergency Planning, 21
Office of Emergency Preparedness, 21
Office of Preparedness, 21
Office of State and Local Government Coordination and Preparedness (see Office for Domestic Preparedness), 28
Ohio Emergency Management Agency, 105; adoption of TCL, 106; creation of Assistance Tool Box, 105; creation of the Ohio Family Preparedness Wheel, 107; deployment of video telecommunication conferences, 106; development of EMA Preliminary Damage Assessment Field Guide, 105; development of the Ohio Response System, 106; distribution of videos for local governments, 107; use of Public Assistance Handbook, 105; use of training courses for local officials, 105
On Common Sense, 15
Operation Safe Jails, 139

Paine, Thomas, 15
Paul, Christopher, 168n48
Pearce, Russell, 124
Pearl Harbor, 18, 26
Pearl Harbor: Warning and Decision, 26
Pentagon, x, 11
Perry, William, 28
Pequot War, 14
Pickering, Leisha, 144
Plum Island Animal Disease Center, 28
Powhatan, 14; his tribe, 14
preparedness, xiv, 28, 29, 78, 79; the new definition of, 72; old emergency management definition, 72
privacy, 50, 126, 139; attack on the dossier system, 130; use of civil liberties groups, 136
Problem-oriented Policing, 129
Progressive Era, 46; adherence to Darwinism and eugenics, 111; impact of national origin quotas on Jews during the Holocaust, 111; leadership of Margaret Sanger, 111; support for discriminatory immigration laws, 111
Prophet Mohammed, 7

al-Qamari, Essam, 6
Quakers, 15
Qutb, Muhammad, 6, 7; as professor in Saudi Arabia, 6
Qutb, Sayyid, 3; death of, 5; intellectual leader of Muslim Brotherhood, 6; interpretation of jihad, 6, 9; Osama bin Laden's reading of, 7; travel to America, 5

Rahman, Omar Abdel, 10
Readiness Quotient, 143
Ready.gov, 14, 143, 186n19
Reagan, Ronald, x, xi, 25, 43; decrease in disaster declarations, 97–98; the problem of government, 44

Real ID Act, 34, 115; funding for, 46; passage of, 46–47
Really Simple Syndication, 149
Reconstruction Finance Corporation, 96
Regional Information Sharing System, 133, 183n47
Republican Revolution, 43; devolution to Republican Corruption, 44; government shutdown of 1995, 44; growth of government, 44; passage of welfare reform, 44
Restatement of the Obvious, xv, 113
Rhode, Patrick, 174n10
Richter Scale, 103
Ridge, Tom, 27, 141; assignment of HSPD-8 implementation to ODP, 73; first reorganization of DHS, 28–29; relationship with Michael Brown, 29, 92
risk, 55; definition of, 55
Robert T. Stafford Disaster Relief and Emergency Assistance Act, 96, 100, 103
Rome, 128; development of decentralized law enforcement system, 128
Roosevelt, Franklin D., 17; expansion of disaster response activities, 96; the federal government as an instrument of unimagined power, 71; threat to pack the Supreme Court, 46
Rules of Survival, 21
Rumsfield, Donald, 12, 55

al-Sadat, Anwar, 6
Saffir-Simpson Scale, 103
Samuelson, Robert J., 51
Sanford, Mark, 47
Sanger, Margaret, 111
al-Saud, Fahd bin Abdul Aziz 8
Saudi Arabia National Guard attack, 11
Schelling, Thomas C., 26
Science and Technology Directorate, 28
Scruggs, Dickie, 57
Seattle/King County Public Health, 88–90; creation of Community Communication Network, 88; creation of King County Healthcare Coalition, 89; creation of Vulnerable Populations Action Team, 88; development of Community Based Standards, 89; development of Pandemic Flu video, 90; designation as an Advanced Practice Center, 90; lessons learned from SARS scare, 88; use of lessons from other jurisdictions, 88–89; use of Regional Medical Resource Center, 89; work of Special Advisory Group, 89
Second Amendment, 16
Second Continental Congress, 15
Second Stage Review, 29; changes not made until after Hurricane Katrina, 93–94
Secret Service, 28
Sector Specific Plans, 35
Secure Border Initiative, 32
Secure Freight Initiative, 33
Senate, 45–46; vote on Real ID Act, 47
Sensitive Compartmental Information Operational Network, 133
September 11, 2001 attack, ix, x, xi, xiv, 9, 10, 11; activation of the plot, 12; eight year gap between first and second al Qaeda attacks, 26; exploitation of weakened security, 130; exploited our freedoms, 127; lessons from the Pearl Harbor attack, 26; reshuffling of federal agencies after, 27; use of flight schools, 12, 127
Seventeenth Amendment, 46
Severe Acute Respiratory Syndrome, 88, 89
Sheehan, Michael, 11
Sixteenth Amendment, 46
South Carolina State Port Authority, 83
Soviet Union, ix, 6, 7, 8, 19, 20; fall of, 22
Spanish-American War, 46
Spartans, 3
Spitzer, Elliott, 181n92
Standard on Disaster/Emergency Management and Business Continuity Programs, 148

State Homeland Security Program, 81; reform of, 81–82
State, Local, and Tribal Working Group, 77
Story, Joseph, 109
Strategic National Stockpile/National Disaster Medical System, 28
Strickland, Ted, 47
Suez Canal, 149
Sullivan, John, 138
Supremacy Clause, 118
Suspicious Activity Reports, 139
Systemic Alien Verification for Entitlements, 121

takfir, 7
Taleb, Nassim Nicholas, 56
Taliban, 8; warnings to the Taliban about al Qaeda, 12
Target Capabilities List (TCL), 18, 27; adoption and use in Ohio, 106; applicable across potential attack scenarios, 167n28; codification by state legislatures, 84; confirmation of capabilities by Hurricane Katrina, 75; delay in finalizing, 77; development of, 74–77; model of true partnership, 49; providing strategic template for defending America, 37; use in allocating grants, 67–70; use in developing NPS, 78; use of cooperative agreements to build, 86
Tenth Amendment, 16, 45, 109, 118, 124
Terrorism Risk Insurance Act, 56–57
Terrorist Early Warning group, 138
Texas, 51; activation of amateur radio network, 52; creation of Border Security Operation Centers and Joint Operations and Intelligence Centers, 52–53; launching of Texas Data Exchange System, 53; Operation Border Star, 52; Operation Rio Grande, 52; Operation Wrangler, 52; partnership with CBP, 53; seizures, 53; steeped in federalism, 51; use of private partnerships in disaster response, 51–52; use of Texas Data Exchange System, 53–54
Texas Seed Act, 95

The 9/11 Commission Report: Final Report of The National Commission on Terrorist Attacks Upon the United States (9/11 Commission Report), 23, 26, 131, 136
The Need for Civilian Protection, 18
Tora Bora, 7
Total Information Awareness, 126
Training and Data Exchange Partnership, 78
Training Information System, 78
Transportation Security Administration (TSA), 28, 31, 32; grants moved to ODP, 28; securing transportation modes, 33
Transportation Worker Identification Credential, 34
Treatise on the Police, 128
Truman, Harry, 19, 20
Tsouli, Younes, 35
Tytler, Alexander, 155

Under Secretary for Preparedness, 29
Under Secretary for Policy, 29
Uniting and Strengthening America by Providing Appropriate Tools Required to Intercept and Obstruct Terrorism Act of 2001 (PATRIOT Act), 27
Universal Adversary, 169n22
Urban Areas Security Initiative (UASI), 49; allocation discrepancies, 67–70; allocation of grant funds, 65–66; creation of "super" UASI jurisdictions, 62; dilution of finds, 80; expansion of eligible jurisdictions, 63, 80–81; political make-up of cities, 64–65; reform of, 80–83
U.S. Army Appropriation Act of 1916, 16
U.S. Army Corps of Engineers, 25, 96
U.S. Chamber of Commerce, 115
U.S. Civil War, xiv, 3, 16, 46
U.S. Conference of Mayors, 17; call for more funds, 48, 73
U.S. Constitution, ix-x, 13, 15, 27, 31; Bill of Rights, 45; checks and balances, 45–46; federal roles and

responsibilities, 32; preservation of, 153; structural changes to, 46; Supremacy Clause, 118
U.S. Department of Defense (*see also* War Department), 11, 19, 30
U.S. Department of Homeland Security (DHS), xiv; allocation of grant funds, 67–70; areas of focus, 32; blamed for FEMA failures, 93–94; budget of, 28; burdensome congressional oversight, 36; comparison to creation of Department of Defense, 30; creation of fusion centers, 132–133; conflict with DOJ and FBI, 40, 132–133; congressional reorganization, 29; creation of, 27; cyber security challenges, 34–35; development of risk formulas, 58–63; expansion of eligible UASI jurisdictions, 63, 80–81; failure to conduct state and local capabilities assessments, 80; financial management challenges, 30; financial oversight and accountability challenges, 30; first reorganization, 28; grant allocation discrepancies, 67–70; grant recipient challenges, 37; merger of components, 28; release of infrastructure plans, 35; Second Stage Review changes, 29; senior leadership turnover, 31; structure of department, 28; unfunded mandates and requirements, 37, 72–73, 85; use of grant allocations to measure risk, 145; use of Investment Justifications, 67–70; use of No Match letters, 115; using the TCL to allocate funds, 67; using effectiveness to allocate funds, 64, 67–70
U.S. Department of Housing and Urban Development, 21
U.S. Department of Justice (DOJ), 39, 137; conflict with DHS, 40, 132; investigation of Chiquita Brands International, 148
U.S. Department of State, 39, 158n38
U.S. embassy bombings, 11
U.S. Government Accountability Office (GAO), 81, 84, 85, 86, 87

U.S. Strategic Bombing Survey Summary Report (Pacific Way), 19
U.S. VISIT, 35
U.S.S. Cole attack, 11, 12
USA on Watch, 144

Van Gogh, Theo, 182n3
Vietnam War, 21, 125
Vigiles Urbani, 128
Volunteers in Police Service, 144
Virgil, 14

Wallace, William, 3
War of 1812, 16, 46
War for Independence, 3, 15
War Department (see U.S. Department of Defense), 19
Wars for Scottish Independence, 3
Washington, George, 15
Weak Horse, 5, 11, 12
Webster, Daniel, 43
Western Hemisphere Travel Initiative, 115
Williams, Anthony, 74
Wilson, James Q., 129
Wilson, Woodrow, 43; belief in societal masters, 46; distaste for constraints of the Constitution, 46
Witt, James Lee, 94; appointment by Bill Clinton, 98; career experience, 98; failure in response to Hurricane Floyd, 94; political use of FEMA, 98–99
Wohlstetter, Roberta, 26
World Trade Center (WTC), 7, 10, 22, 23, 24, 82
World War I, 16, 46, 95
World War II, 19, 22, 83, 125
Wright, Lawrence, 8, 157n6, 158n38

Yousef, Ramsi, 10; Philippine plot, 11; World Trade Center plot, 10, 22

al-Zawahiri, Ayman, 6, 10; fatwa against America, 9; imprisonment of, 6; in Afghanistan, 7; in Pakistan, 6–7; in Saudi Arabia, 6; in Sudan, 7; in the United States, 6, 158–38

About the Author

MATT A. MAYER is President and CEO of Provisum Strategies LLC, as well as Visiting Fellow with The Heritage Foundation and Adjunct Professor at The Ohio State University. He served as Counselor to the Deputy Secretary and as Head of the Office of State and Local Government Coordination and Preparedness in the U.S. Department of Homeland Security. Mayer has written extensively on homeland security, federalism, and other constitutional issues. He was a Lincoln Fellow with The Claremont Institute for the Study of Statesmanship and Political Philosophy and an American Marshall Memorial Fellow with the German Marshall Fund of the United States.